Unbalanced World

The asset stewardship shortfall

David Calver

Biography

I'm a self-funded independent retired finance and business expert with no current affiliation to any organisations or institutions, apart from being a member of Brasenose College at Oxford University (MA hons Mathematics 1980 - 1983) and a member of my professional body which is the Institute of Chartered Accountants in England and Wales.

My previous books are:

"Peak XXXX: Infinite Possibilities on a Finite Planet", and

"People or Planet: Towards a Regenerative Economics"

They are about perspectives on enablers and barriers to creating a just and sustainable future for all of humanity in perpetuity.

This current book takes a similar general direction as its context, but deepens the analysis of the opportunities by using a largely financial lens applied to the topics of natural capital and other assets and liabilities. The main focus throughout is the creation of a World Balance Sheet, something rarely even contemplated by others, and not achieved by anyone until Harald Deutsch's book "World Balance Sheet: Global Assets at a Glance", published in 2020. I build on Harald's work, fleshing out some of the most important assets and liabilities from a sustainability perspective.

ISBN: 979-8702781440

The companion website for the World Balance Sheet concept can be found at:

WorldBalanceSheet.com

The companion website for the Planetary CFO concept can be found at:

PlanetaryCFO.com

Acknowledgements

My gratitude goes to everyone who has crossed my life path in any way whatsoever who has encouraged, supported, inspired and helped me; they are all part of what made me the person I am. And I wouldn't be any other person but myself.

A particular message of thanks and love go to my wife and family, who have supported me spending the time and effort on researching and writing this book.

Quotes underlining the need for a book like this one

"Remarkably, there is no proper balance sheet, and the future consequences of depleting natural capital are simply ignored... our planet should be properly valued"
(Dieter Helm, 2015)

"In order to shift towards an economic model that protects and builds Natural Capital, we need to look at the system as a whole and align our incentive structures to propel us in the right direction. With this in mind, having a common roadmap, standards and metrics would greatly help drive and accelerate common action and scaled results. ... we need to start accounting for Natural Capital on our balance sheets. Without this we cannot tell the true value of our asset base, nor how damaging our operations are on the natural world."
(HRH Prince of Wales, in Costanza et al 2020)

*"We start off with a list of the quantities of all exchangeables possessed by some person or organization. We multiply each by its money price or some equivalent in terms of what might be called a "valuation coefficient"; then we get a money value for each quantity of exchangeables. Five hundred pounds of cheese at $4 a pound will be $2,000. Some of these exchangeables are positive assets with positive money values; some of them are negative assets with negative money values. Negative assets include garbage wastes, pollution, and debts that we owe. Debts have the peculiar property that they are negative assets or liabilities in one [person's] account [ie balance sheet] and positive assets in another [person's balance sheet]. Accountants are fond of showing a bottom line or net worth, which for any particular cluster of assets is the sum of the values of the positive assets minus the sum of the values of the negative assets, though negative assets are not always very well recorded. Net worths can be calculated for individuals, for families, for organizations, for corporations, for nations, **and for the whole world**."*
(Dolfsma et al, 2013, quoting from Kenneth Boulding's "What do we want in an economics textbook?)

I thank you for your overall positive comments on my work. I have thrown a stone in the water by publishing "World Balance Sheet". Everybody who feels competent and entitled, is invited to improve the framework, the calculation, and the numbers. I hope this can diminish the error bars, leading to better results. That you take on this challenge, is greatly appreciated.
(Harald Deutsch, 2020, author of "World Balance Sheet: Global Assets at a Glance")

Preface

This preface sets out two observations from responding to reviewers of the manuscript.

Firstly, as one reviewer rightly pointed out, my book will benefit from describing my Planetary CFO's methodology for the world balance sheet, as this is a key part of the thinking this book offers and has so much impact on how the final produced world balance sheets look. There's a chapter in which I cover this, although I could see that parts of the methodology are also described through the rest of the book, so I did some sorting out to ensure the various techniques are referenced where they appear and described more fully in the methodology chapter. The methodology chapter summary looks like this:

Chapter summary for the methodology chapter:

- Should everything be monetised or is there room for non-financial measurement of economic throughput?
- What should a proper methodology look like – what are the main elements?
- Where does planetary governance fit in?
- What has already been covered elsewhere in the book? (cross-referenced)
- What is missing from the methodology?
- How are the gaps going to be filled?
- Would it be useful to run volumetric measurements (suggested by Murison Smith) _alongside_ financial ones in the world balance sheet, in meaningful ways?
- Accounting frameworks - IFRS (International Financial Reporting Standards) compared with SNA (System of National Accounts) and SEEA-CF (Standard for Environmental and Ecological Accounting – Central Framework

Secondly, the human destructiveness provision (which is a new concept described in the methodology) is another matter raised by a reviewer. It's potentially a hugely significant matter, with immense, very material impact on the world balance sheet, and in particular on how the bottom line looks (eg the asset stewardship shortfall) and on what some of the key messages will be for actions going forward. It is potentially very politically charged. However, I'm not deliberately trying to be "political" in this book. I believe that any ambitions to achieve sustainability transcend politics. I'm very aware that many of the matters I deal with in the book are made political by other people, and this one - human destructiveness provision, with its impact on the net value of human capital - is likely to be one of them.

The value of humanity in solving problems is, of course, very great, but so is our capacity to make problems for ourselves, for others and for all other life on the planet. This latter set of problems (at planetary scale) are unprecedented for humanity and it's not clear what will happen next, given that humanity's power has advanced at a faster rate than its collective wisdom to use that power. I do feel it is a matter of "the jury is out" on whether humanity will pull through currently known environmental crises (transition and pull through the neck of the bottle) or whether our animal basic selves will embroil us in too much denial and conflict, and even world wars over scarce resources, before the solution set has been sufficiently identified, developed and implemented, preventing us from engaging in that implementation. As a species, I think it would be arrogant of us to think that we cannot suffer from societal collapse and even our own extinction. I reference works such as Jared Diamond ("Collapse"), Toby Ord ("The Precipice") and White and Hagens ("The Bottlenecks of the 21st Century") which all give us cause for careful thought about this, given the long history of collapses and crises for humanity. The subject can easily become the focus for an entire book, so my challenge is to decide what my position is as Planetary CFO, to ask myself whether I'm basically optimistic or pessimistic on it. And to relate it to accounting principles, of which there are several that are probably most relevant, and some of which potentially conflict with each other on this matter:

- *Accrual principle*
- *Conservatism principle*
- *Full disclosure principle*
- *Going concern principle*
- *Materiality principle*

Ultimately, the question I need to ask myself is "what will represent a 'true and fair view' of the state of the planet, its assets and liabilities, and its future prospects?"

The new ideas in this book, and especially the World Balance Sheet concept introduced by me in 2015 (as referenced in Calver (2020b)), explored independently and published by Deutsch in 2020 and expanded / adapted by me in this current book, might not take off immediately. This is to be expected. As Groom and Hepburn (2017) say:

> "… sometimes the time is not right for an idea to become policy. Therefore, academics looking for policy impact need to be patient. It may be decades before an idea takes hold. But ideas matter – they are the cogs that drive history (Grayling, 2009). Furthermore, when a policy window opens, the time might be right for an old idea to re-emerge from hibernation, blinking into the light and scrutiny of government processes."

I hope that, if not now, then at some point in the not-too-distant future, the time will be right for the ideas in this book to flourish and bear fruit.

Contents

Chapter 1

Introduction

Taking Stock and the World Balance Sheet ("WBS")

"For there is nothing lost, that may be found, if sought."
(Edmund Spenser, The Faerie Queene)

"Knowing comes from learning, finding from seeking."
(Vaddey Ratner)

"I still have enough faith in language to believe that if I place enough words next to each other on the page, they will start to speak with sounds of their own."
(Dexter Palmer)

Have you ever felt like there was something missing from the world? Something making the world unbalanced? I have, often. When I was training as an accountant, I felt there was something missing from national accounts – a proper balance sheet. When I worked for BP, I felt that there wasn't enough sustainability in the company's future plans and strategies. All these were feelings that could be paraphrased as "hold on - there's something missing here, something unbalanced", or more colloquially as "a WTF moment".

For an accountant, that's one of the most difficult feelings to address, especially if one is to maintain some professional composure.

Part of me wants to scream somewhat despairingly "what have we been doing, and why have we let this happen on our watch!"

Another part of me advises "calm down – it's not over yet, and there's everything to play for, which makes it an exciting time to be alive and to be part of the solution."

Completeness (answering the question "what's missing, what's causing the world to be unbalanced?") is usually the most challenging issue for an accountant to address. How do you know what you're not seeing, if it's not there to be seen? How do you know what you don't know? And how do you fill in the gaps, even if you find them in the first place?

Those questions have been the driving force for this book. It's about finding the gaps and filling them in. Gaps in understanding, gaps in analysis, gaps in what is reported, gaps in what is discussed. But in order to fill in the gaps, you need to know where those gaps are, and why they are important to fill.

I will also blow the lid off (or, to use more professional language, "challenge and question") my profession's inertia or complacency. Accountancy has, for the last few decades, failed to keep accounting rules and practices, especially in national accounting, up to date with the reality of the unsustainability of the current human system of systems. Things are starting to change, for example with the UK government's commitment to include natural capital in the UK's national accounts soon (perhaps in 2021, in relation to the accounts drawn up to the end of 2020). But this process of modernisation and reform needs to be accelerated if we are to avoid the worst of scenarios describing disruption-during-transition.

One of the best places to start in that process of challenge and questioning, one that comes quite naturally for most accountants, is to take stock.

Taking stock is about consciously deciding to stop, and look. To count, classify, evaluate and add up. To consider what we have in our possession and, to some extent, how it got here, what condition it's in and how it's likely to fare in future. The core aspect of the taking stock process is to focus on a snapshot of the state of everything at a particular point in time. That snapshot time for this book is the year 2020.

In the following pages I'll apply this process of taking stock at two very different scales. One is the mega-macro scale of the whole planet and all the living beings on it. The other is the mega-personal scale of one person – myself.

2020 felt like a pivotal year. Two examples of why this is so are Covid-19 and the Sustainable Development Goals.

The first example is the global Covid-19 pandemic, which has given the whole world a shock, and this has caused people everywhere, including myself, to re-evaluate much of our world view and the transient and vulnerable nature of our own part in it. For many, this has meant a taking stock of their own personal position, their past, present and future trajectories and life path. I'm no exception to that.

As a recent retiree, I had already undertaken some important changes in lifestyle before the pandemic arose. The covid-19 pandemic has compounded the nature and extent of those changes. It's a strong part of my motivation to write, driven by a sense of urgency. Call it legacy creation or a sense of one's own mortality. Whatever you call it, if there's a story to be told, now is the best time to tell it. We've been given a wake-up call by Covid-19, reminding us to take our opportunities while we have them.

The second example is the set of Sustainable Development Goals ("SDGs") which replaced the earlier Millennium Development Goals in 2015. It's now 20 years since the change of Millennium, and five years since the SDG's were established and agreed. Now is a good opportunity to start building a picture that can help us to answer some questions about how we are doing against both the original Millennium Development Goals and the newer SDGs.

In the UN Emissions Gap Report 2019, they comment on the relationships, synergies and trade-offs between carbon emission reduction actions and the various aspects of the SDG's that are involved. I include a diagram about this, sourced from that report, as Appendix 4.

Many academics and other authors have been criticising how we currently measure progress, including progress on the SDGs. For example, Costanza et al (2013) encourage us to look at GPI (Genuine Progress Indicator) instead of GDP (gross Domestic Product). I say more about the criticisms of GDP later.

While *GPI* is a better measure of progress than GDP, it can be improved further by setting it in a balanced scorecard of measures, including key metrics from the world balance sheet. Using a balance sheet approach as well as a progress indicator will strengthen the validity and meaningfulness of the results of both types of metrics.

Why we should compile world balance sheets – to help us know how we are doing in squeezing through the bottleneck

In chapter 8, I talk about the bottleneck humanity faces. This draws from White and Hagens (2020). In order to know how much of a challenge we face in "passing through the bottleneck" (to use White and Hagen's very graphic phrasing), we need to know how large the existing stock of natural and other assets is, so that we can compare that with how narrow we think the neck of the bottle is. This requires us to take stock.

One of the best ways to take stock is to record the things we're taking stock of and to put them in a balance sheet. If we're taking stock of all the important things in the world, then we can put these in a World Balance Sheet.

The following is from World Bank (2006):

> "… investments in produced capital, human capital, and governance, combined with saving efforts aimed at offsetting the depletion of natural resources, can lead to future welfare increases in developing countries."

and this is from World Bank (2018):

> "National income and well-being are underpinned by a country's assets or wealth - measured comprehensively to include produced capital, natural capital, human capital, and net foreign assets. Sustained long-term economic growth requires investment and management of this broad portfolio of assets."

Leaving aside for a moment whether long-term economic growth is feasible within a finite planet (which I talk about later in the book) it's clear that the World Bank believes in the importance of managing wealth (which is another word for the capital assets in a balance sheet).

Once we have a World Balance Sheet, we can be better placed to assess whether the things we've taken stock of are adequate, in terms of amounts and condition, and to a lesser extent whether their distribution and availability are adequate, and to assess whether they serve the needs of global populations and communities, now and into the long-distant future. This would turn the expression "the wealth of nations" into "the wealth of the world".

In this tome, I will argue that some of the most important but finite assets on the planet are undervalued and over-exploited. This is one of the key reasons we face continuing degradation of the biosphere and other natural capital, damaging the long-term sustainability of ecological systems and therefore threatening our own ability to survive and thrive in perpetuity. Compiling the World Balance Sheet, and reviewing how its asset and liability values change in future decades, will be an essential cornerstone in action planning for global transition to sustainability.

The subsequent discussions about land, and the closely related concept of natural capital, are of immense importance, because if we get the stewardship of them wrong and let the world's land and natural capital continue to be degraded at the rates currently occurring, these immeasurably useful assets will be lost not just to us but to all future generations.

But before I talk further about assets and balance sheets, I want to say something about the wider sociological and developmental context. Although politics and economics are not core subjects dealt with in any detail in this current book, I feel I cannot ignore them altogether. I'll therefore dip my toe ever so gently into those tumultuous waters, for a short time, just to give a steer about the sort of transition pathway I believe holds the best chance of creating a just and sustainable future while minimising 'collateral damage' along the way.

It has been particularly evident from the responses to the worldwide economic circumstances surrounding the 2008 global financial system crisis, and again in the responses to the global covid-19 pandemic, that there is a strong and vociferous movement for the overthrow and replacement of the currently dominant model of capitalism. A typical example of this argument is expressed by Ann Pettifor, among others, and has given rise to advocacy for "A Green New Deal" ("GND"), especially in the USA and (with some variations) in the UK. This concept takes inspiration from the New Deal in the USA which responded (with some success) to the Great Depression in the USA in the 1930s.

A good summary of what the Green New Deal movement is calling for as its "ask/mission" is given in Pettifor (2019):

> "… we can – and to survive, we must – transform and even end within the next ten years the failed system of capitalism that now threatens to collapse earth's life support systems and with them, human civilisation … end a deeply entrenched system of racialised capitalism … a financialised capitalist economy that deliberately depletes the earth's finite and precious resources."

Opinions differ, even among GND advocates, about whether, in order to create a sustainable and just future, it will be necessary to completely dismantle and replace the capitalist system (and, as a pre-requisite of this, break the suggested stranglehold maintained by the richest 1% of the global population), or whether it will be sufficient merely to reform capitalism in some way. The means to these ends, within Green New Deal narratives, is usually to adjust the balance, between the public sector and the private sector, of their powers over the economy and especially over the global financial and monetary systems. This is to be achieved (in GND narratives) through a new drive for localism at national and sub-national levels, given the failure of global and international accords and processes such as the Conference of the Parties in relation to Climate Change.

While this radical and dramatic GND narrative has some attractions, especially when it comes to rallying people and inspiring action for change, and I have sympathy with many of the desired directions of travel indicated, at a personal level I'm not convinced that the case has been sufficiently proven for **_all_** of the actions and aims in the GND 'manifestos'. As with many movements that have become politicised, polarisation creeps in, and the most extreme proposals for toppling and replacing existing regimes, rules and systems get written into aims and objectives, in order to create an action plan that is distinctive and which has an obvious social group as its scapegoat – in this case, the richest 1%.

Mainstream sources such as the IMF (2020) suggest less radical pathways forward, for example that well planned public policies around such matters as carbon pricing can be used not only to achieve net zero emissions by 2050 (one element of a set of milestones on the transition to sustainability), but also to eliminate the financial impacts of this on the poorest:

> "... whereas carbon pricing would disproportionately affect poorer households, recycling one-sixth to one-quarter of carbon revenues as targeted transfers could fully compensate the poorest 20 percent of households. Fully compensating the poorest 40 percent of households would require recycling between 40 and 55 percent of the carbon revenues. In addition, some limited government spending on low-carbon sectors would support job transitions from high-carbon to low-carbon sectors. Conscious and determined action by governments to build inclusion will be key to enhance the social and political acceptability of the transition."

Rather than blame the richest, I prefer to take the view, as expressed by Helm (2015), that we are **_all_**, in fact, the perpetrators of the problems of unsustainability:

> "... there is little escaping the fact that the villains of the piece are the consumers and shareholders, rather than the easy scapegoat – some large corporate entity [or a rich global elite]. Strictly speaking, companies do not pollute, only consumers and shareholders do. Companies are just our agents – intermediaries doing our bidding."

Helm appears to lean toward something akin to 'lifting the veil of incorporation' in order to attribute the real responsibility to shareholders rather than the corporate entities they might hide behind.

His indication, in Helm (2020) is that the answer is not found in either dominance by the State or dominance by the private sector, but in redressing the balance between them:

"What is needed is a middle ground – combining a model with the State doing what the markets cannot, and the market then sorting out the resulting allocation of resources within the framework the State provides."

While sensible public policy can help push towards sustainability and social justice, I'm not convinced it will be enough to achieve that aim, without other actions by wider civic society.

I say more about economics in chapter 8. For now, let's move on and talk about a category of asset that has, over the last hundred years, lost its prominence in specialist and generalist circles of discourse.

Let's look at land, in brief. Land is a particularly useful concept within emerging methodologies for world balance sheets. This is because:

- there is a finite amount of land on the planet
- we know how much land there is in total
- we are getting better all the time at understanding and measuring "land use" everywhere on the planet (and the impacts of "land use change")
- "land use" can be used (directly and/or as a proxy, if necessary) to classify natural capital into a number of asset sub-categories, for the purposes of reaching natural capital asset valuations for inclusion in world balance sheets

Given its central importance in any balance sheet that contains natural capital, I devote an entire chapter to land and how to account for it.

I will argue that some of the key building blocks for addressing the challenges around balance sheets and sustainability are already in place. All we need to do is link up the disciplines of sustainability, ecology, accountancy and economics in a quest to place proper values on the assets **and obligations** associated with land (and other asset) ownership and stewardship.

It's by taking stock of assets in the World Balance Sheet that we can make a start on a long-term exercise to objectively measure their adequacy in the context of sustainability.

When it comes to measuring the value of a category of assets, there are two fundamentally different approaches, and I apply both of them at various points in the book.

The first way to measure value is a "bottom-up" approach – to multiply an asset count by a value per unit. Then, we can 'impute' a value per unit of the assets from the outputs that are sustainably provided by those assets. This is a specific case of a classic Net Present Value calculation, adding all the discounted cash flow effects of the sustainable outputs through each future year in perpetuity (ie forever). When a sensible discount rate is used, these sums do not equal infinity but instead arrive at a finite result for the value of the assets that produced those outputs. Discounting is explained more fully in chapter 9.

The second way to measure value is a "top-down" approach. A typical method for this is to take a previous balance sheet and use some broad generalisations about what has happened to the assets and liabilities since the date of that balance sheet, and reflect those changes in the new balance sheet.

Each of these methods has their strengths and weaknesses. The ideal is to use them both, and to use them as a means of triangulation and validation to increase confidence that the results arrived at by both methods are robust. In practice, this rarely happens, especially in a subject such as ecological sustainability, and even the supposedly more mathematical discipline of ecological economics. However, it falls quite naturally to an accountant to try such triangulations and so you will see them appearing in this book sporadically. I deal with valuation methods and their application to assets in the world balance sheet, in relevant chapters.

The work of another author, Harald Deutsch, is applauded, and extensively refenced, in this book. Deutsch has recently undertaken what might turn out to be a world first – he has actually created a world balance sheet, including putting all the basic numbers into it. In his 2020 book "World Balance Sheet – Global Assets at a Glance", he outlines a thought experiment in how to sum up (and consolidate) a range of asset types. He then proceeds to do so, from a range of real-world sources of data, and presents the world balance sheet with actual, real-world numbers in it. As far as I'm aware, his was the first ever robust attempt to do this (setting aside Mulhall's efforts in the late nineteenth century as being largely invalidated by his very incomplete and opaque methodology – see further comments about this later on). I will be building on Deutsch's work, extending it and revising it in order to illustrate how this is only the start of a new revolution in how we take stock of the world's assets and steward them for sustainability. I consider Deutsch's work in more detail, mainly in chapter 3.

One of the difficulties I've been finding with my formulating of my approach (ie "the Planetary CFO's approach") to the World Balance Sheet is that it seems to be necessary to draw on multiple accounting standards and frameworks, and to invent new ones, in order to derive a balance sheet that is useful for assessing sustainability of the current human systems impacting the biosphere. The approach I've used is a combination of IFRS, SNA, NPV project appraisal, environmental economics and common sense. I think previous authors have found this as well. This means, for all of us, and any other people working on this topic, that the balance sheets we derive are likely to be a mixture of items, and use a mixture of recognition, counting and valuation techniques, in order to be as complete and comprehensive as we can be in presenting a "true and fair" picture of the state of the world.

Providing our different interpretations of terms and methods don't materially alter the overall pictures we're presenting, that heterodox approach to accounting probably doesn't matter very much to the usefulness and accuracy of the final results of our respective works.

There will be some downsides to this approach, including the potential for lack of consistency between the treatments of various asset classes, as well as potential for the approach and techniques to evolve over time, resulting in difficulties in comparing balance sheets drawn up at different times. It's hoped that these deficiencies are outweighed by the benefits to be obtained from undertaking the drawing up and comparing of world balance sheets – something that has been done so rarely in the past that almost any improvement on what has been done before will be a significant improvement.

As stated in UN (2014):

> "These measurement challenges do not … invalidate the use of accounting frameworks to compile coherent and structured information. Indeed, an important role of an accounting framework is to assist in the identification of data gaps."

Where our obsession with GDP has led us

GDP (Gross Domestic Product) is a measure of throughput. Worse than that, it doesn't distinguish particularly between throughput that is productive and throughput that is destructive (eg damaging natural and other assets).

There are numerous texts that point out the flaws in using GDP as a measure of economic success, rather than looking at nations' (and the whole world's) balance sheets.

For example, Hynes et al (2020) describe very starkly the prevailing approach to GDP and growth in the time since I was born (1962). It's sobering for me, personally, to reflect on the fact this economic reality is the backdrop to my entire life so far:

> "In 1961 the newly-created OECD, encouraged by 'classical' economists, proposed to turbocharge the economy. They championed an unsustainable and delusional new target for something they named "growth", 50 percent over the decade. They also pushed policies for financial liberalisation, although it would take several decades for these changes to be fully implemented. These policies led to a series of credit booms – regarded as 'infinite booms' by for example, traders in sub-prime mortgages and collateralised debt obligations. The situation was one of "all competition and no control", both as regards demand-side measures, such as limits on loans-to-value ratios, and supply-side actions, including lending and interest rate ceilings, reserve and capital requirements, and supervisory guidance. Policy and regulation require boundaries, but finance capital abhors boundaries. The result is an international monetary system run by the equivalent of the Sorcerer's Apprentice. In the absence of the Sorcerer – regulatory democracy – financial risk-takers and fraudsters have, since 1971, periodically crashed the global economy and ruined the lives of millions of people."

One positive way forward that is still evolving is to set alongside GDP a cocktail of other measures. This recognises the deficiencies in GDP and attempts to overcome them, by focussing more attention on the ultimate aims of sustainable development, rather than the economic activity that GDP measures. As Stiglitz et al (2018) reports:

> "Following Sen (1985), and Stiglitz, Sen and Fitoussi (2009), GDP is seen as an input, a means to an end rather than an end in itself …
> - Can we find a single composite index to replace GDP?
> - If not, how big should the dashboard of indicators be and what should be on it?"

How we know we're overshooting with our consumption and drawing down natural capital and the reasons this has happened

A blinkered focus on GDP has led to planetary overshoot. This is covered extensively by other authors. Also, you only need to briefly check out news headlines about Earth Overshoot Day to see more about this. It's why we need to change tack and look at balance sheet approaches to fill some gaps in our knowledge left by our myopia.

This state of affairs has occurred because the dominant economics has for several decades been neoclassical economics, with an emphasis on inexhaustible economic growth as the main aim of macroeconomic policy.

There are alternative approaches. One of the more radical ones, that is gaining traction and entering the mainstream, is ecological economics in general, and Steady State Economics ("SSE") in particular. For example, a key proponent of SSE is Daly (2011):

> "In ecological economics, optimal scale replaces growth as a goal, followed by fair distribution."

I'll return to the economic contexts for world balance sheets in chapter 8, and I include as Appendix 1 a summary diagram charting the main branches of economics through modern history. In the meantime, let's look at a particular example of the planetary overshoot we're currently experiencing.

A small example of planetary overshoot and global drawdown of natural capital - how does the UK's food footprint look?

The following excerpt from GRI (2020) sums it up neatly:

> "The UK is highly dependent on imported commodities. Although 52% of the unprocessed products eaten in the UK in 2016 were produced nationally, estimates of the total area required to grow crops to meet the demands of the UK food system suggest that over two thirds of the UK's land footprint is overseas. A 2017 report identified that seven key commodities – beef and leather, cocoa, palm oil, pulp and paper, rubber, soya and timber– were responsible for the largest proportion of the UK's imported commodity driven overseas land footprint, an area equivalent to over half the size of the UK, over six times the size of Wales. While this is on average less than 3% of total global production for most of these commodities, it is not an insignificant amount, particularly considering the potential to align the UK's actions with efforts in other major producing and consuming economies to create a new global framework for collective action."

This is telling us that the UK has a very significant resource usage beyond its "rightful share". A logical follow-up question is to ask how much of that food footprint is unsustainable, involving drawing-down of natural capital and other assets, unsustainable agricultural practices, carbon emissions and so on.

If the UK is to be in a position to carry some moral authority as facilitator of the international CoP meeting on Climate Change in 2021, it needs to be sure it is doing all it can to lead the way by practically demonstrating the steps it's taking to 'put its own house in order'.

One example is the UK Government's public consultation on "due diligence on forest risk commodities". My views on this initiative are included as Appendix 3.

How a balance sheet approach can help, and must be tried

Numerous academics and researchers have spelled out that one of the reasons human systems are being operated unsustainably is that there has been an over-emphasis on income and expenditure (mostly through the use of the headline numbers for GDP) and that balance sheets, and especially the balance of natural capital assets, have been neglected for too long.

Although controversial, we can draw strength and inspiration, albeit with some caution, from the "Hartwick Rule", as described in Tietenberg (2018):

> "... the 'Hartwick Rule': ... In an early article, John Hartwick (1977) demonstrated that a constant level of consumption could be maintained perpetually from an environmental endowment if all the scarcity rent derived from resources extracted from that endowment were invested in capital. That level of investment would be sufficient to assure that the value of the total capital stock would not decline."

A big advantage of looking at a balance sheet approach, alongside income and expenditure, is that it is giving an opportunity, at every balance sheet date, for a 'taking stock' as part of our stewardship responsibilities. This is such an important concept that it has even entered the English language as a term to be used outside pure accounting contexts. Hence, we talk about taking stock of many things in our lives. This means no less than to undertake a reality-check on whether the state of things is OK, or indeed the extent to which they are not. This is the big win that a balance sheet approach can bring. It enables a taking stock, a standing back and a proper review of where things stand and how they are.

And at the current point in history, this is more significant than it's ever been before. We need to stand back, look at what we're doing with (and to) the biggest assets that support us (for example, the oceans, the forests and the soils) and decide what we're going to do differently going forward.

Tietenberg (2018) goes on to state very clearly how the Hartwick Rule applies to achieving sustainability, at first in a simple example and then applying it to the (global) planetary environment:

> "Consider an analogy. Suppose a grandparent left you an inheritance of $10,000 and you put it in a bank where it earns 10 percent interest. What are the choices for allocating that money over time and what are the implications of those choices? If you withdrew exactly $1,000 per year, the amount in the bank would remain $10,000 and the income would last forever; you would be spending only the interest, leaving the principal intact. If you spend more than $1,000 per year, the principal would necessarily decline over time and eventually the balance in the account would go to zero. In the context of this discussion, spending $1,000 per year or less would satisfy the sustainability criterion, while spending more would violate it.
> What does the Hartwick Rule mean in this context? It suggests that one way to tell whether an allocation (spending pattern) is sustainable or not is to examine what is happening to the value of the principal over time. If the principal is declining, the allocation (spending pattern) is not sustainable. If the principal is increasing or remaining constant, the allocation (spending pattern) is sustainable.
>
> How do we apply this logic to the environment? In general, the Hartwick Rule suggests that the current generation has been given an endowment. Part of the endowment consists of environmental and natural resources (known as "natural capital") and another part consists of physical capital (such as buildings, equipment, schools, and roads). Sustainable use of this endowment implies that we should keep the principal (the value of the natural and physical endowment) intact and live off only the flow of services provided. We should not, in other words, chop down all the trees and use up all the oil, leaving future generations to fend for themselves. Rather, we need to assure that the value of the total capital stock is maintained, not depleted."

I advised caution in using the Hartwick Rule above, because a lot depends on the extent to which someone believes that substitution of produced ("physical") capital for natural capital should be allowed.

It's not clear, for example, whether Tietenberg is using a weak or strong definition of sustainability in the above excerpt. However, the overall message is clear about maintenance of various types of capital in order to secure a sustainable flow of resources in perpetuity. Balance sheets help us to plan for capital maintenance and to monitor if those plans are succeeding. Tietenberg also goes on to state a revised version of the rule if one is concerned about maintaining strong sustainability:

> "[under strong sustainability] … an allocation is sustainable if it maintains the value of the stock of *natural* capital. This definition assumes that it is natural capital that drives future well-being and further assumes that little or no substitution between physical and natural capital is possible."

I say more about the opportunities and difficulties with the Hartwick Rule in Chapters 4 and 9.

Some economists have been concerned about the lack of full balance sheet accounting, for example in Systems of National Accounts (SNA). One example is Stiglitz et al (2018) (the emphasis is mine):

> *"Outstanding issues and new questions*
>
> While the 2008 SNA includes full balance sheets for economic assets and liabilities, many countries are still guided by a very limited (and possibly misleading) approach to sustainability ... comparisons of (gross) public debt to GDP are incomplete measures of economic sustainability. It may be that part of the appeal of using the debt to GDP ratio as an indicator of sustainability is that it is relatively simple to calculate and understand.
>
> However, sustainability has two additional aspects to be considered:
>
> ☐ **A full balance sheet approach** (i.e. taking stock of a broader range of both assets and liabilities, and associated risks [ie not just "economic assets"]), by looking at:
> - o the balance sheets of all sectors (banks, households, etc.) rather than the government alone;
>
> - o both liabilities and assets (e.g. recognising that fire-sales of assets in depressed financial markets may worsen net worth);
>
> - o distinguishing between types of economic capital that add to productive capacity and those that do not (e.g. land), and between changes in volumes and changes in prices
>
> ☐ A long-term sustainability analysis which takes account of the impact of demographic and other factors on the evolution of public finances."

Discussion of data sourcing and the degree of completeness it enables

The UN FAO (Food and Agriculture Organisation) has extensive data collections, and these are referenced extensively in this book. However, many of them are not updated very frequently and some of them are incomplete (which the UN admits). As a consequence, we have sometimes used other sources in preference to FAO, for example to arrive at more up to date numbers. In these circumstances, the FAO data can often be used as a means of providing a reality-check and triangulation on the numbers actually used.

Initial conclusions (further developed as a thread throughout this book)

If humankind could find ways to extract economic values from ecological assets (while remaining within sustainability limits, for example as per Kate Rowarth's "Doughnut Economics"), the resulting future aggregate consumption of humanity could potentially be much higher than it is today. This is comparable to the innovation of domestication (livestock breeding) in the stone age: When the hunters found ways to maintain and to feed the game, the game assets turned into a renewable resource, and suddenly: the more livestock, the better... whereas, as hunters, only the killing counted, not the stocks (herds). This is one of the key arguments for protecting and enhancing natural capital, on which future generations will depend. On the other hand, if we have already passed tipping points for nature, the degradation of natural capital is likely to accelerate and we will have failed in our stewardship of these essential assets.

Chapter 2

Finding the meaning behind the numbers – old precursors

"… to develop a universally accepted strategy to ensure the sustainability of Earth's life support system against human-induced stresses is one of the greatest research and policy challenges ever to confront humanity"

(Steffen et al. 2007, p. 618).

My concepts of what accountancy is about have always included a principle which goes beyond the fundamental principles every accountant is trained to apply. The additional principle is described as follows:

"Look for the meaning behind the numbers"

(source = the author)

This is about building an opinion based on some form of revealed truth, on which the accounting numbers should be shedding some light, not just reflecting a particular, biased view of the world that might be held by the owner or manager who has asked the accountant for their opinions.

The accountancy profession began (hundreds of years ago) because people needed an independent and objective person (the accountant) to "tell me how it is, not how I want to think it is". This function of the accountant can only be fulfilled if they have the ability to find the meaning behind the numbers, so that they can talk meaningfully to the non-accountants who rely on their opinions.

In the current circumstances of almost universal global, regional and local unsustainability, we need this objectivity. We need this quest for a truth. We need accountants, more than ever, to seek the meaning behind the numbers, and to tell it how it is, especially to people in power but also to everyone else, backed up by the numbers in the form of a World Balance Sheet. This resonates with the often-quoted campaign slogan of "talking truth to power".

Looking at the meaning behind some early forerunners / precursors – eg Mulhall

Rarely is there anything in this world that hasn't been tried before. The World Balance Sheet is no exception.

In looking for precedents, we could start by considering the work of Adam Smith. Anyone who has taken even a passing interest in economics will have heard of this early founder of the discipline. We might ask whether Adam Smith's "Wealth of Nations", his world-famous seminal work from 1776, might be a starting point. The title seems to suggest that it dealt with … well … the wealth (ie balance sheet assets) of nations? So, one would naturally expect that there might be some information about assets / wealth. Unfortunately, the title of the book seems to be somewhat of a misnomer, since Smith for the most part only dealt with market forces and product manufacturing output, supply, demand and pricing and included almost no actual numbers. His work was largely theoretical and ideological. The only numbers included were examples used to illustrate the effects of supply and demand on market forces. No balance sheet was produced, not even a national one for his home country, let alone for the world as a whole.

However, just around a hundred years later (from 1881 to 1896) some work that could very loosely be described as the first real forerunner for a world balance sheet was undertaken, in various published works, by George Mulhall, a Fellow of the Royal Statistical Society.

Before assessing Mulhall's work with a critical eye, it's worth just summarising the main numbers he published in his various books. The data he worked with, although very patchy, covers an era running from 1664 to 1896, which roughly corresponds to the pre- , early-, and mid-Industrial Revolution. However, for most of those years only partial data (eg only relating to Great Britain) are shown. Where the aggregate numbers were published for what Mulhall considered to be "the whole world", they relate to the 1880's and 1890's, as follows:

Figure 1 – Summary of Mulhall's 'World Balance Sheet' – key numbers 1870 - 1896

Mulhall's "Balance-Sheet of the World"				
	1870	1880	1882	1896
Capital or Wealth of Nations - "The World" (£ billions)	42.0	46.5	50.7	69.8

Source: gathered from Mulhall's published books (1881, 1884 and 1896 – see references and bibliography) and summarised by the Author

It would be a mistake to simply rely on the above numbers and treat them as "fact" without undertaking a mini-audit of them, with a view to coming to some conclusion about their likely accuracy and usefulness in the current context. For those of you who find this sort of analysis uninspiring, you might want to skip ahead to the conclusions at the end of this chapter.

Mulhall's "Balance-Sheet of the World" in 1881 was a valiant attempt to do the sort of stock taking I'm talking about, during an era which was synonymous with the Industrial Revolution, when it must have seemed that the world's resources were inexhaustible. The task was deemed "easy" by Mulhall, probably because this was a time in history when science, mathematics and statistics (data) were seen to be tools that could achieve anything. What was the 'meaning behind the numbers' Mulhall was looking for? The objectives for doing his work would surely have been very different in 1881 from those of Adam Smith a century before, but not so very different from the objectives for my current work on this topic in 2020. Mulhall (1881) says, of his own objectives:

> "It is certainly as important for us to know every ten years the progress made by nations in the various branches of industry and finances, as to take a census of their population. The task is, in a manner, easy, since it reduces itself to a careful comparison of the statistics relative to commerce, agriculture, manufactures, revenue, and public debt, as exhibited in the 27 Tables (pages 14 to 40), on which the present work is constructed. The diagrams show at a glance the results of the said Tables ..."

It appears that Mulhall was interested in measuring "progress" of nations. He does not spell out what sort of progress he means, but there are some strong hints in his use of language, and in the sorts of data tables he produced, that he meant industrial and economic progress, and in particular Great Britain's progress compared with other nations. Given this intention underlying his work, it's not surprising that in many of the metrics calculated and compared, Great Britain 'comes out on top'. Was there some selective data gathering and analysis? Perhaps that's a strong possibility.

However, his work, predictably, fell very short of modern data standards in a number of other ways. For example, it was not comprehensive geographically. In his own words, in the preface, he states:

> "I may observe that the inquiry is confined to the nations of Christendom, that is Europe, America, and the Colonies of Great Britain. It is hardly necessary to add that in all cases the term Great Britain is used as synonymous with the United Kingdom ..."

The mere fact that Mulhall titled his 1881 book "Balance-Sheet of the World", despite the large number of nations for which no data was collected, speaks volumes of the arrogance that existed among British authors at that time, and the clear and erroneous implication (or inference) that ignoring any nations other than "Europe", "America", and Great Britain and its colonies would not be a significant omission.

Also, Mulhall makes the misadventure of spending most of the 1881 book looking at flows and very little of it looking at stocks. Despite the title of his book, it almost entirely deals with flows of output and consumption. This is the same mistake that was to be continued by many others and would be embedded in measures of economic progress in the middle of the twentieth century, when GDP was adopted as the headline indicator of economic success virtually everywhere in the world.

Furthermore, the "results" Mulhall refers to seem to consist of a series of grand sweeping statements about the ascendency and unassailable superiority of British industrial production and labour efficiency. One wonders whether this was what Mulhall was trying to illustrate all along, with the unsettling fear arising in my mind that perhaps he only looked for data that would confirm this view, and ignored any data that pointed in a different direction.

It is clear that, on some measures that he reported in his later works (eg in 1896), the USA had 'made more progress' than Great Britain and had overtaken Great Britain on some of the metrics. Mulhall made very little mention or comment about this in his later works, compared with the effusive comments about Great Britain's ascendancy in his earlier works.

Perhaps, in that respect, his silence about certain matters speaks volumes in itself. After the turn of the century, Mulhall appears to have produced few relevant publications, and his work seems to have changed direction somewhat, comprising statistical "dictionaries" rather than world balance sheets. Even in his 1896 book, the world balance sheet had become a small table buried deep in the volume, with no prominence given to it and no comment about its meaningfulness.

Nevertheless, if we can set aside our personal feelings on the biased nature of the "results" of Mullhall's work, and his interpretation of them, there is some value in taking a look, objectively, at the information he published. Perhaps we can impute meanings ourselves, knowing what we do about the history of the relevant era.

His methods of presentation of information are notable. In stark contrast to Adam Smith's book (which is almost all prose and virtually no numbers), Mullhall's is packed full of numbers, tables and various pictorial/diagrammatic representations of numbers designed to illustrate comparisons between nations on various types of data presented. The overall impression is that it was (for its time) an extraordinary piece of inventive numerical analysis. It is not unlike a modern set of international financial and operational accounts, intended not only to present financial and operational information, but to make them meaningful to people who are not financially trained. Maybe we would now call what he produced a set of "management accounts" or even an "annual report and accounts" for a large swathe of the world's industrial and commercial activities.

Despite the "snowstorm" effect of the provision of a massive amount and variety of data, Mulhall does come up trumps, in the middle of the 1881 book, by producing a single balance sheet for the world. It appears as if Mulhall might have combined information published in his book with information from other sources (perhaps his records and calculations used in other earlier books of his), because within his book he sets out a single page (his table 18, reproduced below) which he titles "Capital or Wealth of Nations". It lists total assets ("wealth") by nation and gives a total for all nations listed (which he calls "The World"). This is £46,519,000,000 of gross assets, ie about £46.5 billion.

Figure 2 – The earliest known World Balance Sheet? (data for 1870 and 1880)

BALANCE-SHEET OF THE WORLD. 31

TABLE 18.
CAPITAL OR WEALTH OF NATIONS.

	Millions sterling.		Increase. Millions £.	Ratio per Inhabitant.		Do. free of National Debt.	
	1870.	1880.		1870.	1880.	1870.	1880.
Great Britain	8,310	8,960	650	£264	£260	£238	£237
France . . .	7,122	7,417	295	187	201	174	180
Germany . .	5,350	6,075	725*	141	135	137	130
Russia . . .	3,290	3,540	250	44	44	41	36
Austria . . .	2,830	3,050	220†	79	78	69	67
Italy . . .	1,750	1,860	110	66	65	52	47
Holland . .	1,080	1,130	50	303	283	280	262
Belgium . .	900	940	40	178	168	172	156
Spain . . .	1,240	1,373	133	76	82	59	51
Portugal . .	255	272	17	64	65	49	45
Swed. and Nor.	693	738	45	115	113	114	110
Denmark . .	340	350	10	190	178	183	173
Turkey, etc. .	750	760	10	31	31	26	19
Europe . . .	33,910	36,465	2555	£111	£111	£101	£98
United States	6,320	7,880	1560	164	158	151	150
Australia . .	346	490	144	190	172	170	140
Canada . . .	524	636	112	138	148	134	140
South Africa .	71	98	27	80	72	78	65
South America	900	950	50	36	37	30	29
THE WORLD .	42,071	46,519	4448	£112	£113	£102	£101

* Including £280,000,000 for Alsace-Lorraine.   † Including £55,000,000 for Bosnia.

To calculate equivalent World Balance Sheets for years or decades before or after 1870 or 1880 would normally require some ingenious "incomplete accounts" work.

When I was an accountancy trainee, some hundred years after Mulhall published his book, part of my training involved being given an "incomplete accounts" exercise, otherwise known colloquially as a "brown envelope" exercise. This comprised, literally, being given a brown envelope containing various pieces of paper (eg receipts, invoices, bank slips, stock-take records etc) relating to an organisation. The objective of the exercise was to use the information gleaned from the pieces of paper, and some sensible inferences, to construct as full a set of financial statements (both a Profit and Loss statement and a Balance Sheet, or perhaps even two Balance Sheets at two different points in time – perhaps a year apart). Accountants in 1881 would probably have also been familiar with such an exercise. I feel in some way connected with those who would have no doubt worked with Mullhall on his accounting endeavours culminating in the compilation of his book. It's one of the most fundamental skills for an accountant to learn, because it represents a form of "reverse engineering" applied to the financial books and records. When done well, this skill allows the financial picture to be rolled forwards or backwards through time, as if passing a computer mouse forward or backwards along a timeline and seeing the relevant Balance Sheet at each year-end.

We could deploy such incomplete accounts methods to the data in Mulhall, to fill in some gaps. But for now, let's peruse the ultimate culmination of his work and that of his team – the earliest known published World Balance Sheet shown in his table 18 (the figure above).

There are a number of good aspects, and some poor ones, about this balance sheet and the way it is set out, and I list them here as a set of "pros" and "cons":

Pros:

- It is a simple, single-page presentation format
- It shows amounts in total and per-capita (per person)
- All numbers are shown in one currency (making comparisons easier)
- Some comments are made in the accompanying text about comparisons between nations and also comparisons between balance sheet amounts ten years apart

Cons:

- Not geographically comprehensive (many nations not included)
- Not economically comprehensive (many business sectors and types of capital not included, for example natural capital and human capital)
- Not comprehensive technically, eg:
    o just one total given for assets
    o doesn't include totals for liabilities and/or equity
    o this suggests it might not be based on double-entry bookkeeping

- o this creates doubt on basic accuracy of accounting techniques used in the analyses
- Data sources and their likely accuracy were not made clear in the accompanying text – in fact, he doesn't even quote the sources used
- Likely error ranges or statistical confidence intervals are not included

There are some more general deficiencies in his books:

- Inconsistent layout and structure of tables from one time period to another (eg not consistent from one of his books to another)
- Inconsistent ordering of tables, resulting in much casting about to try to find equivalent numbers in books published in different years

Clearly, many of the above deficiencies were addressed when Systems of National Accounts were developed more than half a century later, and it would be harsh to criticise Mulhall too brutally for these faults when his work was almost certainly highly superior in quality, depth and presentation to anything that had preceded it.

Fortunately for us, Mulhall did not stop in 1881, and he went on to produce some more detailed analyses in the following years. In 1884, he published what he called "Mulhall's Dictionary of Statistics". In it, he listed many "statistical" tables (ie tables of data), relating to the latest data then available (for 1882). For example, his table "Wealth of Nations" (on his page 469) in that book showed wealth by nation and also by industrial sector within each nation.

I reproduce it here as figure 3.

Figure 3 – Mulhall's "Wealth of Nations" in 1882

WEALTH.

A.—WEALTH OF NATIONS, IN MILLIONS £.

	Land and Forest.	Cattle.	Railways.	Public Works.	Houses.	Furniture.	Merchandise.	Bullion.	Shipping.	Sundries.	Total.
United Kingdom	1,880	235	770	547	2,280	1,140	350	143	120	1,255	8,720
France	2,930	212	494	590	1,890	945	165	301	15	518	8,060
Germany	2,420	231	467	442	1,470	735	155	108	15	280	6,323
Russia	1,940	345	309	224	880	440	60	34	7	104	4,343
Austria	1,590	205	255	188	770	385	64	20	4	132	3,613
Italy	905	56	108	131	656	328	48	45	9	65	2,351
Spain	740	57	79	60	340	170	22	41	7	77	1,593
Portugal	170	11	12	15	80	40	7	14	1	21	371
Belgium	270	30	61	41	140	70	58	29	2	105	806
Holland	220	33	27	125	116	58	61	17	4	326	987
Denmark	216	31	10	11	44	22	10	3	3	16	366
Sweden	444	42	26	32	62	31	14	4	5	35	695
Norway	173	21	6	13	24	12	7	1	13	12	282
Switzerland	110	21	33	30	70	35	10	7	..	8	324
Greece	112	6	...	7	44	22	4	6	2	8	211
Europe	14,120	1,536	2,657	2,456	8,866	4,433	1,035	773	207	2,962	39,045
United States	2,150	378	1,190	527	2,780	1,385	155	157	60	713	9,495
Canada	230	35	72	30	140	70	18	2	12	41	650
Mexico	125	32	12	12	240	120	20	10	..	67	638
Argentine Republic	122	54	16	6	72	38	12	1	..	13	332
Australia	192	66	58	28	108	54	52	14	4	14	590
Total	16,939	2,101	4,005	3,059	12,206	6,098	1,292	957	283	3,810	50,750

One notable trend from the above data is that the "world" total of assets had increased from £46.5 billion in 1880 to £50.75 billion in 1882, a growth of about 10% in two years, or about 5% per year.

Another interesting observation from Mulhall (1884) is the significant changes of Great Britain's wealth from 1664 to 1882, and the number of different people involved in those valuations, as shown by Mulhall on his page 71 (reproduced below).

Figure 4 – estimates of wealth ("capital") of Great Britain for a range of years

CAPITAL. 71

CAPITAL.

A.—CAPITAL AND INCOME OF GREAT BRITAIN.*

Valuer.	Date.	Capital, Millions £.	Income, Millions £.	Capital per Inhab.	Income per Inhab.
Petty . .	1664	250	42	£45	£8
Davenant .	1701	490	55	90	10
Young . .	1770	1,100	122	153	16
Pitt . . .	1800	1,800	230	170	22
Colquhoun	1811	2,180	250	180	21
Liverpool .	1822	2,600	280	186	20
Pebrer . .	1833	8,750	850	150	14
Porter . .	1840	4,100	480	152	18
Levi, &c. .	1860	5,560	760	195	26
Mulhall .	1882	8,720	1,247	248	85

B.—ELEMENTS OF BRITISH CAPITAL.

	Millions £.		Per Inhab.		Aliquot Parts.	
	1860.	1882.	1860.	1882.	1860.	1882.
Houses . . .	1,160	2,280	£41	£65	20·8	26·2
Railways . . .	348	750	12	21	6·3	8·6
Shipping . . .	42	120	2	4	0·8	1·4
Bullion . . .	95	143	3	4	1·7	1·6
Lands . . .	1,840	1,880	65	53	33·0	21·6
Cattle, &c. . . .	460	410	16	12	8·3	4·7
Merchandise .	210	350	7	10	3·8	4·0
Foreign Loans .	420	1,100	15	31	7·6	12·6
Furniture . .	580	1,140	20	32	10·4	13·1
Roads, Works, &c. .	405	547	14	16	7·3	6·2
Total . . .	5,560	8,720	£195	£248	100·0	100·0

This data suggests that up to 1664, Great Britain's total wealth was, essentially, negligible and not worth recording, and that it rose dramatically from that point through to the 1880s. This gives us an overall indication of the significance of the Industrial Revolution for economic activity, and a very rough timeline for the start of the Industrial Revolution and its significance in balance sheet terms, at least in relation to the types of assets calculated and included by Mulhall in his world balance sheets.

Mulhall (1884) also included some detailed data tables by industrial sector. For example, the following table is from his page 472 and shows, for Great Britain, the breakdown of wealth by sector for various years between 1660 and 1882.

Figure 5 – Wealth of Great Britain by sector 1660 - 1882

WEALTH.

F.—GROWTH OF BRITISH WEALTH.

Year.	Millions £.				Per Inhab.	Kingdom.
	Lands.	Houses.	Sundries.	Total.		
1660 . .	144	46	60	250	£45	England.
1703 . .	270	87	133	490	79	,,
1774 . .	568	184	348	1,100	136	,,
1800 . .	820	240	680	1,740	165	G. Britain.
1812 . .	1,066	355	769	2,190	127	U, Kingdom.
1840 . .	1,680	770	1,580	4,030	150	,,
1860 . .	1,840	1,164	2,556	5,560	191	,,
1882 . .	1,880	2,280	4,560	8,720	249	,,

	Millions £.				Aliquot Parts.			
	1812.	1840.	1860.	1882.	1812.	1840.	1860.	1882.
Land . . .	1,066	1,680	1,840	1,880	48·7	41·7	33·1	21·5
Cattle, &c. .	260	380	460	414	11·9	9·4	8·3	4·7
Houses . .	355	770	1,164	2,280	16·2	19·1	20·9	26·1
Railways .	...	33	348	770	...	0·8	6·3	8·8
Shipping .	15	23	44	120	0·7	0·6	0·8	1·4
Merchandise	50	70	190	350	2·3	1·7	3·4	4·0
Furniture .	180	390	580	1,140	8·2	9·7	10·4	13·1
Bullion .	23	61	105	143	1·0	1·5	1·9	1·6
Loans . . .	105	230	420	1,060	4·8	5·7	7·5	12·2
Sundries . .	136	393	409	563	6·2	9·8	7·4	6·6
Total . .	2,190	4,030	5,560	8,720	100·0	100·0	100·0	100·0

The values of land and houses clearly made up a large proportion of Great Britain's wealth. There are many modern books that have given extensive attention to this feature of the UK balance sheet, together with the advantages and pitfalls of this, for example on the paucity of natural capital, the distributional inequalities and intergenerational inequalities that have been generated. For example, see Ryan-Collins et al (2017).

An example of questionable accounting (perhaps indicating failure to use double-entry accounting) by Mulhall is the inclusion of "loans" of £1,060 million for 1882 in his list of wealth of Great Britain in the figure above.

Whereas a commercial or personal loan is an asset for the creditor (eg the bank making the loan) and the creditor would record it as a debit in its books of account, it is at the same time a liability for the debtor (eg the householder) and the debtor would record it (in the same amount) as a credit in their books of account.

Therefore, in a comprehensive summed national balance sheet, the accounting entries for any such commercial or personal loans that were intra-national would cancel each other out (because there would be equal numbers of debits and credits, in the same amounts) leaving nil value in the national balance sheet for such loans.

Therefore, any figure for "Loans" in the balance sheet of Great Britain could only consist of the government's outstanding loans to other nations, net of any outstanding loans other nations had made to Great Britain. It's not clear from Mulhall's text whether this is the case in his tables. However, the total loans of £1,060 million in figure 5 is inconsistent with Mulhall (1884) page 137, where he shows Great Britain's national debt as £763 million in 1882, as seen in the figure below.

Figure 6 – Debts of Great Britain

F.—WEALTH AND DEBT (GREAT BRITAIN).

Year.				Millions £.		Ratio of Debt.
				Wealth.	Debt.	
1702 .	.	.	.	490	13	2·66
1763 .	.	.	.	1,100	147	18·36
1797 .	.	.	.	1,800	413	22·94
1817 .	.	.	.	2,400	841	35·04
1837 .	.	.	.	3,900	788	20·21
1860 .	.	.	.	5,560	826	14·88
1870 .	.	.	.	7,080	801	11·31
1882 .	.	.	.	8,720	763	8·75

Where does the difference of £297 million (£1,060 million - £763 million, about 39% of the "loans" number, ie 3.5% of the total Great Britain assets) come from? Is this a total of intra-national loans, perhaps, which should have been netted to zero instead of being included in the balance sheet? 3.5% of the balance sheet, for this one item alone, is quite a significant "error" (if that's what it is).

This brief look at Mulhall's statistics illustrates the difficulties and challenges of using data without there being sufficient source referencing and methodology descriptions to support them.

Despite many of the above misgivings about data accuracy, it seems that Mulhall perplexed official statisticians, who he decried, derided and mocked (by use of sarcastic comments in his 1881 book) for being too concerned with precision and unwilling to use estimates. Mulhall used estimates extensively, which was his go-to method where there was uncertainty (not unlike the incomplete accounts methods of modern accountants). The following excerpt from an article Mulhall published in the American Statistical Association's Journal in 1890 gives a fascinating insight into the types of estimations he used to fill in some gaps in official figures. Without the use of such 'guesswork' it's unlikely we would have been given the aggregate numbers I've quoted extensively above and which will give a very useful picture of some very old World Balance Sheet precursors:

" ... A sixth [person] inquires: ' What are the annual earnings of the British nation?' And the official statist replies: 'These are matters beyond the reach of mortal ken, unknown even to experts such as we.' And I reply briefly as follows: 'The earnings are easily ascertained by summing up the following:

UNBALANCED WORLD: The asset stewardship shortfall

1. The rent of houses and lands, or rental valuation.

2. The value of food consumed in the year.

3. The value of cotton, woollen, linen, etc., goods consumed.

4. The cost of fuel, gas, and kerosene.

5. The amount paid for transport, say double the railway earnings.

6. The sums expended in national and local taxes.

7. Three per cent on the above gross sum, for learned professions.

8. The annual accumulation of wealth.

These make up 1,260 millions sterling.'

… A ninth [person] asks ' What is the wealth of the United Kingdom, France, and the United States?' The official statist replies as before: ' There are some things forbidden for man to weigh or estimate, and this is one.' And I answer: ' Public wealth consists of ten items, all of which can be measured to a nicety, except one, the value of public works. Land, for example, is worth thirty times the assessed animal rental valuation. Houses are worth eighteen times the rental. Furniture (according to insurance agents) is always worth half the value of the house. Cattle, railways, and shipping offer no difficulty. Merchandise may be taken at six months' imports and exports; and as for public buildings and works, we find churches cost £10,000 each, schools £1,000, and high-roads £500 per mile. The values thus summed up show:

United States	£13,600 millions sterling.
United Kingdom	£9,600 ditto
France	£9,100 ditto"

Mulhall did some updating and summarising of his work, as revealed by his 1896 publication "Industries and Wealth of Nations"

The following figure is the updated World Balance Sheet.

Figure 7 – Wealth of Nations in 1896 – from page 51 of Mulhall (1896)

Wealth.—The aggregate wealth of nations is almost 70 milliards sterling, or six times as much as the earnings. Real estate (that is lands and houses) represents $32\frac{1}{4}$, personal property $37\frac{1}{2}$, milliards; in other words, real estate forms 46 per cent., personal property 54 per cent., of the total. The principal items are shown approximately as follows :—

Millions £ Sterling.

	Land.	Cattle, &c.	Houses.	Rail-ways.	Merchan-dise.	Sundries.	Total.
U. Kingdom .	1,686	391	2,490	985	805	5,449	11,806
France . .	2,580	513	2,159	663	601	3,174	9,690
Germany .	1,977	531	1,755	555	677	2,557	8,052
Russia . .	2,113	597	1,019	349	515	1,832	6,425
Austria . .	1,473	324	719	371	367	1,258	4,512
Italy . .	1,180	219	503	184	223	851	3,160
Other States [1] .	2,803	543	1,189	392	666	2,102	7,695
Europe . .	13,812	3,118	9,834	3,499	3,854	17,223	51,340
United States	3,314	828	4,446	2,260	1,563	3,939	16,350
Brit. Colonies [2]	466	231	319	325	191	547	2,079
Total .	17,592	4,177	14,599	6,084	5,608	21,709	69,769

Source: Mulhall 1896 (NB: His term "milliards" is what we would call (UK) billions today)

By 1896, the total of assets in Mulhall's World Balance Sheet was £69.8 billion, having grown from £50.75 billion in 1882, a growth of some 37.5 % in 14 years.

That is an average compound annual growth rate of about 2.3 percent. We can glean from this that the annual rate of growth of the world balance sheet assets had slowed considerably in about two decades (from about 5% per year in the early 1880s to something less than 2.3% per year in the late 1890's).

Something else that was noteworthy about Mulhall (1896) was the inclusion of detailed tables about forests and forest products, something that was conspicuous by its absence in his earlier works.

Figure 8 – "World" Forestry Assets in Mulhall (1896) – in acres rather than £ sterling

The following table shows the actual forest area, the weight of timber cut yearly, and the possible yield :—

	Forest. Million Acres.	Cutting. Million Tons.	Cwt. per Acre.	Possible Yield. Million Tons.
Russia	498	130	5	374
Scandinavia . . .	64	18	6	48
Other States . . .	146	82	11	110
Europe . . .	708	230	7	532
United States . .	466	600	26	350
Canada . . .	218	48	4	164
Total .	1,392	878	12	1,046

Where afforestation is carefully attended to, the product (between firewood and timber) may reach 15 cwt. yearly per acre without diminishing the forest area. Thus Europe could yield more than double what the forests now produce. On the other hand the United States are rapidly consuming their forest capital, the actual felling of timber being 70 per cent. more than the normal growth ; hence it will be necessary in

He went on to suggest a conservation objective for US forests, as follows, for the time period 1896 to 1996:

> "… hence it will be necessary in the coming century to take measures to limit the destruction of [US] forests, and preserve a minimum of 200 million acres, that is, 1 acre per inhabitant of the probable [US] population one hundred years hence."

It seems that Mulhall was one of a growing number of people, even in 1896, who were advocating maintaining forests at a certain level, in what would now be called a capital maintenance approach concerning an important part of natural capital – the forests of the world.

Mulhall (1896) described both the forestry and fishing industries world-wide. However, from looking at the ways he described them, and the ways he provided financial data about their productive output, but in particular the way he did not publish the value of the _capital assets_ of forests and fish populations, it seems unlikely that he included asset values for either of them in his world balance sheets.

According to Wikipedia, before European settlement of the USA, its forest area was nearly 1 billion acres, and by 2016 it had declined to about 800 million acres. Although this is more than the 200 million acres Mulhall predicted would be needed to support an anticipated US population of 200 million people in 1996, the US population is about 330 million today (in 2020). The current forest cover of the USA therefore represents an amount of just over 2 acres per head of population, compared with the 1 acre per head of population Mulhall predicted would be an adequate level of forest capital asset in the current modern era. Given the amount of time that has passed since Mulhall did his work, and the immense changes that have happened in human history in those 124 years, his predictions seem to have been extraordinarily accurate.

As an aside, the extent of remaining forest cover in the USA is encouraging. It's a testament to the efforts of conservationists and legislators (who, for example, created large national parks such as Yellowstone).

However, it's disappointing to note that national and international accounting has not yet been put in place that would provide an essential element of ensuring that an adequate level of forest cover will exist in another 100 years' time. This is the natural capital that was missing from Mulhall's world balance sheets, and is still largely missing from national balance sheets today. Natural capital will need to feature strongly in any world balance sheets going forward, in order for these to be meaningful in the context of objectives for sustainable development and human progress.

I'll now take a short detour, to explore the trends in global forest cover over time. This will be one of the building blocks for a new world balance sheet, to fill in one of the most obvious gaps left by Mulhall.

How much forest cover has there been, globally, through history, by year, decade, century or era, what are the trends and what does this tell us about the future of this part of natural capital?

It might have been hard in Mulhall's time to get reliable data about the extent of forests and the trends in deforestation, and that might be one explanation for why he omitted forest assets altogether from his world balance sheets. But, today, it's not hard to find that data. This has been a hot topic for several decades. One example of a reliable source is the website "Our World in Data". The figure below is an example.

Figure 9 – Amounts of deforestation pre-1700 to 2010 - From Our World in Data

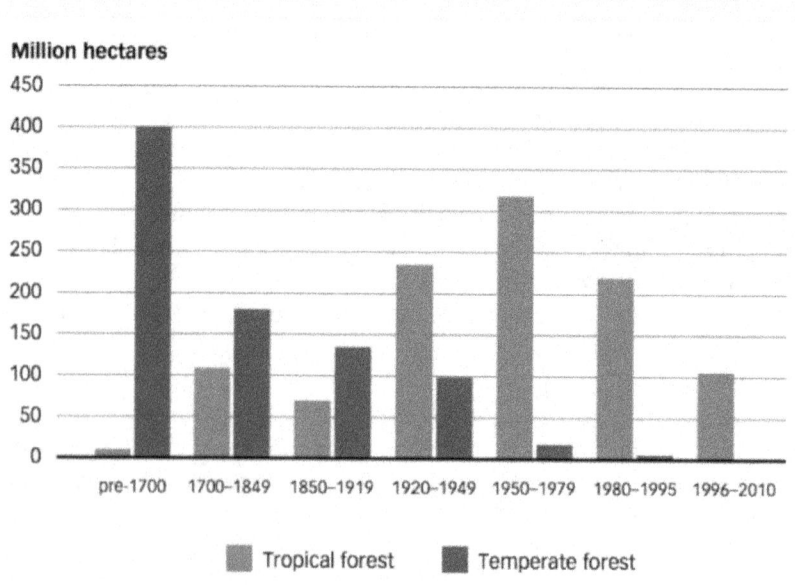

Estimated deforestation by type of forest and time period, pre-1700-2000 – FAO (2012)[5]

Original Source: FAO online

We can see a snapshot of recent forest cover by nation (as a percentage of the land of each nation) in the following figure, also reproduced from Our World in Data.

Figure 10

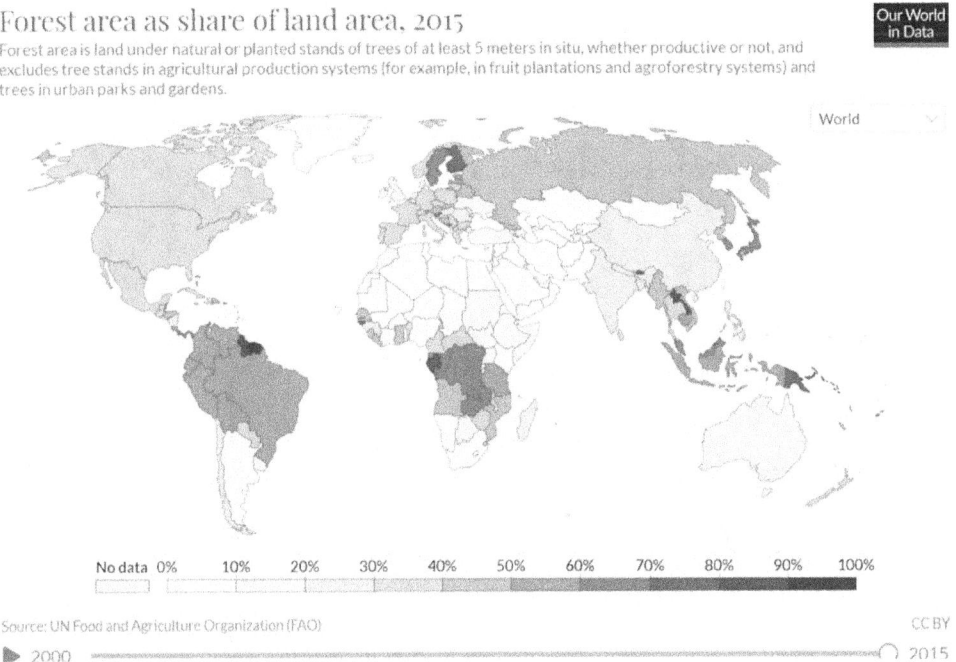

This is supported by a data spreadsheet (available from the same website) of forest cover as proportion of land area for each country in the world. We could compare this with land area data to get total hectares of forest cover, and compare this with the recent rates of deforestation.

However, the FAO has done some of this work already and the following figure is downloaded from their website.

Figure 11 – World - Area of tree cover 1992 to 2018

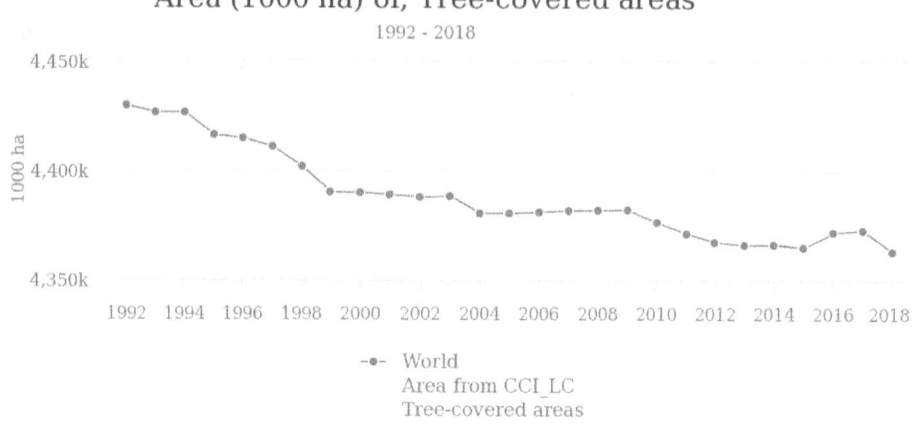

Area (1000 ha) of, Tree-covered areas
1992 - 2018

-•- World
Area from CCI_LC
Tree-covered areas

This figure tells us that worldwide tree cover in 2010 was about 4.37 billion hectares, and in 1996 it was about 4.43 billion hectares.

We can see from figure 11, therefore, that the worldwide area of tree cover fell by approximately 40 million hectares between 1996 and 2010.

Comparing this with figure 9, in which tropical forest deforestation was about 100 million hectares over the same timespan, we need an explanation for the difference.

A fairly obvious potential explanation would be if some of the tropical forest included in the deforestation numbers in figure 9 was actually converted into other types of tree cover (not classified as tropical forest) so it still counts towards the totals of tree cover in figure 11.

We can see from figure 9 (by adding all the bars together) that total deforestation recorded throughout human history was about 770 million hectares. Adding this back to the 2010 number for total tree cover (of 4.38 billion hectares, from figure 11), we arrive at a pre-historical level of tree cover of 5.15 billion hectares.

A summary of these data and what they are telling us – the meaning behind the numbers

Through these simple calculations carried out using the FAO data, we see that worldwide tree cover began before human history at 5.15 billion hectares and reduced by 0.77 billion hectares (ie about 15%) through the whole of human history to 2010. The rate of deforestation in modern times has averaged about 15 million hectares per year (1980 – 1995) which is about 0.29% of the pre-historical area, and even more recently it has averaged 7.5 million hectares per year (1996 – 2010) which is about 0.15% of pre-historical area.

If deforestation was to continue at its current rate, it would take only about 560 years to completely deforest the whole earth and leave no trees alive.

We can triangulate the statistics for tree cover by looking at the equivalent data at Our World in Data. On their website, they include data about global land use for food production. Their data, originally sourced from the UN FAO, gives a figure of 39 million square kilometres for forests in 2019, which is 3.9 billion hectares. This is not so very far from the 4.38 billion hectares of tree cover in 2010, allowing for some deforestation between 2010 and 2019.

It seems quite obvious that it is difficult to get a precise and accurate number for the amount of land with tree cover. However, we could give a broad sense of it if we say that it used to be about 5 billion hectares before human history began and is now about 20% less at 4 billion hectares.

If we were to draw up a world balance sheet for a pre-historical year, and a world balance sheet now (2020), we could include 5 billion hectares of tree cover (at an appropriate average value per hectare) in the first of these and 4 billion hectares (at an appropriate average value per hectare) in the other.

We could also, with some use of estimation, work out values for worldwide tree cover to add to Mulhall's world balance sheets of the late nineteenth century, to fill in some of the gaps in his work and provide amended versions of his balance sheets.

This short digression about forests has given just a glimpse of what's possible. With some information gathering, and some estimation, we can do this – we can create a world balance sheet which will be so much better, and tell us so much more, than Mulhall's balance sheets have done.

I'll come back to forests later in the book, to produce some actual numbers for inclusion in an actual world balance sheet. That balance sheet will include numbers to fill in other gaps as well.

In the meantime, I need to conclude this section by revisiting Mulhall's work and what has been gleaned from it, before moving on to discuss a much more recent world balance sheet compiled from very different sources in a very different era.

Conclusions about Mulhall's work

Despite the obvious deficiencies in his work, there's no doubt that Mulhall provided a rich set of data and infographics that tell us an immense amount about the overall story of growth in global economic activity over a timespan of about two hundred years including the early Industrial Revolution. There is less information about the impacts this had on the balance sheets of nations and of the whole world. Despite his valiant efforts to draw information together and present it to the world, we must treat it with a high degree of caution, and treat it as only representing broad estimates of an incomplete range of world-wide assets and liabilities. Of significant importance is the omission of natural and human capitals, and of large swathes of the earth's geography where much of the natural capital resides.

It's been over a hundred years since Mulhall published his major works. Although he omitted natural capital altogether from his world balance sheets, he made comments about the opportunities to maintain various types of natural assets at levels commensurate with supporting future generations (a hundred years into his future).

We've been very slow to build on his obvious suggestions. We're only now really beginning to act on some of these issues through the introduction of natural capital accounting into Systems of National Accounts in various parts of the world.

Is this a matter of "better late than never", or an indication of a tragic failure, on a massive scale, of our collective stewardship of the planet and its natural resources?

Conclusions from this chapter

Old sources such as Mulhall give us some general sense of trends at various snapshots in historical time. It shows us some of the tangible signs of the growth of produced capital (ie assets made by people) but very little about the depletion of natural capital that was associated with this.

There are a lot of caveats around accuracy and relevance of the data in the associated world balance sheets produced by Mulhall. Before placing any reliance on what they are telling us, we need to triangulate with other sources, and in particular look for more recent information which is likely to be far more accurate and reliable, because of modern data collection and analysis methods.

Another reason for looking at modern data is that they are likely to be maintained and improved going forward, which means they can be used in constructing accounting frameworks for future world balance sheets, whereas it would be problematic to try to do that with the older data sources.

Chapter 3

Modern forerunners / precursors – World Bank, Deutsch and derivations from Costanza et al (2011 and 2014)

"... wealth should be used as an indicator of sustainability to complement GDP, which measures only current income ... the comprehensive wealth approach provides a useful, indeed essential, lens for viewing a broad set of development concerns - the sustainability of development " *(World Bank, 2018)*

"We cannot manage what we do not measure. Therefore, we need to measure the world's capital." (Deutsch, 2020)

The World Bank "Changing Wealth of Nations 2018" report contains what is, in effect, a summary world balance sheet as follows (although it stops short of calling it that).

Figure 12 – World balance sheet from the World Bank (2018)

TABLE 2.2 Global Wealth, by Type of Asset, 1995 and 2014

	1995		2014	
	Billion US$	Percent	Billion US$	Percent
Produced capital	164,781	24	303,548	27
Natural capital	52,457	8	107,427	9
Forests and protected areas	14,515	2	18,290	2
Agricultural land	25,859	4	39,890	3
Energy resources (fossil fuels)	11,087	2	39,094	3
Metals and minerals	997	<1	10,154	1
Human capital	475,594	69	736,854	64
Net foreign assets	−2,890	<1	−4,581	<1
Total wealth	689,942	100	1,143,249	100

Source: World Bank calculations.
Note: Figures are in constant 2014 US dollars at market exchange rates.

In the commentary, the World Bank notes that a significant proportion of the assets comprise human capital, which is "... estimated as the net present value of the population's future labor earnings." They also say that, in their work, "Natural capital is measured as the discounted sum of the value of the rents generated over the lifetime of the asset." Discounting is explained more fully in chapter 9.

As a first step triangulation on the above data, compare the global total assets ("wealth") of USD 1,143 trillion in 2014 with the USD 1,497 trillion in the Deutsch 2018 world balance sheet (reviewed later in this chapter). Accounting for some growth between the two years, the numbers are not completely out of kilter.

What the World Bank (2018) says about the state of the 2014 world balance sheet

Their overall conclusions include:

> "... the wealth accounts also indicate areas of concern. Some low-income countries - especially in Sub-Saharan Africa - saw a decline in per capita wealth as rapid population growth outpaced investment. We also see that in 12 countries the percentage of people living in extreme poverty has jumped over the last decade. Looking at this disturbing trend through the lens of wealth accounting shows that the 'demographic dividend' from population growth can be realized only with rapid investment in infrastructure and education, and by managing the natural asset base sustainably in the long run."

The following excerpt from the report summarises their more detailed views on natural capital.

> "Natural capital increased its share from 8 percent to 9 percent, largely because of an increase in subsoil assets. Energy resources are the largest component of subsoil assets, but metal and mineral resources, starting at a low base, increased very rapidly. The value of renewable [natural capital] assets - agricultural land, forests, and protected areas - increased, but not fast enough to maintain the same share ... ([from] 6 percent [in 1995], down to 5 percent in 2014) ... getting rich is not about liquidating natural capital to build other assets ... Development is about more efficient use of natural capital, and its sustainable management in the case of renewable natural capital, bringing to bear other assets to increase productivity, together with the strong institutions and policies that make investment attractive."

This is largely a normative set of statements, especially in relation to sustainable management of natural capital, rather than being descriptive. World Bank includes various comments about practices, policies and approaches that they would like to see more of, and to some extent they assume that these will be put into place universally across the world in the near future. This is, in my view, an optimistic assessment of future direction. It's by no means clear that countries around the world will properly invest in, maintain and protect their natural capital.

Deutsch's work

Deutsch (2020) makes an ambitious step forward by publishing what is, as far as I'm aware, the first ever published World Balance Sheet worthy of using that title. It goes so much further than Mulhall did, or even the World Bank, and Deutsch spends most of his book talking through the methodology he has used as well as providing the numbers.

Deutsch sets out his own objectives for the world balance sheet:

> "Thus, why is a World Balance Sheet important?

> Firstly, in a real economy, global assets are the world's production factors that generate all economic outputs. What is the importance of these production factors and their relative contribution? Do we see changes, potentially declines? What does it take to promote them? Do we see structural changes that we need to address with structural answers?

> Secondly, from a political-economic perspective, the world's assets encompass everything around us – our house and the streets surrounding it, our car, the company we are working for, our children's school, and the work of our hands. Are all of these in good order? Are there issues to be politically addressed?"

He says relatively little about sustainability, and excludes much natural capital from his work, for reasons of practicality, although he does point out that the state of various natural assets he has excluded is of some concern, and he hints at the issue of depletion of natural capital:

> "Services not considered as standard are excluded due to a lack of specialized data and limited relevance. These nonstandard services include those related to tourism, renewable energy (e.g. wind, solar), and water supply ... Furthermore, even more complex ecological advantages of land cannot be measured yet. These potential advantages may include water and soil retention, cooling, carbon storage, and wind modification, which are not yet covered by SEEA-CF. More work of the international community is required to establish commercially viable measurements of ecological rents ... here is a visible tendency to forest depletion ...Fish stocks are overexploited ... The net results are negative rent streams ... the fishing rent stream and fishing values of the seas are negative ... Ecological services are in principle not included in our study. The World Bank also does not set up hypothetical value streams beyond fishing ... High increases of consumption are only possible due to divestments, particularly depletion of natural resources."

The main thing Deutsch brings to the table is a logical and well-reasoned methodology for compiling a world balance sheet.

The methodology comprises, in brief, taking the national balance sheets of all nations, and the balance sheets of all non-governmental entities (eg companies, banks, institutions, households etc), adding them together and cancelling some items as part of that consolidation process. The cancellation of items on consolidation is an accounting process to prevent double-counting or misleading overstatement of numbers. If this was not done for some types of assets and liabilities, the resulting balance sheet would show vastly overstated numbers and would be subject to significant manipulation by unscrupulous vested interests.

The technical device (and thought experiment) behind this consolidation process is to conceive of a new entity, that Deutsch calls "World Inc" that one can imagine acquiring all the assets and liabilities of all the nations, all the companies, all the households and all the other entities. This is what enables all the assets to be added up to provide numbers for all the assets in the world, and for a similar process for all the liabilities.

He cancels out all debts on consolidation. This is both an elegant and attractive device from the perspective of keeping resulting balance sheets simple. It is theoretically justifiable, from Deutsch's stated method, because the final entity in his thought exercise is both the lender and borrower in all the debts in the world, so it can simply cancel them all and be neither better off nor worse off as a result. From a sustainability and limits to growth perspective, it is attractive because interest-bearing debt is one of the key drivers of economic and throughput growth which has caused us to be in the position of planetary overshoot in which we currently find ourselves.

Deutsch is at pains to point out that he in no way proposes that such an entity as World Inc be created, or that it acquires all the assets and liabilities in this way. This is simply a logical way of thinking through how the process of consolidation could be undertaken, purely for the purposes of producing a world balance sheet in a way that is technically correct and justifiable as a thought experiment. This is a necessary suspension of disbelief in order to get to the end result. I follow this approach myself in compiling the Planetary CFO's world balance sheets (see later in this book). If we did not take this leap of imagination as part of the process, we would have to face a plethora of difficulties with the process of getting from actual reality of ownership of assets and liabilities in the real world to the end point of all the world's assets and liabilities being owned by one global entity (essentially on behalf of all of humanity).

As just one example of those difficulties, if interest-bearing debt is cancelled, it is not just the principal indebtedness that is cancelled (which prevents that principal being used for capital asset construction), but also the future stream of interest payments, and the liquidity that this provides to the lender (eg for capital asset repair, protection and maintenance). These losses of opportunity apply equally to natural capital assets as to other types of assets. I take the view that money / debt / liquidity is not inherently 'evil' as some of the most fundamental environmentalists / sustainabilitarians believe, but rather it is the use to which it is put that varies on a spectrum from angelic / philanthropic at one end to demonic / destructive at the other.

There is a danger here (in cancelling all debts) of 'throwing the baby out with the bathwater' and stifling our ability to perform a proper stewardship of the world's natural assets, which might be especially pertinent given their current state of damage, depletion and proximity to unsustainable thresholds in some instances. Return on (natural) capital might be a key performance indicator in the generations to come, and debt financing might be a valid instrument for optimising it. However, this is a somewhat moot point for the time being, as this book is primarily about the world balance sheet and I will avail myself of the benefits arising from the simplicity of the debt-cancellation decision made by Deutsch, which I carry forward into my methods for the Planetary CFO's world balance sheet. Sometimes, it's better to get a perspective on the world, and then if that perspective turns out to be attractive, work out how best to translate that into real-world change.

So, we have avoided such real-world difficulties, for the time being, by simply pointing out that the end-point is more important than the transition, for the purposes of arriving at a world balance sheet in the first instance. It will be for others (or ourselves in later works) to address how a process might be constructed that improves upon this leap of imagination and deals with any practicalities that arise.

Let's get started, then, with building on the work of those who have preceded us. The following figure is a summarised version of Deutsch's 2018 world balance sheet.

Figure 13 – Summary of the key numbers from Deutsch's world balance sheet 2018

Deutsch's World Balance Sheet 31 December 2018 (USD trillions)		
Assets		
Fixed Assets		
Property		
Land	132.09	
Subsoil Assets	51.91	
Subtotal Property		184.00
Plant		
Dwellings	119.84	
Other buildings	140.43	
Subtotal Plant		260.27
Equipment		
Commercial equipment	41.98	
Military equipment	8.74	
Subtotal Equipment		50.72
Intangible assets		
Goodwill	117.63	
Intellectual property	20.76	
Brand value, licences	5.60	
Subtotal intangible assets		143.99
Current assets		
Inventories		46.90
Cash and cash equivalents		1.64
Human Capital		809.94
Total assets		1,497.46
Total liabilities and equity		1,497.46

Deutsch has been specific about the data sources he has used. They include major respected and credible organisations such as the World Bank, IMF, UN, European Union, OECD, Systems of National Accounts, various NGOs and so on.

Deutsch's world balance sheet is clearly a much more comprehensive financial statement than Mulhall's. It's noteworthy that, wherever possible, Deutsch has used international accounting standards, to ensure consistency and transparency of methods.

He notes, however (about SNA):

> "... global data show gaps; that is, the SNA's fixed asset classes are not reported by many countries on a global level ... therefore, they are .. only part of .. the second-tier reporting level... these data, on which all major studies rely, face serious accuracy issues."

He goes on to describe how many of the asset values in SNA are not measured by direct stock-taking, but are instead calculated from other flow-based (throughput) measures. In particular, these calculation methods are highly sensitive to small changes in key parameters and assumptions.

Additionally, in relation to natural capital in particular, Deutsch points out:

> "... the World Bank observes that 'natural capital per person in high-income countries is [in SNA] three times that in low-income countries, $19,525 versus $6,421 in 2014, even though the share of natural capital in high-income OECD countries is only 3 percent.' (Lange, Wodon and Carey (2018) p. 9)."

This hints at the existence of large inconsistencies in how natural capital is being included in (and valued in), or omitted from, the SNA (System of National Accounts) for each country.

Despite the difficulties Deutsch himself notes in accounting for natural capital and ecosystem services (see also the excerpts further above from his book), within his values for Land, Deutsch includes USD 2.69 billion for forests (therefore forests represent only 0.18% of the total global assets, within the category of land which is itself only 8.8% of total assets). It seems intuitive that this must be a very significant under-valuation of natural capital, and this is something I'll return to later in this book.

By way of rough triangulation, how does Deutsch's total assets value of 1,497 USD trillion in 2018 compare with Mulhall's total assets value of £ 69.8 billion in 1896?

At today's currency exchange rate of about 1.3, Deutsch's 2018 total assets, expressed in sterling, are about £ 1,152 trillion.

This is a ratio of 16,504 between the 1896 total assets and the 2018 total assets.

This represents an average compound growth rate, in the 124 years since 1896, of about 8%.

How much of this is due to price inflation? According to Inflation.EU (with original data source being the UK Office for National Statistics) CPI inflation index numbers between 1957 and 2019 were a ratio of about 21 for those 62 years.

Extrapolating the same average inflation rate for another 62 years earlier than 1957 would give a ratio of about 42 for the effects of inflation between 1896 and 2019.

Therefore, on this estimate the nominal ratio of the balance sheet total assets between 1896 and 2018 (ie after adjusting for inflation) would be about 393. This would represent annual average nominal compound growth rate of 4.95%.

This seems to fall within a realistic range, given what we know about the historical picture of steady advancement and economic growth in certain types of capital assets since 1896, only punctuated by occasional crises or growth spurts, and given the fact that the 1896 Mulhall balance sheet was woefully incomplete and therefore understated.

However, before we get too carried away by this result about the average nominal growth rate, there are a number of factors that frustrate comparisons between the two balance sheets and throw significant doubt on the validity of this result. The 1896 balance sheet excluded large parts of the world, and almost all natural and human capital, goodwill and intellectual property. There were also significant doubts about the basic data accuracy and lack of transparency about the data collection and aggregation methodology of the 1896 balance sheet.

Let's move on from the general growth statistic, and look at other aspects of the Deutsch balance sheet, to see what it might tell us about what the situation is now regarding the assets of the world.

Many of the data problems that related to the Mulhall balance sheets, such as incomplete geographical coverage and lack of recorded methodology, have been dramatically improved upon in Deutsch's balance sheet. That's a good start in giving us confidence to draw some inferences from it.

However, despite the obvious improvements over Mulhall's efforts, some features of Deutsch's balance sheet nevertheless make it difficult to interpret what it is telling us from a sustainability perspective. I list these features here:

- He does not use distinct asset classes for the main types of capital, namely natural capital, produced capital, human capital and financial capital (although he does at least show human capital separately) – this is a deficiency in the International Accounting Standards he has used as a framework
- No trends over time are shown (because he has only produced one balance sheet so far, and no previous year comparatives are included)
- He makes little comment about the state of the assets and their ability to support humanity going forward in perpetuity, except to posit that assets are currently sufficient to support a 1.13% compound annual growth in aggregate human consumption in perpetuity (this is discussed more fully below)

Natural capital is known to be under threat and is being depleted, throwing doubts on the future sustainability of the human support systems that depend on it. See Helm (2015) and Helm (2019) for an extensive discussion on why this is so and what is being done in the UK to address it, for example through the work of the UK Natural Capital Committee up to 2020 and its successor organisation, the Office for Environmental Protection (OEP), from 2021 onwards.

Deutsch does comment about human consumption patterns, with a view to concluding on whether the assets in the balance sheet today are sufficient to provide for the global population's anticipated consumption into the future. He computes an average future consumption growth rate of 1.13% per year (forever), being the growth rate at which "consumption and total assets are balanced".

Deutsch describes the method he has used as being based on those set out in World Bank (2006), with some modifications by himself, the former of which he says has subsequently not been repeated by the Bank in later years. It is reached using two different methods for arriving at total assets, and then reconciling them. The first is the World Bank 'bottom-up method, which is essentially counting assets and giving them a value per counted unit (to arrive at a number for the asset side of the balance sheet). The second is to look at a "top down" method, reviewing human population trends and performing a net present value of all future consumption needs for all future forecast population numbers (from World Bank data as well). This is a method for arriving at the total for the liabilities or commitments side of the balance sheet.

World Bank described this methodology, and hints at some of its most obvious deficiencies, in 2006 as follows:

> "Total wealth, in line with economic theory, is estimated as the present value of future consumption. Produced capital stocks are derived from historical investment data using a perpetual inventory model (PIM). Natural resource stock values are based upon country-level data on physical stocks and estimates of natural resource rents based on world prices and local costs. Intangible capital, then, is measured as the difference between total wealth and the other produced and natural stocks. The estimates of natural wealth are limited by data - fish stocks and subsoil water are not measured in the estimates - while the environmental services that underpin human societies and economies are not measured explicitly."

Deutsch essentially uses both methods (which he describes as top-down and bottom-up), and notes that, as the World Bank has concluded, if there is no further addition to the balance sheet, there is a shortfall of assets to provide for those future human needs. The Word Bank therefore makes up an amount for the difference, to add an amount to the assets side of the balance sheet, describing it as "intangible assets" to make the balance sheet balance. Deutsch has used the same method, although he has highlighted the weaknesses inherent in this approach.

My interpretation is that, in using this method, the World Bank have created a tautology. They have assumed that both sides of the balance sheet must be in balance currently, on the basis that the world's assets currently provide the needs of the currently existing human population today (albeit sub-optimally, as evidenced by the extent of undernourishment of a significant number of people).

At first, the World Bank compares the total assets with the total liabilities, from the bottom-up approach and the conclusion is as follows (as described in Deutsch 2020):

"… the identified assets cannot support the world's known consumption as the shortfall accounts for approximately 78% of total wealth."

The World Bank goes on to assume that both sides of the balance sheet must be in balance currently, so there must be some other assets to add to the balance sheet (the balancing number). They infer that this must be the value of as-yet-unidentified "intangibles" such as human capital and intellectual property.

They justify their approach to consumption by reference to Hamilton and Hartwick (2005):

"A proof that the current value of wealth is equal to the net present value of consumption can be found in Hamilton and Hartwick 2005."

Going forward, Deutsch has estimated an annual compound growth rate for the human population's needs for consumption and then applied the same growth rate to the other side of the balance sheet (the assets). Both sides will then continue to be 'in balance', by definition rather than by independent estimation of each side of the balance sheet.

Is this perhaps drawing on Malthusian approaches – ie assuming that resources and the size of human populations are in lock-step in times of limited resources (eg through population collapses in times of scarcity of food)?

The World Bank's approach, as adapted by Deutsch, is, I fear, a very over-simplified way to tackle an assessment about whether the assets are sufficient to support the global human population in perpetuity. In particular, the above approach doesn't address two important issues:

1) Whether any such growth in consumption (and assets) is sustainable (eg in relation to the Limits to Growth agenda, and Kate Raworth's Doughnut Economics – eg see Raworth (2017))

2) Whether substitution of natural capital for other forms of capital will continue, resulting in insufficient natural capital to sustain the expected future human population, even if the aggregate value of all forms of capital in total continues to grow as population (and its need for consumption) grows

3) Whether there might be reasons why human population consumption and assets are growing (or being depleted) at different rates from each other, regionally and in aggregate, resulting in a widening "asset shortfall" without equivalent increases in "intangibles" to plug that gap, resulting in what I am calling a "stewardship shortfall" (the equivalent of a funding shortfall in a pension fund). This 'gap' might be currently bridged by drawing down on natural capital assets, essentially turning capital into income to meet the short-term human needs

The tool that the World Bank is (perhaps) using as a "get out of jail free" card is to assume that:

> "… investments in produced capital, human capital, and governance, combined with saving efforts aimed at offsetting the depletion of natural resources, can lead to future welfare increases in developing countries."

Within this statement is an assumption that natural capital will be maintained and enhanced going forward, which flies in the face of historical empirical evidence to the contrary, ie the vast amount of data and information showing that nations, and the world in aggregate, are not in fact maintaining natural capital in this way. The World Bank appears to be looking at the future through 'rose-tinted glasses'. I'll return to the topic of natural capital extensively later in the book.

Deutsch expresses some significant doubts about the validity and accuracy of the World Bank's approach. In chapter 4, I explore some of these deficiencies and try to address them within the Planetary CFO's world balance sheet.

I've already mentioned that Deutsch has stated that natural capital is being depleted. It's not clear whether he has included such effects in either his balance sheet values or his assessment of adequacy of total assets going forward. He has made it clear that quite a lot of "ecological services" are excluded altogether from his analyses, on the basis that the science that studies them (including ecological economics) is currently underdeveloped and that accountancy does not have robust methods to value and account for them. I think this is a significant omission and one which I attempt to address by using some conventional and some unconventional methods in the emergent subject of natural capital.

What's missing here is (among other things) a comparison of world balance sheets, prepared on consistent bases and with sufficient detail, over time, to see the extent to which capital asset substitutions and maintenance, enhancements and depletions are taking place, especially regarding natural capital. We will need to produce world balance sheets on a consistent basis for a number of years to come (perhaps even a few decades) to get a clearer view on some of these matters.

I've talked about different types of capital in this chapter, and it forms a key plank of the technical foundations for the next world balance sheet I'll show you, which is the Planetary CFO's (Planetary Chief Financial Officer's) world balance sheet, in chapter 4. For some people, those foundations will benefit from some further explanation. Chapter 5 deals with this. If you'd like to explore the fundamentals before the discussion of the balance sheet itself, you might want to take the next two chapters in reverse order – and read chapter 5 before chapter 4. On the other hand, if you are already well-versed in the fundamentals of accounting, then you might want to read on through chapter 4 next and skip chapter 5 altogether when you come to it.

Triangulating balance sheet values for natural capital from Santos et al (2001), Costanza et al (2014) and Spencer (2013)

Figure 14 - table of ecosystem services values produced by Santos et al:

Annual return values from environmental (ecosystem services) functions (1) and natural capital (2) of different ecosystems.

Ecosystems	(1) US$/ha/year	(2) US$/ha	References
Estuaries of the east coast of the USA	10,000	200,000	Gosselink et al., 1974
Charles River Basin, Massachusetts, USA	28,000	560,000	Thibodeau & Ostro, 1981
Atlantic *Spartina* sp. Marsh	3,600	72,000	Hair, 1988
Ecosystem complexes on Dutch Waden Sea	6,200	124,000	De Groot, 1990
Galapagos, Ecuador	120	2,400	De Groot, 1988
Ecological Station of Jataí, SP, Brazil	708	14,160	This study
Cananéia, SP, Brazil	395	7,900	*Grasso et al.*, 1995*

* Related only with average WTP value to preserve mangroves located at Cananéia, SP.

Some triangulation here might help us to get a handle on the 'rightsizing' of the overall numbers, per unit of natural capital and in total for the whole world.

Let's start with Santos et al who produced values of ecosystem services per hectare per year, for a range of types of natural settings in Brazil, and compared them with equivalent values, as per the figure above, in other regions of America and elsewhere. They translated this into a capital value for each unit of the relevant natural capital by multiplying by 20 (valuing those services as if they continue each year at the same level forever, discounted to the present time at a 5% discount rate).

It can be seen that these various elements of natural capital had capital values in a very wide range, from USD 2,400 per hectare for the Galapagos to USD 560,000 per hectare for the Charles River Basin in the USA. This at least provides some triangulation in terms of understanding the range of unit values of natural capital.

Costanza et al (2014) went further and looked at a global scale. They produced some numbers for global ecosystem services that can also be used as triangulation.

Although Costanza et al did not translate flow values into natural capital values, nor complete a whole balance sheet for the world, we can use their work as a cross-check on the value of natural capital included in world balance sheets that have been produced (eg by Deutsch in figure 13). This can be done by a derivation method typically used in investment circles, that relies on the project appraisal technique of discounted net present value. Discounting is explained more fully in chapter 9, within a discussion that arrives at the discount rate of 2% that I use in many parts of the Planetary CFO's world balance sheet.

All we need to do is take the flow value, assume the flow is maintained each year forever and then discount each of those future flows back to the valuation date. The net present value is the sum of all those discounted flow values and this represents an economic assessment of the value of the natural capital that produced all those flows, in the sense that a rational economic agent might be prepared to pay that value for the natural capital (if it was for sale) in order to secure all those future flows of ecosystem services from that natural capital.

Costanza et al (2014) calculated the annual global flow of ecosystem services in 2011 (in 2011 USD) at approximately 125 trillion USD.

According to Spencer (2013) "the value provided by the Earth to the global economy" was US$51 trillion in 2011 in 2011 prices. Spencer derived this number from data from the World Bank, Earth Policy Institute and Robert Costanza.

Clearly, there is a large range of possible values for annual flow of benefits nature provides. For prudence, let's take the smallest of these numbers – the one from Spencer (2013) - which is US$ 51 trillion, and see where it leads us.

Using my general discount rate of 2%, that translates into a discount factor in perpetuity of 1/0.02 (ie 50) and therefore a balance sheet value of for natural capital of 50 x 51 trillion USD ie US$ 2,550 trillion. If we did the same calculation for the Costanza data, the result would be even higher.

These values are clearly a lot higher than the US$ 184 trillion of value for "land and soil" in the Deutsch world balance sheet (figure 13).

It's not at all surprising that such valuations vary considerably, given that valuing natural capital and the beneficial flows derived from it is a new and emergent field of analysis. They are based on values calculated for ecosystem services which themselves are subject to much debate as to their relevance and meaningfulness.

For example, Anderson et al (2018) comment on this.

> "So, for me the key issue to debate is not whether monetary valuation is 'accurate', 'complete', or 'true', but rather 'under what conditions is monetary valuation useful?' Let me conclude with an example. The Costanza et al. [1997] global valuation exercise is a popular punchbag, even amongst economists—the general reaction was 'these numbers are largely nonsense' but often also 'wish we'd thought of doing this'. And that is actually a pretty sensible reaction, because while nobody considers their ecosystem service valuation 'right', the authors did largely achieve their aim of demonstrating that even a partial accounting of nature's gifts would show huge sums. But my main point is about their update [2014]. The 1997 estimate for the global value of ecosystem services was c.$46 trillion/year in 2007 $US. The 2014 study updated the unit values and took account of land use/land cover change from 1997 to 2011. The new estimate is c.$125 trillion/year, but this does not imply that things have improved - it derives from an increase in unit values, not physical services. Rising values are not always a good sign: unit values will increase when a good or service becomes scarcer, and the net impact depends on elasticities. A revaluation of the 1997 services using 2011 values would be c.$145 trillion/ year. So the repeated exercise showed the loss of eco-services from 1997 to 2011 due to land use change could be estimated at about $20 trillion/year. A meaningless number, or a powerful way of combining and communicating the combined impacts of a wide range of degradations that might otherwise be difficult to grasp and compare with other priorities?"

I'll return to the subject of valuing natural capital later in the book, as this is such an important topic and a simple comparison of the above examples shows very graphically how different authors can easily come up with very different answers. In chapter 7, I set out a theory of value for natural capital, in an attempt to help describe how methods differ and to provide a framework around which appropriate values can be derived for particular purposes for the world balance sheet.

Chapter 4

Mind the gap! - The Planetary CFO's World Balance Sheet

*"We define **planetary stewardship** as the active shaping of trajectories of change on the planet, that integrates across scales from local to global, to enhance the combined sustainability of human well-being and the **planet's** ecosystems and non-living resources."*

(NCBI definition of planetary stewardship, 2012)

Chapter summary

- The Planetary CFO (as described in Calver (2020b) creates a World Balance Sheet
- Addressing the shortcomings of previous world balance sheets, while building on their foundations
- Minding the gap - how to address the "assets shortfall" issue – for example is it goodwill, intellectual capital or negative equity?
- Showing and discussing the Planetary CFO's world balance sheet and what it tells us
- Debunking decoupling as a solution to sustainability challenges

OK, let's cut to the chase.

The Planetary CFOs World Balance Sheet broadly takes the approach of the World Bank, as adapted, enhanced and updated by Deutsch, but addresses some important weaknesses by making the following amendments to the method:

- Separating out the main types of capital, so that the sufficiency of each can be assessed independently, including the state and adequacy of natural capital (while recognising this is inconsistent with existing international accounting standards)

- For reasons of prudence, restating human capital and some other types of intangibles in the balance sheet, for example by setting new provisions against them to reflect the propensity for humanity to mis-manage them (this builds on the precautionary principle)

- Treating the shortfall in assets (the balancing number) as a deduction from equity rather than an addition to assets – and dealing with the question "what happens if there is negative equity?"

- Considering rebasing or adjusting some asset valuations (retrospectively) in order to reflect the true state of those assets, and forecasting their ability to support the human population going forward

- Updating as many of the numbers as possible to represent a 2020 stock-take and snapshot, based on what we currently know about the state of the world, using reasoned estimates where accurate bottom-up data is not available

Here, I'd like to describe the third bullet above (the asset shortfall) rather more technically for a moment (for those of you who are so minded). The Planetary CFO takes an approach similar to that of accounting for "goodwill", but with immediate writing off of the asset shortfall to income and expenditure, ie without an option to depreciate it over time.

In the methodology outlined in Deutsch (2020) the process of creating the world balance sheet includes a step where all the world's assets are (ultimately) acquired by a fictional entity called World Inc.

When an acquisition of one company by another happens, if the amount paid by the acquiring company is more than the book value of the net assets being acquired, the difference presents an issue. This is because when the acquiring company in that scenario puts the relevant entries into its balance sheet to reflect the acquisition, the cash outflow is recorded (a credit), the net assets acquired are recorded (a net debit) but, as just mentioned, there is a difference between these two amounts – the net assets were less than the cash - so if no further entries are recorded, the balance sheet would be out of balance by the amount of that difference. For a long time, accountants argued about how to resolve this. Some people wrote the difference off to income and expenditure immediately, while others tried to justify putting a value of "something" as a new asset in the balance sheet, carried forward there from one year to the next.

Eventually, a solution was to create a new accounting concept of "goodwill". This solution put that difference into the balance sheet as an additional new asset called goodwill. Essentially there was no more solid basis for its existence, or its amount, than to make the balance sheet balance (which it has to, in order to maintain double entry accounting) and to explain it away as some form of 'economic value generating thing' that the company now had as a result of the acquisition and which it didn't have before the acquisition. To salve the consciences of any accountants who objected to this accounting treatment, some rules were set up to ensure that the goodwill would be depreciated (written off to the income and expenditure statement) over a reasonable timespan, usually no more than 20 years. Later, the requirement to depreciate the goodwill was dropped – it became optional to do so rather than compulsory.

As an example of how the debate in accountancy circles about how to account for goodwill still rumbles on, the following is from Fuller (2018):

> "In the good old/bad old days, goodwill – the difference between net assets, or equity, and the purchase price – was written off … On the plus side, an investor in the acquiring company did not have to worry about goodwill turning to sand through their fingers. The disadvantage was that this flattered return on equity. So, Lloyds Bank's acquisition spree under the late Brian Pitman looked great – until cannier analysts added back goodwill.

> Then we tried amortising all goodwill. This was particularly amusing during the TMT (technology, media and telecoms) bubble, which peaked at the turn of the millennium when Vodafone made its biggest acquisition – of Mannesmann for more than £100bn. Weighed down by an £11bn amortisation charge and other acquisition related costs, Vodafone reported what was then the biggest pre-tax loss in UK corporate history: £13.5bn. The company was dismissive of the accounting losses, and many observers had some sympathy."

Now, here is the 2018 world balance sheet the Planetary CFO has come up with, as an initial starter-for-ten proforma, prepared using some of the above technical enhancements, but before doing any asset revaluations. This is therefore a stepping stone towards a better balance sheet, but it's not yet the finished article.

Figure 15 – The Planetary CFO's Proforma World Balance Sheet 2018

Planetary CFO's World Balance Sheet 2018 (USD trillions) unrevalued		
Fixed Assets		
Property		
Renewable NC (Land)		
Cropland	26.45	
Pasture land	16.06	
Forest	2.69	
Barren/wild land	1.00	
Urban land	85.89	
Oceans	0.00	
Subtotal renewable NC		132.09
Non-renewable NC (eg Subsoil non-living)		51.91
Subtotal Property		184.00
Plant		
Dwellings		119.84
Other buildings		140.43
Subtotal Plant		260.27
Equipment		
Commercial equipment		41.98
Military equipment		8.74
Subtotal Equipment		50.72
Intangible assets		
Goodwill		117.63
Intellectual property		20.76
Brand value, licences		5.60
Subtotal intangible assets		143.99
Current assets		
Inventories		46.90
Cash and cash equivalents		1.64
Human Capital	809.94	
Human Capital destructiveness provision	-809.94	
net Human Capital		0.00
Total assets		687.52
Liabilities		
Human welfare commitment	1,497.46	
Unfunded human welfare commitment	-809.94	
Equity of humankind		687.52
Total liabilities and equity		687.52

A Brief explanation of the methodology used for the Planetary CFO's World Balance Sheet

The starting point for the construction of the Planetary CFO's World Balance Sheet in the figure above was the 2018 world balance sheet published in Deutsch (2020). Let's assume, for the time being, that the number Deutsch uses for human consumption in perpetuity is still valid. We can include this as "Human welfare commitment", ie this is the level of human consumption, in perpetuity, discounted back to 2018, so that if we have enough assets summing to this total, we could say that the balance sheet was "sustainable". I'll return to the human welfare commitment later on, to consider how valid the number actually is, given that it uses certain assumptions about, for example, compound annual growth of consumption and assets, forever. Discounting is explained more fully in chapter 9.

The following adjustments were then made to the other numbers in the Deutsch balance sheet:

1) Created a provision against the human capital asset, to reduce its value, to reflect the fact that humanity has clearly shown itself to have massive destructive capabilities, which it has used to create pollution, cause climate change and significantly reduce both the quantity and quality of natural capital. As a starting point, the provision is equal and opposite to the asset value of human capital, so that the net effect of the two entries added together is to cancel human capital out in the final adjusted balance sheet

2) Reclassified and split out "Property" into a relevant amount of detail, to separately show natural capital – and show separately both renewable natural capital and non-renewable natural capital. A simplifying assumption is that we can describe all renewable natural capital as "land" (with a particular sub-category being "oceans"). Where the renewable natural capital comprises entire ecosystems, they are associated with either a geographic area of land or an ocean, and are included in the relevant category in that way.

3) Split out the total liabilities and equity into more detailed categories, to include not just human equity but also a human welfare commitment (as per Kate Raworth's doughnut of the safe and just operating space for humanity). If the commitment to provide for the consumption of humanity in perpetuity at a basic acceptable level is larger than the human equity, then the unfunded element will show as a negative amount in the total liabilities section (ie the equivalent of negative equity, or a deduction from equity – there is more than one way of showing this)

This enables us to arrive at a world balance sheet that has used essentially the same numbers as the Deutsch world balance sheet, but with some technical changes that consolidate, adjust and present them in a way that draws out the relationships between the assets, the liabilities and the commitments from a sustainability perspective, and which takes a much more prudent approach to the subject of human capital.

The bottom line on this world balance sheet is that the stewardship shortfall, amounting to nearly USD 810 trillion, is finally revealed and given a monetary value.

This is a very different conclusion from that of Deutsch, who concluded that the assets matched the future of all human consumption at a certain level of compound growth.

We're not done, though, because we have not yet fully addressed the important topic of natural capital and its proper contribution to human survival.

***

The next step is to critically appraise and re-evaluate the natural capital and see what changes or adjustments we need to make to the numbers in the proforma world balance sheet to reflect this.

The purpose of this step is to uplift the asset value for various categories of renewable and non-renewable natural capital, to reflect the fact that the Deutsch balance sheet (as he admits) undervalues natural capital and, indeed, leaves a lot of natural capital out altogether.

Revaluing various elements of natural capital

The three main categories of natural capital that need to be revalued are oceans, forests and agricultural lands (comprising cropland and pastureland). I'll take each of these in turn and provide a rationale and some asset uplift or reduction numbers.

To help in a number of calculations which will be relied upon, the total land expressed in percentages, millions of hectares and millions of square kilometres are approximately as follows (derived from Our World in Data, 2019):

	Percent of land	million hectares	million sq kms
Forest	26.3	3,900	39.0
Pasture	27.3	4,000	40.0
Cropland	8.2	1,100	11.0
Barren/wild/glacier	37.5	5,750	57.5
Urban	0.7	150	1.5
Total	100.0	14,900	149.0
Ocean surface area		36,100	361.0
Total surface of the Earth		51,000	510.0

The above table agrees in total land area with a total quoted by Deutsch (2020), on his page 57. However, it differs considerably from some detailed numbers for the breakdown of FAO data on the same page of his book. The biggest differences are in the "Barren etc" category, where the FAO data suggests 33.2 million square kilometres, whereas the table above shows 57.5 million for this category, and in the "Pastureland" category, where the FAO data suggests 30.6 million square kilometres, whereas the table above shows 40 million. In both these categories, the FAO data is well short of the Our World in Data numbers. In another important category, "Forest", however, the difference is the other way round, with FAO suggesting 49.0 million square kilometres, whereas Our World in Data suggests 39.0 million. There are such large differences between these two sources, it's difficult to know straight away how to proceed. However, as Deutsch points out, "FAO and MODIS … cannot track 100% of the world's land." As a result, the FAO/MODIS data Deutsch was referring to only analyse about 85% of the world's land.

Given that our approach fundamentally attempts to attribute a value to *all* natural capital, by associating it with areas of land, it seems sensible at this point to use the numbers for land area from Our World in Data, to ensure that we are at least representing all the land surface and not missing any out in our calculations. So, this is what we'll do.

Before diving in and undertaking the revaluations, I'll set out a number of items that will be used again and again in the calculations. They are therefore important and are worthy of special attention at this point. This will serve a number of purposes.

Firstly, it means there is a place in the book where these items can be found easily, for example when they come up in calculations later in the book and you wonder where they came from or how they were derived.

Secondly, it will enable you as a reader, and me as the author, to cross-check and calibrate to some extent, and what I mean by that is that it will be easier to assess whether the methods used to arrive at a particular value, for example a unit value per hectare of a particular type of land, are "consistent" with methods used to arrive at unit values for other types of assets.

Finally, it serves to remind us all that the world we live in can be described in many different ways, even when taking an essentially scientific approach to measurement. The ways we choose to do the calculations and the variables we choose to deploy, can have an immense impact on the conclusions we reach. It's therefore extremely important to set out, and critically examine, some of the things that could otherwise pass as invisible assumptions. By making these things visible, other people (if such is their inclination) can unpick them, pore over them, pull them apart and rebuild them, to satisfy themselves about the validity and applicability (or otherwise) of the methods and variables used. This way, the scientific method improves the results over time.

Some key variables used in the calculations are as follows (all in global aggregate averages unless otherwise stated):

Table 1

Table of variables (2018)

(for derivations, see text below table)

"Carbon sink" value of oceans	USD 1,000 per tonne of carbon absorbed
Economic value of harvested fish	USD 1,000 per tonne of fish harvested
Value per hectare – forests (carbon sink method)	USD 1,000 per tonne of carbon absorbed
Value per hectare – cropland	USD 19,300 (Deutsch, page 60)
Value per hectare – pasture	USD 5,245 (Deutsch, page 61)

***

We have derived the carbon sink value per tonne of carbon as follows.

Archer et al (2020), for example, give us USD 100,000 per tonne, which they describe as follows:

> "… the ultimate cost of carbon is a first approximation of our potential culpability to future generations for our fossil energy use, expressed in units that are relevant to us."

This, however, seems like an extreme "outlier".

There are much more modest suggestions for a carbon price. Another example is a more moderate carbon price of USD 97 (£75) per tonne, as per the Climate Commission (2020). Another example is a range of up to US$ 443, in Raihan et al (2019), sourced from Abenezer et al (2014), with the particular figure of US$ 443 originally from Manley et al (2005). Another example is Burke et al (2019):

- "A shadow price consistent with a net-zero target would start at £50 per tonne of carbon dioxide (tCO2) (with a range of £40–100) in 2020.
- Complete decarbonisation will require the use of negative emissions technology, which, at the scale required, could cost in the order of £160 (£125–300) per tCO2 in 2050. The shadow carbon price should rise steadily towards this level."

From Burke (2019):

"… an international expert commission led by Joseph Stiglitz and Nicholas Stern recommended a global carbon price of US$40–80 (£30–60)/tCO2 by 2020 and US$50–100 (£38–76)/tCO2 by 2030 (Carbon Pricing Leadership Council, 2017)."

From Manley et al (2005):

"Pautsch et al. (2001) estimated the effects of a variety of subsidy schemes on the adoption of conservation tillage, demonstrating that a subsidy could lead to the sequestration of more than 2 Mt C [Carbon] yearly for a period of many years in Iowa alone. However, in their model, this target could be achieved only at a cost of $550 per tonne of carbon (tC), and then using only the most efficient or carefully discriminating policy. If Carbon uptake is purchased using less efficient policies (e.g., paying the same price for all land used to sequester carbon), the minimum cost rises to over $700 per tC."

Many of these 'medium-range' prices for carbon are arrived at as "a robust but politically feasible approach to carbon pricing" (to quote Burke et al, 2019). They reflect political realities, the main one being that if very high carbon prices were to be set, industry and corporate lobbies would object strongly and the public would be so unhappy with the impacts on the prices of many household goods and services that any government would soon be voted out of power. These prices also usually exclude "embedded carbon emissions" in their calculations. Even if they include some element of carbon offsetting to reflect this, there are some serious concerns about offsetting (eg lack of confidence in its additionality, concerns about leakage etc).

Most of the prices in that middle range are set in order to achieve short to medium term policy objectives, for example net zero carbon in the country setting them by 2050. One major difficulty with the approaches underlying most of them is that they are calculated on a marginal basis.

I'll explain this in a bit more detail, as it's quite a fundamental deficiency when taken in the context of potential thresholds and tipping points for natural systems. Take the example of carbon sequestration by reforestation / aforestation (which could also apply, with some amendments, to other methods of capturing the carbon). One could start by comparing the cost of planting each tree (which is very small – a few USD) and compare that to the damage caused by a tonne of carbon that would occur if that carbon was not sequestered by the tree (representing, therefore, the benefit derived from planting the tree). The difference is usually in the range of a few dollars to USD 100, as we have seen from the examples already quoted. This calculation also applies the other way round – ie to calculate the economic cost of chopping down an existing tree (being the amount of economic benefit from the extracted wood minus the damage caused by the carbon no longer sequestered by the tree).

However, both of these are marginal cost and marginal utility calculations. There are difficulties with this approach. This arises from the fact we are nearing some of nature's thresholds and tipping points. From Helm (2020):

> "It is not just the cost-benefit comparison of what the land is used for now with the alternatives, but it is also the benefits that natural capital yields *for ever*, provided it is not driven to such a low level that it cannot replicate itself going forward ... Eliminating a species is *for ever*, and we do not know [the full extent of] all its future potential benefits. The permanent loss of a natural asset is a much greater risk to take than merely the loss today."

As Helm has pointed out in recent public talks, the marginal cost and marginal benefit calculation prevalent in many carbon price discussions is only valid when it is OK to assume an inexhaustible supply of existing trees, and an infinite capacity of the atmosphere to absorb carbon, neither of which is actually the case. When the level of exploitation of forests nears a sustainability threshold (which might well be the case today), the cost of the damage to ecosystems (and therefore natural capital) would be much higher – orders of magnitude higher – because the loss of entire forests and ecosystems could have huge consequences, and might not be capable of reversal through reforestation by simply planting a few trees. Indeed, it might not be possible at all, for example, if significant numbers of species of trees and animals have been made extinct in the process of deforestation, and/or the soils and climate have been degraded to the point where new forest growth is no longer viable at scale. That near-threshold example might help explain and support a valuation at the upper end of the range, ie of the order of USD 100,000 per tonne.

This can be illustrated with S-shaped supply and demand curves instead of classic straight supply and demand lines in economics.

The classical supply-demand curves are often drawn to look like a criss-cross of a straight supply curve and a straight demand curve, as in this example from Beheshti (2018):

Figure 16

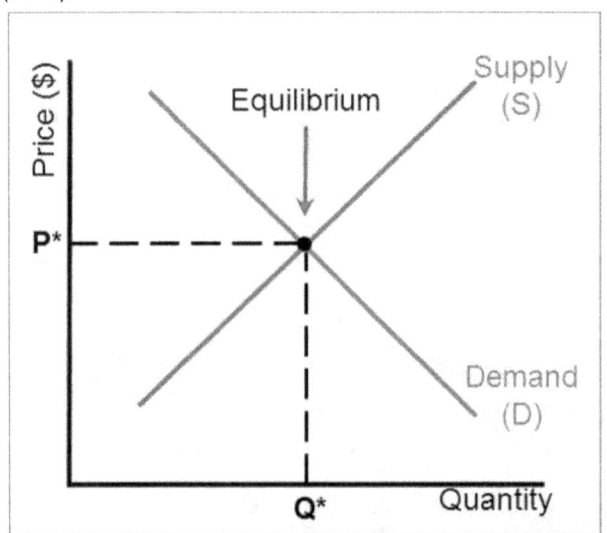

The result is that the market price is P* and the quantity of product sold is Q*, assuming a 'perfect market'.

However, the straightness of those lines assumes raw materials are in inexhaustible supply, and therefore any increases in demand (eg through consumerism) can be satisfied by increasing supply, at the same cost per unit (at constant marginal cost, to use the technical economics terminology) and this can be done by increasing the capacity of the supply chain all the way back to the extractive industry sector that supplies the raw materials.

Most of the classical economists explained that this result was only valid for certain ranges of values for quantities and prices of supply and demand (which could be described mathematically as "relevant ranges"). Beyond the relevant ranges, even the classical economists told us that rates of resource usage might approach sustainability limits (although they would probably have used terms like resource extraction limits rather than using the term sustainability). As volumes of supply approach those limits, they would become more expensive to extract (eg because they become rarer, they might only be available in more distant places and in forms that are more difficult to deal with, to extract and to use as materials).

When materials, in those circumstances, become more difficult (and expensive) to extract, the supply curves are no longer straight, but start to bend, to reflect the fact that every additional unit of resource extracted costs more than the previous one did. Similarly, when considering a much wider range of values for price, the demand curves bend in various ways. The aggregate supply and demand curves now look more like the following example, from Mechanical Markets (2017):

Figure 17

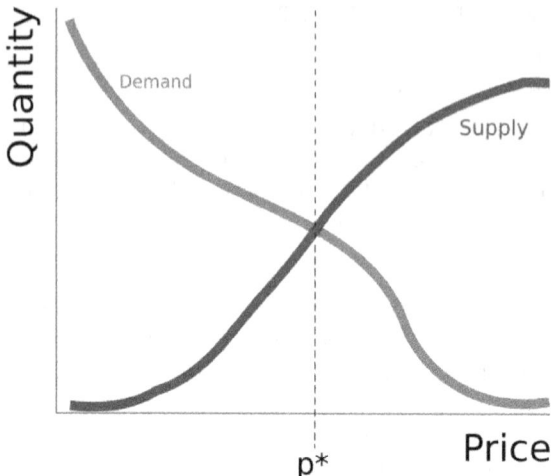

This effect on the supply and demand curves can be seen in some very early economists' drawings, in fact, right back to some of the very first known supply and demand curves. The first time that the idea (of supply and demand) was presented *graphically* came from Fleeming Jenkin. The following famous graph appeared in Grant (1870):

Figure 18

called the *demand curve.*

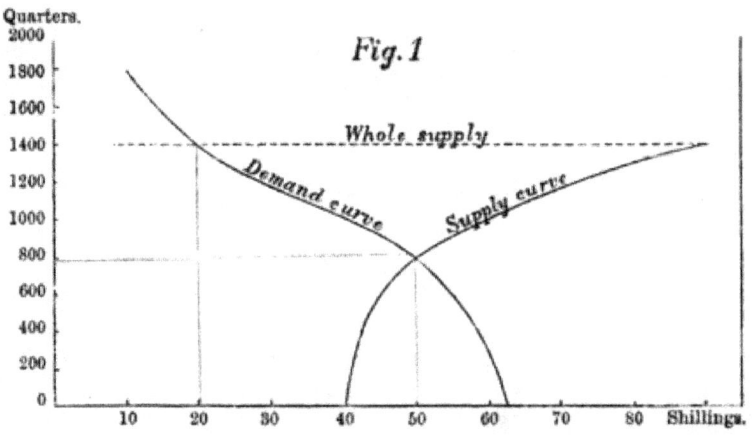

Fig. 1.—First Law of Supply and Demand.
Whole supply for sale at any price, 1400 quarters of wheat.
Price at which whole supply would be sold, 90s.
Price at which whole supply would be bought, 20s.
Market price, 50s.
Price below which no sale could take place, 40s.
Price above which no sale could take place, 62s.
Quantity which will be sold, 800 quarters.

Fig. 1 shows a pair of imaginary demand and supply curves for corn. At 60s. per quarter, the supply is 1000 quarters ; at 55s. the supply is 900 quarters; at 50s. only 800 quarters; at 45s. only 600 quarters; at 40s. the supply is nil.

At 62s. the demand is nil ; at 55s. only 600 quarters ; at

Jenkin wrote in Grant (1870), by way of introduction:

"Supply at a price denotes the quantity which at a given price holders would be then and there willing to sell. Supply at a price is also mensurable. Demand at a price denotes the quantity which then and there buyers would purchase at that price. The supply at a price and the demand at a price in any given market will probably vary with the price they may be said to be functions of the price."

"Let a curve be drawn the abscissae of which represent prices and the ordinates the supplies at each price. This curve will be called the supply curve. A similar curve constructed with the demand at each price as ordinates will be called the demand curve."

Although most classical economists understood this consequence of the shape of the supply and demand curves at volumes outside the normal 'relevant range', most *neo-classical* economists ignored this and assumed we were still operating within the relevant ranges mentioned above for straight-line supply and demand curves, ie nowhere close to ecological limits. That view leads to over-exploitation of natural resources, often beyond sustainability limits.

If, in contrast, as well as assuming a perfect market, we also assume that all externalities are included effectively in the price (eg through carbon taxation and other measures) then the closer the volume of aggregate supply gets to ecological (sustainability) limits, the more the supply curve will bend. There comes a point at which no additional unit of the resource can be supplied, at any price, because the cost of the externality included in the supply price would be so high as to prohibit it completely. That, after all, would be the policy objective of pricing in the externalities, so we have to assume that the policy is designed effectively and is implemented well.

With externalities properly built into pricing (eg with carbon taxes on polluters), the aggregate supply and demand curves would look like the following.

Figure 19 (source – the author)

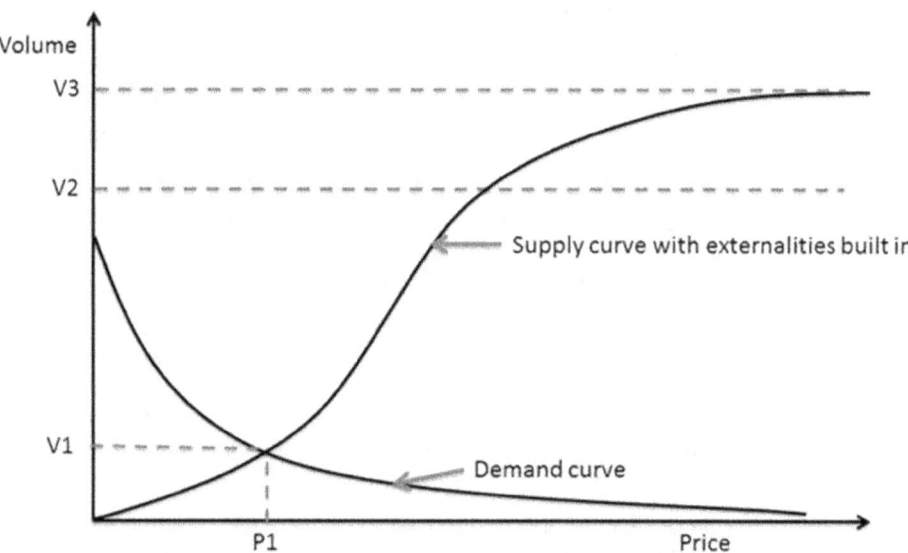

P1 and V1 are market equilibrium price and volume
V2 is volume at which (reversible) bio-capacity impacts would start to occur
V3 is volume at which bio-capacity would be irreparably damaged

It can easily be seen from the above discussion that when we get close to sustainability thresholds, the price of carbon will be orders of magnitude different from currently discussed "politically acceptable" and pragmatic prices such as those in the middle range of about USD 100 per tonne.

In order to proceed, however, and given that the range between the two outlying figures discussed above (USD 100,000 and USD 97) is so wide, I'm inclined to use one somewhere between them, at, say, USD 1,000 per tonne. This seems both challenging (when most real-world carbon prices have been under USD 100) and at the same time only one order of magnitude different from real-world prices, so not an impossible stretch of the imagination by any means.

The gross economic value per tonne of fish is assumed to be similar to the landed price of the fish. The UK Sea Fisheries Report 2017 gives a value of £980 million to a total landed catch of 724,000 tonnes, from which the unit value is seen to be £1,350 per tonne, ie about USD 1,750 per tonne.

This is the value of fishing by UK registered fishing craft, however, and these fish are destined generally for affluent markets where the economic value will be highest. If we factor in that most of the world's fish are consumed in much less affluent markets, and if we deduct an estimate for the costs of fishing and processing the fish, then a global aggregate estimate of USD 1,000 per tonne seems more reasonable.

It's worth reflecting on these two numbers for just a minute or two to gain some perspective.

For every tonne of fish we take out of the oceans, we derive about USD 1,000 of net economic value after the direct economic costs involved in the food supply chain. And for every tonne of carbon the ocean absorbs we derive about the same amount of economic value (because that carbon is not then going into the atmosphere where it would contribute to global warming). In effect, the ocean is protecting us from USD 1,000 of damage by absorbing that tonne of carbon for us. Each of these activities provides about the same benefit per unit (tonne).

But how many units are we talking about each year for each type of activity?

According to Our World in Data, global seafood production is about 155 million tonnes annually. As we found for the data on land cover, Our World in Data shows much larger numbers than the UN FAO. The FAO gives the total worldwide catch from marine fisheries as about 80 million tonnes per year (see page 111 of the UK Sea Fisheries Report 2017). However, this is only a part of the fish harvested – a significant, and increasing, part of the harvest is from aquaculture and inland fisheries. FAO (2011) indicates these other sources of fish produce about the same quantities of fish as the marine fisheries do.

As with the data on land coverage, we use the numbers from Our World in Data, as this is likely to be more complete, and more up to date, than the data from the FAO.

The American Meteorological Society's 'State of the Climate in 2017' report tells us that, in 2017, the ocean absorbed a net 2.6 billion (2,600 million) tonnes of carbon from human activities.

This tells us that the scale of these two activities is very different. Carbon sink activity is approaching 17 times bigger (in quantity terms) than fishing. Because the value per unit is similar, this means that the economic benefit of the oceans as a carbon sink is about 17 times their benefit as a source of harvested fish.

This does not imply that we should focus all efforts on the carbon sink problem and ignore the unsustainability of fisheries management altogether. But it does flavour discussions about relative priorities and the proportions of efforts and resources that should be put into each, if there are limited resources and choices to be made.

***

Now for the revaluation calculations, for each of the main types of natural capital assets in the balance sheet.

1) Oceans

The value of ocean ecosystems (eg fish relied upon to feed billions of people and carbon absorption which provides a dampening effect on climate change) are not given a value in Deutsch's balance sheet. However, this is not for the same reason that ecosystem services are excluded from his values for forest, cropland and pastureland. As with those other types of natural capital, he draws on calculations of direct economic net present values (ie economic rents) for oceans. However, because of widescale overfishing, he concludes that the economic rents of fishing are currently **negative in aggregate**. This implies that oceans should be valued at less than zero in the world balance sheet, ie as a liability instead of an asset, purely on economic value terms.

The theory behind this requires a little explanation, as fisheries management has some complexities, both scientifically and economically.

An important enabler for such an approach is the concept of the Maximum Sustainable Yield ("MSY"). MSY is essentially a theory, worked out mathematically and applied in the farming and fishing industries. It calculates a level of aggregate yield, for a farming or fishing season, that is the largest yield that can be extracted as harvest without forcing the population or stock of the natural 'product' to decline dangerously towards thresholds to unsustainability and its collapse within the relevant ecosystem. Usually, the level of fishing ("level of effort") associated with MSY is well below the threshold to unsustainability and collapse.

The figure below (World Bank's figure 10A.1 from World Bank, 2018) shows the level of fishing effort at which the economic rents are positive, and those at which it is negative, and where these are in relation to the fishing effort associated with MSY.

Figure 20

FIGURE 10A.1 Catch, Fishing Effort, and Rents

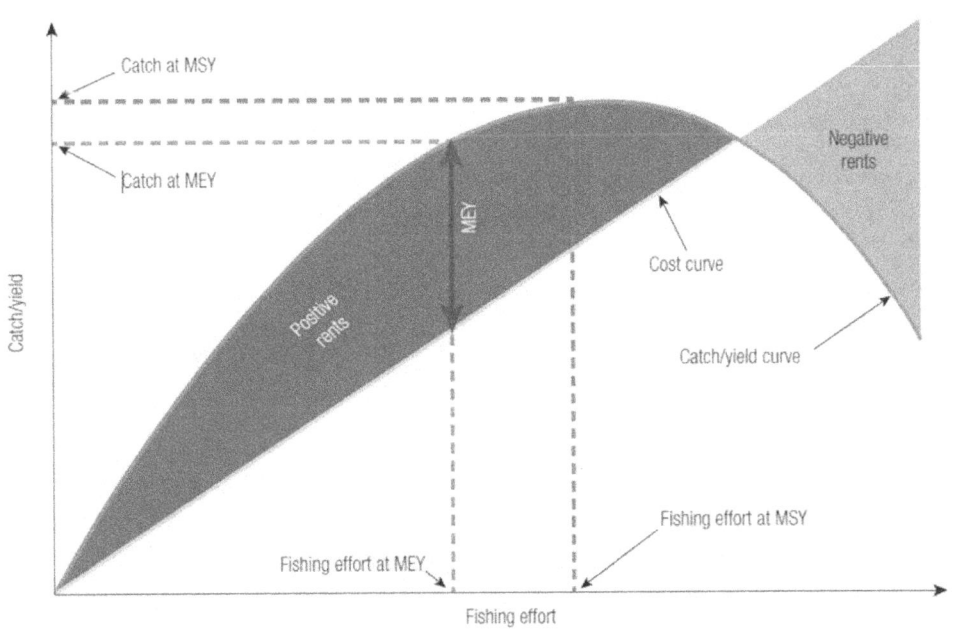

Source: World Bank and FAO 2009.
Note: MEY = maximum economic yield; MSY= maximum sustainable yield.

Rather than follow this method to its logical conclusion and insert a negative value into the balance sheet, however, Deutsch follows a principle of "functional neutrality" instead and ascribes a value of exactly zero to the oceans.

The Planetary CFO is inclined to observe the accountant's prudence principle, which aligns quite well with the sustainabilitarian's precautionary principle, and therefore to recognise a negative value representing damage to the current state of the oceans, as suggested by Deutsch's workings, but to use this as a provision against the value of the ocean's fisheries rather than as an asset value for the fisheries themselves.

However, in order to show a balance sheet that is intuitively "right", I will deploy a similar approach to that used for human capital. I will give a gross value for the oceans (reflecting both their potential economic value regarding sustainable fish production and the value of their ecological services in perpetuity) and then set against that gross value a provision for the current cumulative damage (the negative economic rent value as suggested by Deutsch). This will ensure that the true sustainable potential of the oceans is not forgotten. The net of the two amounts might or might not be negative, but it is hoped that investments in restoring the oceans will, over time, improve the net value and result in increasing ocean value year by year until it reaches its optimum sustainable value.

The oceans can be given a gross value (before accounting for damage) by adding the economic value of the sustainably harvested fish to an amount representing their value as a carbon sink.

Let's therefore start by looking at the value of the oceans as a carbon sink.

As I mentioned above, the American Meteorological Society's 'State of the Climate in 2017' report estimated that the oceans absorb about 2.6 billion tonnes of carbon from human activities per year.

Let's do some basic triangulation on this number.

According to Bellassen et al (2014) the oceans absorb about 2 petagrams of carbon per year (ie 2 billion tonnes of carbon per year).

From Gruber et al (2007):

> "… we estimate a global oceanic anthropogenic carbon dioxide (CO_2) sink for the period from 1800 to 1994 of 118 petagrams [billion tonnes] of carbon … [and] 37 petagrams [billion tonnes] from 1980 to 1999."

That means that from 1800 to 1994 the average was 0.6 billion tonnes per year. The rate accelerated in more recent times, and the average from 1980 to 1999 was just under 2 billion tonnes per year. It seems likely, therefore, that the current rate is between 2 and 3 billion tonnes per year.

Let's use the estimate, from the American Meteorological Society's 'State of the Climate in 2017' report, that the oceans absorb about 2.6 billion tonnes of carbon from human activities per year, assuming that the rate is still approximately right now.

At USD 1,000 per tonne (from our table of variables), and using a discount rate of 2% for future years, and if we multiply this unit value by the number of tonnes absorbed annually by the oceans, we get a "carbon sink" net present valuation which is:

USD 1,000 x 2,600,000,000 x 50   ie USD 130 trillion

Let's then add to that an amount for the economic value of sustainably harvested fish. Global seafood production is about 155 million tonnes annually. If the economic value of this food (net of fishing and food processing costs) is, say, USD 1 per kilo, ie USD 1,000 per tonne, then the annual global seafood production is worth a net economic benefit of USD 155 billion.

Again, if we discount this at 2% for future years, this would give us a net present value for current seafood production of the oceans of:

USD 155 billion x 50, ie USD 7.75 trillion

We need to make an adjustment to this, to get to a gross value of oceans before setting provisions against it.

To reflect the value of theoretical optimal sustainable fish harvests rather than the actual harvests, we know that a significant proportion of marine fisheries are over-fished (see, for example, FAO 2011). Also, the following is from World Bank (2018):

> "... the FAO assessment of the biological state of fish stocks indicates that approximately 90 percent of the world's fisheries likely were subject to economic overfishing in 2011."

If we assume, very broadly, that the optimum (and sustainable) fish harvesting would be, say, about 10% more than the actual, then we should add USD 7.75 trillion x 10%, ie, say, USD 0.78 trillion, to get USD 8.53 trillion, to arrive at a gross valuation before accounting for cumulative damage to date.

Adding these two sums together (the carbon sink value and the gross fishing grounds capital value), we get a gross asset value for the oceans (before degradation) of USD 138.53 trillion.

The gross value of the oceans is then USD 138.53 trillion.

If this is the gross value, then clearly the amount we set for the damage provision is hugely important, as the net value is likely to be one of the most significant and material numbers in the world balance sheet, alongside human capital and its associated destructiveness provision.

We have already noted that many fisheries are overfished, and we added a sum of USD 0.78 trillion for this effect. Therefore, our provision for ocean damage should start with this amount in it.

The oceans, and their ability to absorb carbon, are damaged and depleted as a result of global warming. CO_2 is less soluble in warmer water; thus, warmer oceans absorb less CO_2, meaning more CO_2 remains in the atmosphere. The oceans, which have absorbed 27.9% of the anthropogenic CO_2 in the past 200 years (IPCC, 2013), play a crucial role in the global carbon cycle.

We calculated the gross carbon sink value of the oceans (above) as USD 130 trillion.

Let's say that the provision for damage to this asset as a carbon sink is 10%, ie USD 13 trillion.

We could also look at adding to this some damage from plastic pollution. However, this is likely to be immaterial in the overall scale of the oceans. So, let's park that for further analysis at a later date (or to be included in another book).

This now means that we've arrived at an ocean damage provision of USD 0.78 trillion (fisheries damage provision) plus 13 trillion (carbon sink damage provision), ie USD 13.78 trillion.

Therefore, the gross value of the oceans is USD 138.53 trillion (as calculated earlier) and the net value is USD 124.75 trillion after accounting for the damage provision.

2) **Forests** (39 million square kilometres, 3.9 billion hectares, 26.3 % of the land)

I present below three alternative methods for valuing forests (a "swap" method, and a "carbon sink" method and a "restoration cost" method). I settle on the carbon sink method for use in the Planetary CFO's world balance sheet. However, I include discussions of the other two methods, as a demonstration of the variety of methods that are possible, and to allow for healthy debate about whether the method I have chosen is valid, useful and appropriate to the objectives of the world balance sheet. I invite this debate in this emerging area of enquiry and analysis, in relation to this section and all other sections of the book more generally.

Before we get into the specific valuation methods, let's take a little time to set the scene in terms of the biophysical extent, condition and characteristics of forests.

We saw earlier (in chapter 2) that the area of forest cover globally was about 3.9 billion hectares in 2019, and that it has been reducing by at about 0.15% (7.5 million hectares) per year up to 2010.

According to The World Counts, the rate of deforestation has been about 20 million hectares per year since about 2011 (about 0.39% of the pre-industrial level), 28 million hectares per year since 2016 (about 0.54% of the pre-industrial level).

Let's use an approximation, therefore, for 2020 forest cover, of 3.9 billion hectares minus 0.54% (ie 3.88 billion hectares), and for 2018, 3.9 billion hectares plus 0.54% (ie 3.92 billion hectares).

Now we have the extent of forest for each of the two balance sheet years we are working on, what average value per hectare should we use? Chapter 7 gives us a summary of the Planetary CFO's theory of value. What value should we choose, and what data is there to provide a starting point for such a value?

As a sustainabilitarian, it seems intuitive that forests should be valued at a higher unit value than other types of land, probably even the highest of all land types, because it is the richest ecologically and the most difficult (and costly) to replace as and when it is lost, damaged or converted.

Alongside that, we need to reflect the current state of forests, either on a global average basis, or by sub-categories that are classified (and valued) by the extent of their degradation.

This is by no means a trivial exercise. Indeed, many commentators (including Helm) have suggested that, even with modern scientific and ecological knowledge, it might in fact be impossible at the current time (but might be possible at some time in the not-too-distant future).

Accepting that these calculations are not going to be accurate with precision, can we at least come up with some sensible and rational estimates, in order to put an approximate and useful value on the forests instead of valuing them (precisely) at zero?

Deutsch undertakes a "probabilistic approach" and arrives at a value of about USD 55,000 per square kilometre. What do we think of this?

Well, for a start, Deutsch admits that his approach to valuation is based on direct economic benefits to humans and he selects it in order to provide consistency with existing international accounting standards.

His valuations therefore do not include ecological services (for example, nutrient recycling, water services, habitat/species protection and human recreation), because they "conflict with the IFRS standards". There is a fuller discussion of IFRS in chapters 7 and 9. However, to summarise, my main contention here is that the Planetary CFO's World Balance Sheet should go beyond IFRS in order to present a more useful picture of the world's assets and liabilities.

Deutsch includes direct economic outputs from forestry (eg wood and wood products) and some non-wood forest products (eg nuts, and other types of food and food additives). But it could be argued that these are a tiny proportion of the actual indirect value of forests, so the Planetary CFO makes an adjustment for this.

A) A "swap" method of valuation for forests

One angle to cut through the Gordian Knot on this is to consider opportunity cost. This would see the value of a unit of forest being as large as the best value alternative use of that unit of forest. Is that best alternative use high-value cropland, for example, at a unit value of about USD 1.9 million per square kilometre (minus a very small amount of cost of conversion from forest to cropland – how much does it cost, after all, to slash and burn a square kilometre of forest?). Why would we value the forest at anything less than that, and wouldn't we consider only USD 55,000 (the value suggested by Deutsch) derisory?

Note that this argument can also be made the other way round, implying a very low value for cropland because it would be very difficult, time-consuming and expensive to convert cropland into old forest. If we apply it to a valuation of cropland, its unit value would be very small, being the net of USD 1.9 million per square kilometre (the direct economic value), minus the considerable costs of conversion from cropland into old forest (or something at least equivalent to it in ecological terms capable of providing ecosystems supporting human and other life), which could itself run into millions of dollars per square kilometre. If you are shocked by this suggestion, simply take a few minutes to familiarise yourself with the Biosphere 2 project, where an entire ecosystem (including man-made forest) was created to support a small human "crew" for only two years at immense cost.

This suggests, perhaps, that we should, in fact, as a first-order estimate, swap the values per unit of forest and cropland, giving the first of these a value of USD 1.9 million and the other one a value of USD 55,000. This draws from the "policy objective" idea in the Planetary CFO's theory of value elsewhere in this book, as a means to use a public policy approach to end existing perverse incentives driven by purely economic value calculations.

Can we justify this "swap" approach in any other way, given that it seems to largely cancel out the direct economic value of cropland? I think we can, as follows. The typical economic value calculation (a net present value calculation) does not currently take into account externalities such as contributions to climate change, other pollution, and degradation of nature caused by that economic activity. Some commentators suggest, for example, that a very high carbon price should be implemented to address this. Suppose we envisage a world in which such environmental externalities are priced in, with the effect of reversing the trends towards deforestation and providing incentives, instead, for afforestation. Swapping the unit values of cropland and forest, as above, would provide this reversing of incentive, and the economic incentive for afforestation would then be as strong as it is currently for deforestation.

This makes a lot of sense for tackling (and reversing) one of the most serious and worrying trends affecting our future sustainability – deforestation. If we make this change, every square kilometre of cropland converted into forest would add about USD 1.8 million to the natural capital assets in the world balance sheet, and every conversion the other way round (from forest into cropland) would reduce the natural capital assets by the same amount.

The adjustment required to the USD 2.69 trillion forest value shown in Deutsch is to multiply it by the ratio 1.8 million over 55,000, giving USD 32.73 trillion, an uplift of USD 30.04 trillion on Deutsch's value.

Before deciding whether to use this method for valuing the forests, let's consider the alternatives I mentioned above.

B) A "carbon sink" method of valuation for forests

Would a carbon sink valuation of forests (ie similar to the one for oceans, included above) be easier to justify than the above "swap" method? Let's 'do the math'.

What is the value per tonne of carbon for the sequestration by forests?

If we use the same number as for oceans, it is about USD 1,000 per tonne, although, in fact, we won't even need to use this number here, for reasons that will quickly become obvious.

How much carbon sequestration do the forests do?

According to Harris et al (2021)

> "We estimate that global forests were a net carbon sink of −7.6 [billion tonnes per year], reflecting a balance between gross carbon removals (−15.6 [billion tonnes per year]) and gross emissions from deforestation and other disturbances (8.1 [billion tonnes per year])"

However, there are some quite significant error bars on the above estimates. Let's look at another source. According to Bellassen et al (2014) the forests absorb about the same amount of carbon as the oceans, at about 2 petagrams of carbon per year (ie 2 billion tonnes of carbon per year).

Therefore, we could, as a first-order approximation, use the same value as we have used for the oceans. This gives us a gross value for the forests of USD 130 trillion, an uplift of USD 127.31 trillion on Deutsch's value.

As an aside on forestry management techniques that improve both the value of the forests as a carbon sink and improved sustainability from the use of harvested wood, Bellassen gives some simple tips:

> "… forest-management techniques that increase both the amount of wood produced and the carbon stock retained in the forest should be prioritized. When not in conflict with other forest uses, replacing dying or low-productivity stands, protecting young sprouts from damage after harvest, planting tree mixes that are more resilient, and optimizing fertilizer use and tree growth by adding nitrogen-fixing species in afforestation projects, will contribute to climate-change mitigation no matter how the global carbon sink evolves."

C) A third alternative - a "restoration cost" method of valuation for forests

There is some interest in establishing restoration costs for forests. However, it appears this is mostly out of curiosity rather than as a serious attempt to value forests this way.

From UN (2014), with my emboldening:

> "A particular issue arises in the case of ecosystem assets, since it may not be appropriate to apply valuation approaches developed in the context of produced assets (such as buildings and machines) to ecosystems which are complex assets, have the potential to regenerate over time, provide multiple services, and may experience varying degrees of use over time. ….
> A related question is whether the valuation of ecosystem degradation should be based on analysing forgone income due to the reductions in the current and future flows of ecosystem services, or if valuation of ecosystem degradation should be based on the costs of restoring the ecosystem to a previous state … Use of a restoration cost approach is associated with a range of contentions, for example, that the implicit price does not reflect a market price, that it is unclear whether the ecosystem should or could be restored to a previous condition, and that the use of an aggregated approach is not conducive to a full allocation of costs to relevant economic units. At the same time, this direct approach to the estimation of a possible value of ecosystem degradation resembles the approach commonly used in the estimation of the value of public goods in the national accounts. Further, **even if they are not used to value degradation, estimates of restoration cost may still be of interest in their own right.**"

Just exploring this briefly, if we were to find a cost of restoring degraded forest to its previous state from a currently degraded state, this approach could be extended to provide a total value for the forest as comprising a total cost of restoring it from a zero stocks position to a full (and fully restored) forest asset.

We immediately run into a difficulty with this approach, however, because of lack of time to implement the restoration. By which, I mean that a standing forest, once cut down, takes many years, decades, centuries (perhaps even longer) to regrow into the rich habitat that it once was. If we aren't confident that the funds, the commitment, the actual resources (in terms of people and equipment), and suitable conditions, will prevail for that length of time, then there is doubt about the feasibility of this restoration project.

Setting aside the time it takes for restoration, the regrowth to maturity might (if the conditions are favourable) be done by nature itself, in which case the cost of restoration would be quite low. However, I don't think we can assume that nature will do this restoration work. At some point, nature will become so compromised by human activities that its restorative capabilities will be significantly damaged, at least in timescales that make practical sense to human planners.

I therefore parked this method for now.

Conclusion on forest valuation

After completing the above analyses, the carbon sink method was a clear winner for use in the Planetary CFO's world balance sheet.

The carbon sink method of valuation gives a better uplift than achieved by the "swap" method above (so better meets the "policy objectives" criterion), and is generally easier to explain and justify. The "restoration cost" method currently lacks robust data, and has insufficient availability of implementation timescales, to sustain it.

3) **Cropland and pastureland** (combined 51 million square kilometres, 5.1 billion hectares, 35.5% of the land)

We use the World Bank method, described in their 2018 report as follows:

> "... to value cropland, land rents are measured as the value of crops produced at local prices minus the economic cost of production (input costs including labor plus an assumed "normal" return on capital). The value of agricultural land then equals the present value of all the rents associated with agricultural production in local prices. This value is converted to [2014] US dollars."

Deutsch takes the 2014 numbers published by the World Bank in their 2018 report and uplifts them to reflect changes in land cover and agricultural productivity between 2014 and 2018, to arrive at the values per hectare included in my table 1 above.

Applying these unit values to the amount of land cover given by Our World In Data, the values of cropland and pasture land for 2018 for the Planetary CFO's world balance sheet are as follows:

Cropland (USD19,300 x 1,100million ha)   USD 21.2 trillion

Pastureland (USD5,245 x 4,000million ha)   USD 21.0 trillion

These represent an adjustment of approximately USD -5.2 trillion and +4.9 trillion respectively to Deutsch's valuations. The net effect on the bottom line is negative but quite small.

4) Barren/wild land

This is in some ways a neutral category of land, because barren or wild land is probably marginal land that is remote and difficult to change one way or another. At the same time, humans probably derive very little aggregate benefit from it, directly or indirectly (even if the local benefit for the relatively small number of people living there is significant to them because it provides them with nearly everything they need). The value we give it is likely to be small and insignificant in the overall picture. Therefore, following again the accounting principle of materiality, the Planetary CFO is going to ascribe zero value to this category of land.

***

Now, let's make all those revaluation adjustments to the world balance sheet, and see what happens to the numbers.

Figure 21 – The Planetary CFO's World Balance Sheet 2018 - *revalued*

Planetary CFO's World Balance Sheet 2018 (USD trillions) revalued			% total assets
Fixed Assets			
Property			
Renewable NC (Land)			
Cropland	21.25		
Pasture land	20.96		
Forest	130.00		
Barren/wild land	1.00		
Urban land	85.89		
Oceans	138.53		
Ocean damage provision	-13.78		
Subtotal renewable NC		383.85	
Non-renewable NC		51.91	
Subtotal Property		435.76	46.4%
Plant			
Dwellings		119.84	
Other buildings		140.43	
Subtotal Plant		260.27	27.7%
Equipment			
Commercial equipment		41.98	
Military equipment		8.74	
Subtotal Equipment		50.72	5.4%
Intangible assets			
Goodwill		117.63	
Intellectual property		20.76	
Brand value, licences		5.60	
Subtotal intangible assets		143.99	15.3%
Current assets			
Inventories		46.90	5.0%
Cash and cash equivalents		1.64	0.2%
Human Capital	809.94		
Human Capital destructiveness provision	-809.94		
Net Human Capital		0.00	
Total assets		939.28	100.0%
Liabilities			
Human welfare commitment	1,497.46		
Unfunded human welfare commitment (-ve) ie asset stewardship shortfall	-558.18		
Equity of humankind		939.28	
Total liabilities and equity		939.28	

Commentary on the figure above – the revalued 2018 world balance sheet

It becomes obvious that the "bottom line" on this sustainability-focussed style for the world balance sheet, ie the stewardship shortfall, amounting to nearly USD 560 trillion, has been improved (from over USD 800 trillion in the first version in figure 14). This improvement has arisen through revaluing existing natural capital, despite its depleted and damaged state.

46% of the total assets are now shown to be natural capital in the Planetary CFO's world balance sheet, compared with only 6.5% in the balance sheet shown by Deutsch.

The message is clear – we need to properly protect, maintain and enhance our natural capital in order to support humanity in perpetuity. In 2018 we were already in deficit on that objective.

In doing the revaluations, I've left intangible assets (other than human capital) untouched so far. It's worth pointing out that the "goodwill" in the balance sheet is of dubious value in a sustainability context. However, rather than write it off in one year, the Planetary CFO would prefer this goodwill to be depreciated over, say, 20 years, to smooth the effects of this change rather than take it all in one hit.

***

Let's try to triangulate the above Planetary CFO's calculations of value with other sources.

In chapter 3, we saw that there are a wide range of ecosystem service values derived by various researchers. In one example, they ranged from USD 120 per hectare per year for the Galapagos to USD 58,000 per hectare per year for the Charles River Basin in the USA.

In UNEP (2018b), Van der Ploeg and de Groot (2010) are referenced as providing a value of forest non-timber annual benefits of USD 2,091 per hectare of temperate or boreal forest, USD 2,990 per hectare of tropical forest. Looking at the diagram itself (the figute below, from TEEB (2013), it in fact gives a more comprehensive range of the potential total economic value (TEV) for various types of biome.

Figure 22 (their figure 2.2) – range of ecosystem service values – from TEEB (2013)

Figure 2.2 Range of values of all ecosystem services provided by different types of habitat

(Int.$/ha/yr2007/PPP-corrected)[6]

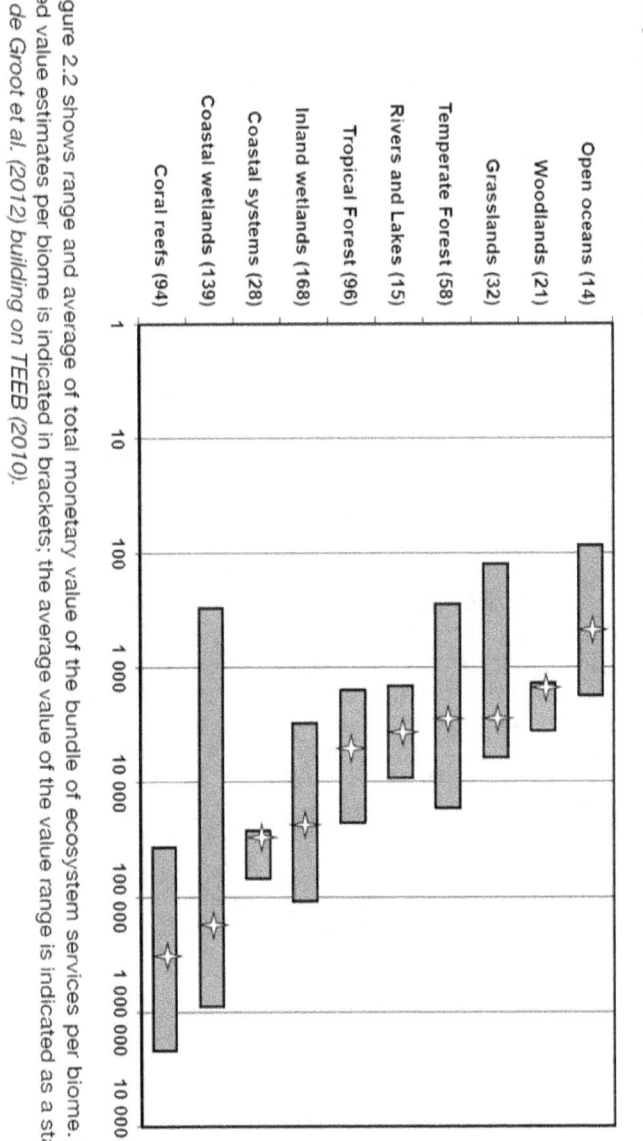

Note: Figure 2.2 shows range and average of total monetary value of the bundle of ecosystem services per biome. The total number of published value estimates per biome is indicated in brackets; the average value of the value range is indicated as a star sign.

Source: de Groot et al. (2012) building on TEEB (2010).

If we take 3.9 billion hectares of forests and multiply by an average TEV of USD 3,000 per hectare (estimated from the above figure), this gives us a value of annual ecosystems services from forests of USD 11.7 trillion (in 2007 USD).

At a discount rate of 2% (used elsewhere in my calculations), this gives an asset value of USD 585 trillion for the forests. This makes my USD 130 trillion asset valuation for forests in figure 17 look dramatically underestimated.

Van der Ploeg and de Groot (2010) do explain some of the data and valuation difficulties in this area:

> "For large scale assessments, like TEEB [The Economics of Ecosystems and Biodiversity], big ranges of original values are part of the game. There are several causes for this.
> - First, case studies of valuation studies come from a wide variation of locations and countries.
> - Second, a wide variety of valuation methods has been used to obtain monetary values of ecosystem services.
> - Third, the different case studies that we selected for the combination of an ecosystem service and biome describe a variety of sub-biomes (ecosystems) and sub-services.
> - Fourth, the monetary values of services which the selected case studies provide are carefully selected to suit their specific location and time and are in general part of a total value analysis. Therefore, it is sometimes difficult to interpret these service values without taking into account the benefits of the other services.
> - Fifth, aggregation of data implies that the nuance of the original case studies is blurred"

The results of my various triangulations have been to confirm that my Planetary CFO's valuations are not necessarily outliers, but fall in a quite wide range of values produced by various researchers.

***

Let's consider the potential to provide a more up to date Planetary CFO's World Balance Sheet, to try to make trends over time visible.

Unfortunately, actual data for 2020 (the most recent year) is quite sparse. For example, up to date UN FAO land use data is not available yet. Even in the Planetary CFO's 2018 world balance sheet, we had to use older data and project forward to 2018.

In the absence of actual data, we are left with the prospect of making estimates of rates of change since 2018. This is far from satisfactory. It would be much better to use actual data for asset values in the more recent years. However, if there is no realistic alternative, then projecting into the future is what we are left with, and the best we can hope is that our estimates are not too far out of wack.

Luckily, the numbers we are talking about are huge (because the earth is a big place) and at a global scale, in proportion to the size of the earth, they are changing by relatively small proportions each year. This means that it will probably not stretch our margins for error too much to do some straight-line projections from 2018 to 2020.

For forests, it was already noted above that the extent of forest cover was 3.92 billion hectares for 2018 (3.9 billion hectares plus 0.54%), and 3.88 billion hectares for 2020 (3.9 billion hectares minus 0.54%). All other things being equal, the value of the forests should therefore be reduced by the ratio of those numbers, and therefore the 2020 value should be USD 130 trillion x 0.99, which is USD 128.7 trillion, a reduction of USD 1.3 trillion.

Cropland and pastureland will probably not change as much as forests do. Given their much smaller contribution to the total assets value, I suspect we would lose the net changes of each of these in the roundings.

When it comes to the oceans, the increase in their absorption of carbon (from there being slightly more carbon in the atmosphere in 2020 versus 2018) will be somewhat offset by the slightly reduced ability of the oceans to absorb carbon in 2020 versus 2018. Even without doing the maths, it is likely (as with the cropland and pastureland) that the net effect of these is a small change in the value of the oceans, which might be positive or negative but is likely to be immaterial in the overall scale of the numbers.

When it comes to other assets, for example produced capital assets such as buildings, commercial equipment, infrastructure, there are two counteracting factors affecting these between 2018 and 2020. On the one hand, there has been some economic growth (ie increased economic activity). On the other hand, the covid-19 pandemic has caused economic shocks and reduced some economic activity levels around the world. Again, it is difficult to know the extent to which these two effects will counteract each other, but it's entirely possible that the resulting net effect will be small in the overall scale of the world balance sheet.

The updated world balance sheet is shown on the next page, with very small adjustments made for the above effects.

Figure 23 – The Planetary CFO's World Balance Sheet 2020

Planetary CFO's World Balance Sheet 2020 (USD trillions)			% total assets
Fixed Assets			
Property			
Renewable NC (Land)			
Cropland	21.25		
Pasture land	20.96		
Forest	128.70		
Barren/wild land	1.00		
Urban land	85.89		
Oceans	138.53		
Ocean damage provision	-13.78		
Subtotal renewable NC		382.55	
Non-renewable NC		51.91	
Subtotal Property		434.46	46.3%
Plant			
Dwellings		119.84	
Other buildings		140.43	
Subtotal Plant		260.27	27.7%
Equipment			
Commercial equipment		41.98	
Military equipment		8.74	
Subtotal Equipment		50.72	5.4%
Intangible assets			
Goodwill		117.63	
Intellectual property		20.76	
Brand value, licences		5.60	
Subtotal intangible assets		143.99	15.4%
Current assets			
Inventories		46.90	5.0%
Cash and cash equivalents		1.64	0.2%
Human Capital	809.94		
Human Capital destructiveness provision	-809.94		
Net Human Capital		0.00	
Total assets		937.98	100.0%
Liabilities			
Human welfare commitment	1,497.46		
Unfunded human welfare commitment (-ve) ie asset stewardship shortfall	-559.48		
Equity of humankind		937.98	
Total liabilities and equity		937.98	

A triangulation between the Planetary CFOs world balance sheet and IMF or World Bank numbers for economic activity

The IMF (2020) have published a number of years' world GDP and some projections for 2021 and 2025 (including the effects of the Covid-19 pandemic in 2019 – 2020).

The IMF predicts global GDP rising (in real terms) from USD 75 trillion in 2012 to USD 84 trillion in 2020 and then to USD 113 trillion in 2025.

If we compare this with the above 2020 world balance sheet (where total assets are about USD 938 trillion), we see that 2020 GDP is, at USD 84 trillion, expected to be a return on capital of 84/938 ie about 9% (rising to about 12% by 2025, using the same calculation).

I would conjecture that the GDP numbers are being swelled by some element of output that is in fact a drawing down of capital rather than renewably generated output from a stable stock of capital. This is in spite of the fact that we are also in a situation where there is already an existing deficit of capital to satisfy the human welfare commitment (see more about this commitment to humanity below).

When calculating return on capital, it might be better to look at consumption numbers rather than GDP, because of the deficiencies of GDP as a measure of activity. The following figure shows consumption numbers from the World Bank.

Figure 24

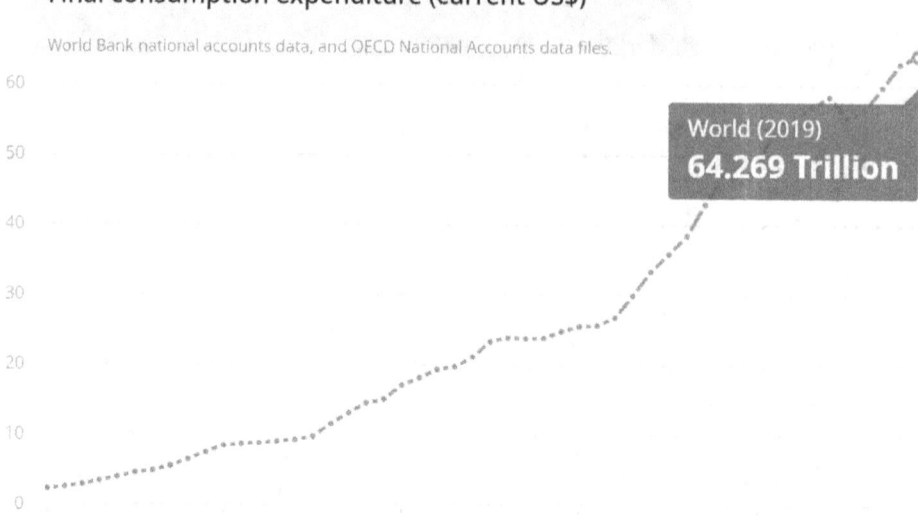

Final consumption expenditure (current US$)

World (2019)
64.269 Trillion

(source = data.worldbank.org – chart downloaded 21 January 2021)

We can now modify our calculation, using consumption instead of GDP, in 2019, of USD 64.3 trillion, and divide this by USD 938 trillion of capital assets (in 2020, but only a small error from timescale), giving us an approximate return on capital of 7%.

Both these calculations (based on GDP and consumption respectively) seem to produce figures for return on capital that are very high for an enterprise (the whole earth) which is not only reaching saturation point in many sectors, but which is bumping up against some planetary limits and exceeding others.

As an aside, Deutsch (2020) finds the return on capital on his world balance sheet, based on a calculation also using consumption, much lower; at 3.2%, which he points out is more in line with general theory.

Commentary on the Planetary CFO's 2018 and 2020 World Balance Sheets

The main, obvious differences between the Planetary CFO's world balance sheet and earlier precursors (eg World Bank and Deutsch) are that:

- Natural capital now represents a more prominent proportion of the assets (nearly 50%)

- There is a recognition of the human welfare commitment – the obligation on all of us to provide the basic means of a decent life to all humans on the planet

- We are clearly failing in our collective stewardship of the planet, as illustrated by the size of the existing asset stewardship shortfall in (USD 560 trillion in 2020)

This final point is such a significant one that it's worth drawing out for particular emphasis. The assets are not currently sufficient to provide for the needs of humanity into the distant future (let alone in perpetuity - ie forever - which should be our ultimate goal). We're short of assets, and the remaining assets are shrinking rather than improving each year. By looking back in time, we can see a long pattern of deterioration in natural capital. Even though we don't have very reliable historical world balance sheets (showing the health of our natural capital over time) to support this assertion, we know it to be true, and that it's a serious depletion of our life support systems. If this was a business, the board of directors would be hauled over the coals by *all* the stakeholders. They would be grilled with questioning about what they were going to do about it.

We know some things are being done about it. We know about the Conference of the Parties process for dealing with climate change. We know about the increasing uptake of Natural Capital Accounting. We know that Governments are increasingly concerned about deforestation and are implementing plans for afforestation. Will enough be done to avert the worst of disasters?   In the short term, it's difficult to tell if any actions already taken are having the desired impacts. This is part of the quandary we're all in. The planetary systems are so large, and some of them operate on such long timeframes (the carbon cycle, and the water cycle, for example) that it will be many decades, even centuries, before the full impacts of actions taken today are fully reflected in the state of the earth's biosphere.

My hope is that the World Balance Sheet is there, from year to year, decade to decade, century to century, letting us know whether we are having some positive impact on the direction of travel, and how big the remaining challenge is, in order to pass through the bottleneck.

A word about incrementalism

The changes from 2018 to 2020 in the Planetary CFO's world balance sheet are proportionately small. This is perhaps no surprise, since the world is a big place, and we know that sustainability challenges such as climate change are insidious and creeping ones. This is what the history of environmentalism has taught us already – that the problems caused by carbon emissions have been building steadily for decades. It's only by looking over longer timeframes than individual years, and sometimes even longer than decades, that the patterns have become clear, the causality has been established, and the alarm bells have started to be heard.

On reflection, it seems that updating the world balance sheet from 2018 to a 2020 version has not produced much by way of new, strong inferences or conclusions and is a futile exercise.

In chapter 10, however, I'll do some crystal ball gazing using scenarios into the distant (but still imaginable) future, which is necessary in order to escape the obvious incrementalism of looking into a future too near to make a big difference. By looking longer term, we can see more clearly the potential trajectories which either move us towards a sustainable future, or further away from such a future.

Sustainability and decoupling

Decoupling (of economic activity and its growth) from material throughputs, or environmental impacts, has been touted by some as a solution to the problem of inadequacy of natural capital assets. However, recent research reviewing the evidence so far gathered about this gives little confidence that it provides even some of the answer to the basic problem. The following is from Vaden et al (2020):

> "We found that 170 articles presented cases of relative decoupling and 97 articles cases of absolute decoupling. Out of the 97 cases of absolute decoupling, 74 articles concern impact decoupling and 23 concern absolute resource decoupling. Out of these 23 we concentrated on eleven articles that present evidence of economy-wide and at least national level absolute resource decoupling. We found that none of those articles claimed robust evidence of international and continuous absolute resource decoupling, not to speak of sufficiently fast global absolute resource decoupling. This result in no way undermines the importance of the environmentally desirable outcomes, such as national level absolute decoupling between land and blue water use, reported in the articles in the survey. However, it points out that with regard to the goal of ecological sustainability, the empirical evidence on decoupling is thin."

A further examination of the human welfare commitment (USD 1,497 trillion in 2018) and the asset stewardship shortfall (USD -600 trillion in 2018)

Let's just remind ourselves where the human welfare commitment came from. This is what Deutsch (2020) called "human consumption", which was derived by him from the World Bank's (2006) approach to discounted total future human consumption, updated for 2017 data on world consumption, then fed into a net present value calculation to reflect future consumption over the next 25 years, using a formula from Hamilton et al (2005).

The total assets in the Deutsch world balance sheet (USD trillion 1,497 in 2014) are thought, by Deutsch, to be sufficient to support consumption growing at 1.13% compound annual growth rate in perpetuity, the consumption to be met in each future year from production generated from those assets. It's not clear how Deutsch has made this calculation, but he has stated that he has not relied on the Hartwick Rule being met, but has relied on other aspects of World Bank calculations. (see box 1 for more about the Hartwick Rule)

He notes that this 1.13% growth rate for consumption is lower than the historical growth rate of consumption over recent history (2.74%), and that if current consumption trends continue, the existing value of assets (as calculated by him) would not be sufficient to meet that consumption and the expected future consumption would have to be met by depleting "natural resources" (ie drawing down natural capital each year to ensure that year's consumption needs were met).

Deutsch was right to point out the capital asset 'drawdown' effect from current high rates of growth in consumption, but assumes that the rate of consumption growth can be reduced (from current and recent historical levels) so that it falls within a sustainable range when compared with the assets. How realistic is this assumption?

There are some aspects of the World Bank approach that concern me. The World Bank references the Hartwick Rule (see box 1) and this is not without its difficulties. For example, in Hartwick (1977), it's assumed that:

- the initial stock of exhaustible (ie non-renewable) resource is precisely sufficient to sustain the economy over infinite time and
- the technology used for extraction and conversion is assumed to exhibit constant returns to scale

Both of these assumptions could be incorrect, especially if rates of consumption are mismatched with the amounts of initial stocks. This is something the World Balance Sheet approach should help us to start to assess.

Box 1 – The Hartwick Rule applied to natural capital

The Hartwick Rule basically says that (economic) sustainability can be obtained if capital assets are maintained by reinvesting sufficient amounts of the profits from liquidations (ie economic rents) of other capital assets back into new or existing capital assets, thus maintaining those assets at, or restoring them to, a sustainable state.

From Hartwick (1977):

"If in this sense the stock of productive capital is not being depleted, what can one say about the time path of current output and current consumption per head? For the case of per capita consumption remaining constant over time, one could say that no generation was better off than another. Intergenerational equity was being achieved."

Interpreting this, its usefulness can become clear if applied to investment in (ie maintenance of) a specific class of capital assets, ie natural capital, with no substitutability of this type of capital for other types of capital (which is one definition of sustainability). The Hartwick Rule then describes natural capital being maintained in a sustainable state in perpetuity, by reinvesting the capital profits (or economic rents) from exploiting renewable resources (ie natural capital) back into renewable natural capital.

As noted in Hamilton et al (2005):

"The Hartwick Rule (Hartwick 1977) offers what Solow (1986) termed a 'rule of thumb' for sustainability in exhaustible [ie non-renewable] resource economies – a maximal constant level of consumption can be sustained if the value of investment equals the value of rents on extracted [non-renewable] resources at each point in time. For countries dependent on such wasting [ie non-renewable] assets this rule offers a prescription for sustainable development, a prescription that Botswana in particular has followed with its diamond wealth (Lange and Wright 2004)."

There are criticisms of the applicability of the Hartwick Rule when trying to establish sustainability.

From Asheim et al (2003):

"If … natural capital has to be conserved in order for utility to be sustained (i.e., the world is as envisioned by the proponents of 'strong sustainability'), then – it is claimed – the Hartwick rule for sustainability does not apply … The analysis … thus reinforces the message of Toman et al. (1995, p. 147), namely that the Hartwick investment rule cannot serve as a prescription for sustainability. It is not enough to know whether the current investment in man-made capital in value makes up for the current depletion of natural capital, since the Hartwick result only says that following the Hartwick investment rule will entail constant consumption for an interval of time. This is neither sufficient nor necessary for development to be sustainable. Rather, a judgement on whether short-run behaviour is compatible with sustainable development must be based on the long-run properties of the path and the technological environment."

The following is from Bazhanov (2020):

"This [work] offers an expression for accounting price of a natural resource that arises from a condition guaranteeing sustainability of production possibilities. Estimation of this price needs specification of extraction path and production function, which supports the claim of Hamilton and Ruta (2017) that "accounting prices can only be measured with respect to the assumed allocation mechanism . . . And [this mechanism] needs to be fully specified." This claim should be even stronger because the assessment of sustainability may depend, besides allocation mechanism, on specification of technology and initial conditions."

Note in particular Bazhanov's focus on initial conditions and technology in the above excerpt. This backs up the need, if the Hartwick Rule is being relied upon, to assume sufficient initial capital assets exist and a sufficiently successful set of technologies are deployed for its increasingly efficient extraction so that its extraction can continue forever (extracting smaller and smaller amounts each year but still enough to meet consumption needs). This is at least questionable if applied as a policy position for sustainability, and might well conflict with the laws of thermodynamics, as argued by ecological economists such as Daly.

Drawdown

In fact, the Planetary CFO's world balance sheet shows that the drawdown and depletion of natural capital (renewable and non-renewable), has already been occurring, and has led to a cumulative asset stewardship shortfall up to 2018 of about USD 560 trillion.

The Planetary CFO not only does not rely on the Hartwick Rule for any of the valuations, but also does not use the World Bank's assumption about a 'balancing figure' to make up the assets with froth and conjecture (eg "intellectual capital") but instead seeks to evaluate by how much the assets we **do** know about (with reasonable confidence), are short of what is required for a sustainable situation to ensue without further action.

How this asset shortfall is to be addressed is at the core of sustainability debates, although it has generally not been talked about using the terms introduced here by the Planetary CFO.

To briefly touch on one aspect of the solution space, some people would argue for limiting human populations as being a necessary part of routes to sustainability. However, in my view this is at best premature and at worst unnecessary. I say this based on a large body of research suggesting demographic trends are likely to result in global population peaking at some point during the next 100 years and then reaching a more stable, lower level after the peak. For example, see McFalls (2007). I talk about this in more detail later.

Discounting, as applied to "discounted total future human consumption" in the above paragraphs, is explained more fully in chapter 9.

Other matters of interpretation of the world balance sheet

Just because something (for example some forest within the number for natural capital) has been given a value, this doesn't of itself mean that the right outcomes and objectives will be achieved. One of the most ardent critics of the natural capital concept, Anderson (2018) gives an example of the difficulty of moving beyond capital valuation to stewardship of the capital via management of a sustainable yield (where this latter step might be missing):

> "Suppose someone did the calculations and handed the results to the Indonesian Government (and this has been tried), proving that the forests have a greater value left standing than can be extracted by chopping them down and selling the timber, coal, palm oil, and so on that are currently being exported from Indonesia. I doubt that this would persuade them to change course. They would see the economists' figures as interesting and those who provided the figures probably as well-meaning, but then ask: where is this money? If we could really get what is currently this theoretical money, our plans and policies would change. But we have people to feed and an economy to develop, and we know that selling timber, coal, and palm oil actually brings money in."

However, Anderson omits any discussion of the Maximum Sustainable Yield (MSY) concept. This is the yield of (for example) forest products that could be extracted but which would enable the capital value of the forest to be maintained **while still producing that yield of forest products**. This concept is one that many environmental economists have written about, explaining the extent to which over-exploitation of natural capital in the short-term, however pressing the short-term consumption needs, results, in the longer-term, in even more serious asset shortfalls and even more serious pressures for satisfying basic needs.

The example of the political attitudes in Indonesia quoted by Andersen are, of course, responding to real issues of poverty and basic needs provision. The answer, however, does not lie in addressing the short-term needs through local drawdown of natural capital, but by working together internationally and globally to ensure that, at a global level, natural capital is maintained and enhanced, and that local short-term shortfalls of assets (compared with needs) are addressed through countries cooperating regionally and globally.

Costanza et al (2014) set out a very clear and (in my view) persuasive rebuttal of Anderson's criticisms of valuing ecosystem services and Natural Capital:

> "It is a misconception to assume that valuing ecosystem services in monetary units is the same as privatizing them or commodifying them for trade in private markets (Costanza, 2006; Costanza et al., 2012; McCauley, 2006; Monbiot, 2012). Most ecosystem services are public goods (non-rival and non-excludable) or common pool resources (rival but non-excludable), which means that privatization and conventional markets work poorly, if at all. In addition, the non-market values estimated for these ecosystem services often relate more to use or non-use values rather than exchange values (Daly, 1998). Nevertheless, knowing the value of ecosystem services is helpful for their effective management, which in some cases can include economic incentives, such as those used in successful systems of payment for these services (Farley and Costanza, 2010). In addition, it is important to note that valuation is unavoidable. We already value ecosystems and their services every time we make a decision involving trade-offs concerning them. The problem is that the valuation is implicit in the decision and hidden from view. Improved transparency about the valuation of ecosystem services (while recognizing the uncertainties and limitations) can only help to make better decisions."

Valuation of natural capital is dealt with in more depth in chapter 7.

Chapter 5

Types of capital – an introduction

"National income and well-being are underpinned by a country's assets or wealth - measured comprehensively to include produced capital, natural capital, human capital, and net foreign assets [financial capital]. Sustained long-term economic growth requires investment and management of this broad portfolio of assets … Just as a company measures its value by looking at both its income statement and balance sheet, a look at comprehensive national wealth signals if GDP growth can be sustained over the long run."
(World Bank 2018)

In previous chapters, I've set out a lot of numbers. I've frequently used the term "capital" in the text that has gone alongside the calculations. Now is probably a good point to look at this term in more detail, and explain the meanings behind it.

Later in the chapter, I proceed to an analysis of the various different types of capital.

This is all useful context, as it is at the root of the definition of "capitalism", a concept that is itself at the heart of much debate surrounding sustainability, eg as phrased in questions about whether "natural capitalism" can co-exist with "capitalism" or whether the former is, in fact, an oxymoron. It also sets the scene for a discussion of ringfencing of capitals, which features in chapter 6.

What "capital" is

Arguments about what capital is, and what elements of it are most important, have been around as long as the discipline of economics itself. Here is an example from Solow (1963):

"A man from Mars reading the literature on capital theory would be inclined sometimes to think that capital consists mainly of stocks of consumer goods to maintain workers until their output can be sold; sometimes he would think that the earth is given over to the maturing of wine and the growing of trees, so that capital consists largely of goods in process; sometimes he would realize that most of what we think of as capital consists of durable assets like buildings and machinery, or what we call fixed capital. He would perhaps wonder why Wicksell, in the course of a careful analysis of a model with fixed capital in the form of axes, did not pay any attention to the age of the trees being cut down (though he had done so 30 years earlier), whereas Bohm-Bawerk, who seemed to be thinking mainly about the age at which trees should be cut down, seemed to worry too little about the implement to be used in felling them. He [the Martian] would be a little uncertain whether gestation periods matter a lot or not, whether production is like making elephants or making mosquitoes. The truth, of course, is that all these aspects of capitalistic production are important, that it is useless to try to represent all of them by any one of them, and extraordinarily complicated to deal simultaneously with them all."

One way of explaining capital is that it is as both a resource and liability originally fed into an entity when the entity is first created but before anything has happened. This initial capital might typically have been introduced as a cash asset (as a debit) and equity (as a credit owed to the original funder) in the balance sheet. Over time the cash gets converted into assets, but the initial equity can largely stay intact on the other side of the balance sheet. Assets then get bought and sold, replaced, generate profits etc. Sometimes, the proceeds from the sale of one type of asset are used to buy assets of a different type. This can constitute a substitution of one form of capital for another. Because of double entry bookkeeping, in theory, it's possible to track, or associate, a collection of assets on one side of a balance sheet with a capital fund (or a subset of "equity") on the other. However, in practice the equity credit in the balance sheet is rarely (if ever) subdivided into various types of capital. Despite this, it's sometimes useful to imagine that the equity has been subdivided in that way, for example in order to ringfence particular amounts, or types, of capital. I talk about ringfencing of capitals in a later chapter. In the meantime, and for the purposes of the current explanations, it's sufficient to simply lump all types of capital together on the credit side of the balance sheet as "equity" and focus on the different categories of assets on the debit side as representing a variety of types of "capital".

As Stiglitz et al (2018) state:

"The definition of capital should … include more than produced (economic) capital, to encompass social, human and natural capital. Measuring capital requires constructing and examining balance sheets for different types of capital, for each country and for the whole planet, and assessing their changes over time."

The figure below shows a modern illustration of the main elements of capital "wealth", makes a distinction between natural capital and other types of capital and gives some illustrative examples of each.

Figure 25 – Types of capital (from DFID, Crown copyright)

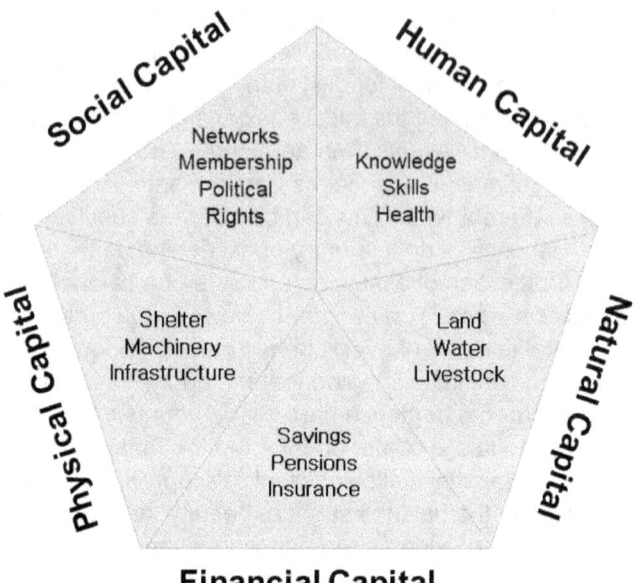

Source: DFID Sustainable livelihoods Guidance Sheets

(NB: Physical capital is also described as produced capital or man-made capital).

The following figure shows a version of the above framework used by McCoy et al (2013), adapted to apply to an agricultural setting in Africa.

Figure 26 – from McCoy et al (2013) - The Sustainable Livelihoods Framework adapted for women farmers in Iringa, Tanzania.

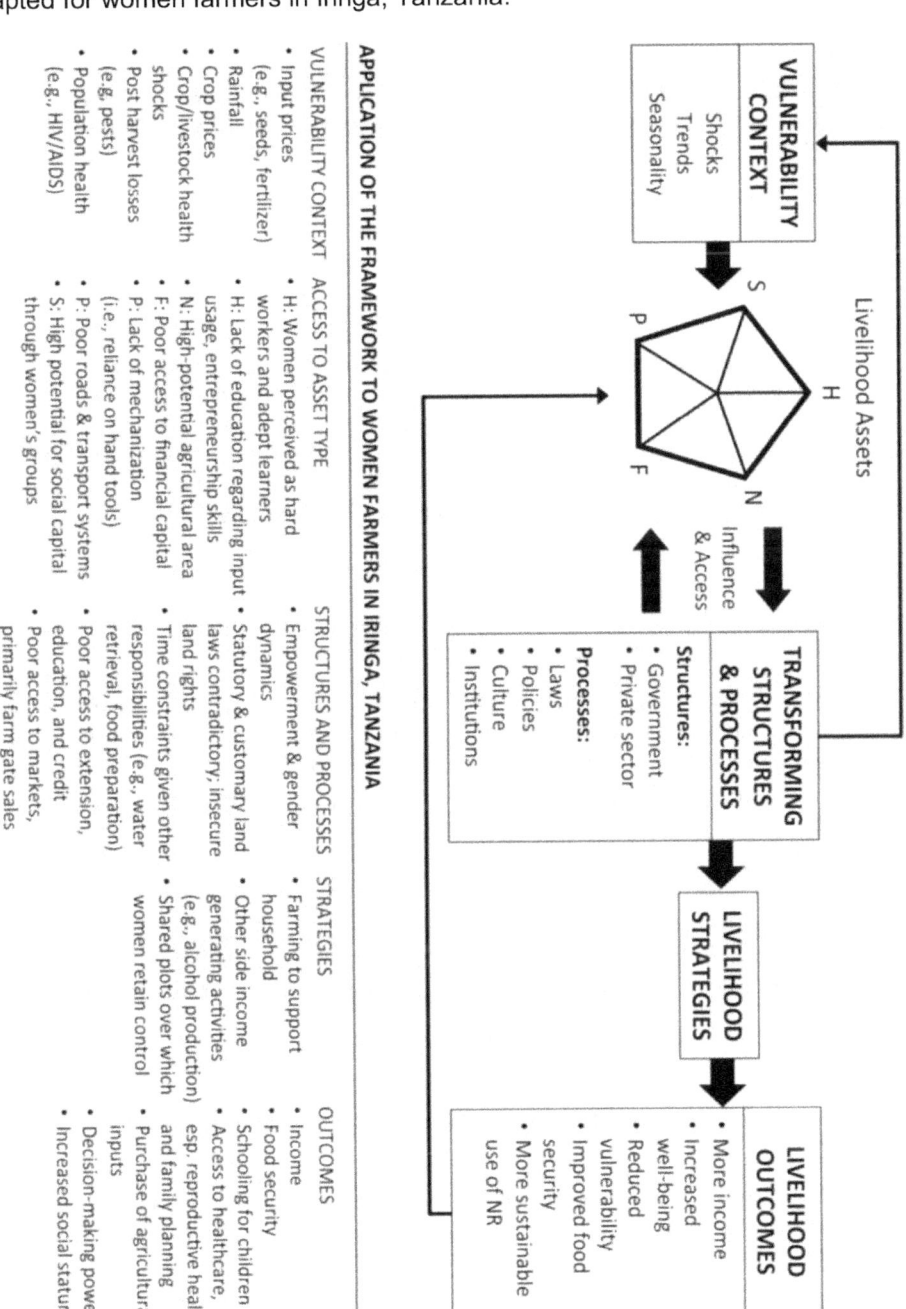

The main 'takeaway' from the use of these models is that they can be used to assess how the various capitals impact on livelihoods and wellbeing, but are in turn impacted by many factors including how those livelihoods are maintained over time and the institutions and processes involved.

***

Stiglitz et al (2018) highlights that not everyone puts a monetary value on capitals:

> "The capital approach builds on the notion of preserving or increasing the different stocks (capital) that drive our welfare and well-being. This "stock" approach to sustainability can either look at variations in each stock in physical terms or convert all these assets into a monetary equivalent. So, the capital approach could evolve in two directions: either as a "mainstream economic approach", determining all types of capital and monetising them; or as an "organising framework" with physical indicators covering all the main assets."

One proponent of taking the non-monetary route is Fraser Murison Smith, for example in "Economics of a Crowded Planet (2019):

> "The perspective [of the book] on the economy is from the outside looking in… to provide a rationale for an economics of a crowded planet. That rationale begins with the material scale of the economy as a bounding condition for individual preference. It is predicated critically upon certain propositions about individual motivations and norms within a stable society on a crowded planet."

I'll discuss the interplay between monetary and non-monetary perspectives on capitals later. In the meantime, let's consider Natural Capital in more detail.

I've already referred to natural capital extensively so far in this book. But what exactly is it?

The concept of natural capital has been around for a long time. As Fenichel and Abbott (2014) point out:

> "Treating natural resources as capital in economic theory goes back at least 200 years to classical economists such as Ricardo and Faustmann (Gaffney 2008), with modern treatment beginning with Hotelling (1931)"

With apologies in advance for the multiple nesting of the following short quotes, Zhang (2015) has published work on developments in natural capital valuation in economics. Quoting from Gaffney (2008) and Ricardo (1821), Zhang points out that this is an under-developed area of economics practice:

> "As pointed out by Gaffney (2008),

"Most economists today live in a two-factor world: There is just labor and capital. Land, so central to classical political economy, has been swallowed into capital and "disappeared.""

Determination of land values and dynamics of land values are important in contemporary market economies. ... It is obvious that determination of land values involves taking account of nonlinear dynamic interactions among many variables. It may explain why economics still lacks profound theories to deal with [the] dynamic of land values. In fact, [this is an important omission because] land use is a central concern of classical economics.

[As] Ricardo (1821: preface) pointed out:
"The produce ... is divided among three classes of the commodity, namely, the proprietor of land, the owners of the stock or capital necessary for its cultivation, and laborers by whose industry it is cultivated. But in different stages of the society, the proportions of the whole produce of the earth which will be allotted to each of these classes, under the names of rent, profits, and wages, will be essentially different; depending mainly on the actual fertility of the soil, on the accumulation of capital and population, and on the skill, ingenuity, and the instruments in agriculture."

What Ricardo (1821: preface) observed [a] long time ago is still relevant today:

"To determine the laws which regulate this distribution, is the principal problem in Political Economy: much as the science has been improved by the writings of Turgot, Stuart, Smith, Say, Sismondi, and others, they afford very little satisfactory information respecting the natural course of rent, profit, and wages."

In Ricardo's statement there is no reference to land value (price). The traditional Ricardian theory does not determine land price dynamics. Nevertheless, price dynamics are important variables of modern economies."

There are particular challenges with identifying accounting values for natural resources, especially non-renewable ones (but also, to a lesser extent, renewable ones, if they are pushed beyond sustainable limits so that their stocks/levels become unsustainable). For example, dealing with the potential for an infinite valuation is an issue which might hinder acceptance of such values into balance sheets or economic models. As Hotelling (1931) points out:

"Problems of exhaustible assets are peculiarly liable to become entangled with the infinite. Not only is there infinite time to consider, but also the possibility that for a necessity the price might increase without limit as the supply vanishes. If we are not to have property of infinite value, we must, in choosing empirical forms for cost and demand curves, take precautions to avoid assumptions, perfectly natural in static problems, which lead to such conditions."

Hotelling gave some insights into the types of natural assets that he thought would be important:

> "While a complete study of the subject would include semi-replaceable assets such as forests and stocks of fish, ranging gradually downward to such short-time operations as crop carry-overs, this paper will be confined in scope to absolutely irreplaceable assets"

Before moving on to discuss calculations involving those irreplaceable assets, however, Hotelling says a little more about natural assets that should be considered in economics, and the same could apply to them being considered within scope for accounting in balance sheets and profit and loss statements:

> "The forests of a continent occupied by a new population may, for purposes of a first approximation at least, be regarded as composed of two parts, of which one will be replaced after cutting and the other will be consumed without re-placement. The first part obeys the laws of static theory; the second, those of the economics of exhaustible assets. Wild life which may replenish itself if not too rapidly exploited presents questions of a different type."

Hotelling's use of the term "semi-replaceable" is what we would recognise as the term "renewable" in more modern texts. It's interesting that, in discussing those assets, he makes the distinction between the part of those assets that are "replaced" and the part that is "consumed" (without replacement). This gives a sense that there is an opportunity to see some part of a natural asset (what we're now calling Natural Capital) being maintained sustainably and which could be included in balance sheets at some fairly steady permanent value. The other part (the part consumed) could be included in a profit and loss account as a cost (e.g. cost of goods sold).

Interest in this type of capital asset has increased in recent times and this has led to work being done to overcome barriers to its adoption in mainstream accounting practices.

I build on this context in the next chapter, where I delve more extensively into definitions of natural capital in particular, given its central significance in the Planetary CFO's world balance sheet.

Chapter 6

The significance of natural capital accounting and substitutability

"Strong sustainability assumes that the environmental capital [natural capital] and [other forms of capital] are complementary, but not interchangeable [ie not substitutable]. Strong sustainability accepts there are certain functions that the environment performs that cannot be duplicated by humans or human made [produced or financial] capital."

Wikipedia, 2020)

Chapter summary

- Definitions of natural capital
- Should it include only the direct economic benefits to humans or some of the indirect benefits?
- How to value natural capital
- Substitutability of natural capital

Definitions of Natural Capital

The following, from King et al (2019), leads us towards it, but doesn't quite get us to a definition of Natural Capital:

> **"Nature as nature:** This relates to the way that stocks of habitats and biodiversity are perceived by people (either in-situ or remotely). They include public preferences for maintaining the extent and condition of key habitats and addressing species population loss because they value its existence for themselves and/or wish the benefits biodiversity provides to be available to others (bequest value) now and in the future."

This does at least point us in the direction of considering stocks of habitats and living organisms (ie treating both of them as capital assets).

Hawken et al (2010) get us a lot closer, by using a systems (asset) perspective:

> "Natural capital can be viewed as the sum total of the ecological systems that support life... "

The following figure is adapted from European Union 2017 (see references), to break down natural capital into sub-categories that are used by the European Union in relation to Natural Capital Accounting.

Figure 27 – natural capital and its main constituent parts:

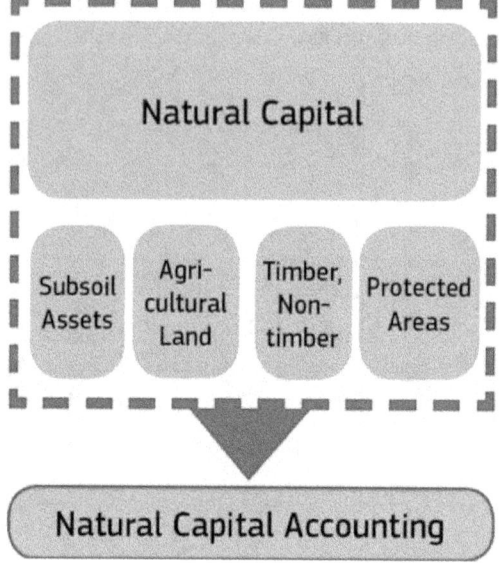

While the picture and classification above is rather simplified, a question that it prompts is where living animals fit in, for example livestock on land (and, indeed, fish in the oceans and the habitats in which they live). Land will be examined in more detail in the next chapter.

Natural capital can be further classified as either **non-renewable natural capital** (such as minerals, fossil fuels etc) which can only be used once, are exhaustible and cannot be replaced in anything faster than long geological timescales, and **renewable natural capital**, which will continue providing outputs forever (as long as it's not allowed to fall below safe thresholds through capital maintenance).

Anderson (2018) gives a good account of the many current debates about the use of natural capital in economics and national accounting. One of his key statements highlights that, although this is a topic of increasing interest in the mainstream, there are many aspects to be settled and a lot of work yet to be done in compiling robust numbers for use in world balance sheets:

> "One of the ongoing challenges is the need to go beyond merely raising awareness of the interdependence of ecosystems and human well-being. There is an unprecedented urgency for advancing the fundamental interdisciplinary science of ecosystem services, and 'implementing this science in decisions to restore natural capital and use it sustainably'... While natural capital has played an important role to date in engaging the key stakeholders it has not, as yet, delivered the real change to practice that is demonstrably needed."

Substitutability of capitals is an important issue, and so I'll now set out what this means and some of its implications.

Substitutability of capitals

Figure 28 - From TEEB (2018):

Source: Own representation, building on Laure Ledoux in ten Brink et al. 2012 and MA (2005) www.maweb.org/en/index.aspx and TEEB National

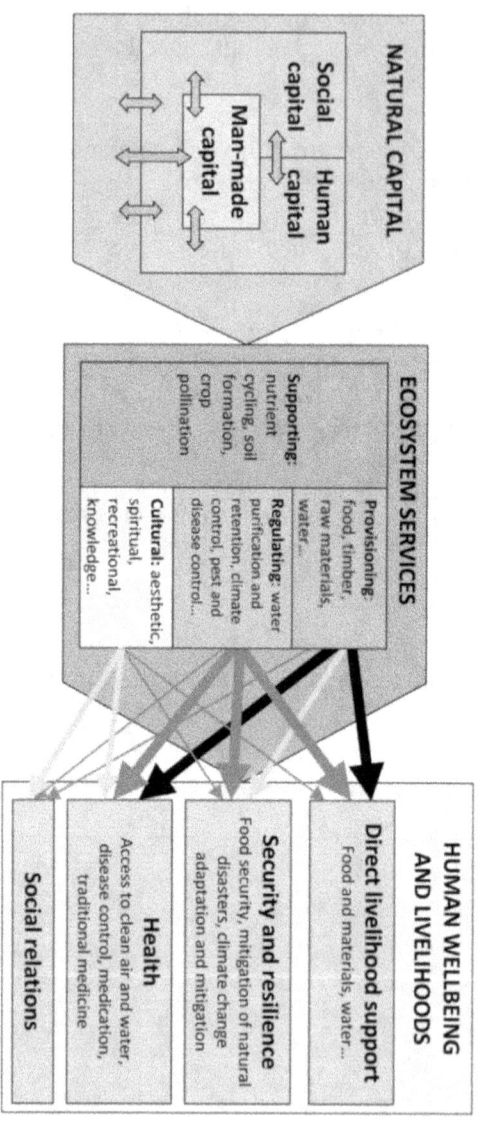

Key to the above figure: as in the Millennium Assessment 2005, the colour of the arrows presents the potential for mediation by socioeconomic factors (i.e. substitutability): the darker the arrow the more opportunities for substitution. A light colour implies less potential for substitution. The arrow's width presents the Intensity of linkages between ecosystem services and human well-being.

The following definition of substitutability is from TEEB (2018):

> **"Substitutability:** The extent to which human-made capital can be substituted for natural capital (or vice versa) …
>
> … A frequent concern about the use of monetary values is the implication that all asset classes are substitutable, and that so long as overall per-capita capital grows in a country, all is well. This is sometimes referred to as "weak sustainability" (Pearce et al. 1989). In reality, ecosystems and biodiversity are subject to major non-linearity such that some degree of substitution may be tolerated, but beyond a point, phase changes occur with significant consequences as entire ecosystems cross *thresholds* or 'points of no return'."

Lawn (2001) indicates that, because of the different roles of natural and produced capital ("human-made capital") in the production processes, these two forms of capital at least are not in any real sense substitutable:

> "… human-made capital and natural capital are fundamentally different elements of the production process. Natural capital, and the low entropy it provides, constitute the material cause of production. Human-made capital, as low entropy resource transforming agents, constitute the efficient cause of production. More of an efficient cause of production produces nothing without the input of the material cause of production."

Cohen et al (2018) talk extensively about some of the challenges surrounding assessing the degree of substitutability of natural capital:

> "The extent to which natural capital can be substituted with physical [produced] or human capital in production is one of the main concerns for the possibility of long-run sustainable economic development…. The degree to which the same output can be obtained with a different combination of inputs depends on the elasticity of substitution between inputs (Slutsky, 1915; Hicks and Allen, 1934; Arrow et al., 1961; Samuelson, 1974; Blackorby and Russell, 1976, 1981, 1989; Stern, 2011). We show that most of the estimates of the elasticities of substitution between natural, physical and human capital are either unreliable or uninformative for key issues in economic development, such as climate change mitigation or sustainable agriculture. Most estimates are based on old studies using econometric methods that are not able to deal with pervasive endogeneity issues, including the simultaneous determination of the output and the inputs used in production, measurement error, input-neutral technical change (Griliches, 1967)."

However, they do go on to provide some steer:

"... our empirical analysis presented in Cohen et al (2017), subject to the caveats above, suggests that overall substitutability of natural capital, in the aggregate, is either low or moderate. There are further reasons for caution here:

> • Any point estimate of the substitutability of nature relates to a specific geographical scale. At the national level, data on aggregate natural capital is generally available. However, the process of aggregation renders the entire exercise somewhat questionable – subsoil assets such as oil and gas are simply not the same sort of production input as climatic conditions or water purification from a forest; adding them together does a disservice to their different functions.

> • To address the challenges created by aggregation, analysis can proceed to a more granular level by exploring the substitutability of natural inputs at the industry or firm level. The challenges here are that granular data on natural capital inputs is frequently unavailable, at least beyond energy and materials.

We conclude that many of these estimates suffer from serious bias and estimation problems, making them an unreliable basis for policy. To the extent that tentative conclusions may be available, they are that – at present levels of natural capital – substitutability is already relatively low, implying that further reductions in natural capital are likely to harm economic output."

From Read (2014, the emboldening is mine):

"... the possibility of exchange between different forms of capital is a fundamental source of contention and is definitive of one's approach to sustainability. A 'weak' definition of sustainability accepts substitution between 'natural' and other forms of capital, whereas a 'strong' definition of sustainability would insist that natural capital is different in kind and cannot be compensated by money ... We would suggest that a basic condition for an adequate definition of sustainability is that **nature cannot be substituted for by other types of 'capital'** – and that this insistence, moreover, marks the distinction between 'weak' and 'strong' definitions of sustainability ... those who subscribe to strong sustainability argue... that we must maintain the stock of natural capital – that is to say, the value of the earth itself – because there are no substitutes for the natural systems that we depend on."

Ringfencing of capital and of capital maintenance funds as a means of enforcing non-substitutability of natural capital

I'll now make a brief mention of a technical development in accounting theory, relating to capital theory, that might help us construct a supporting argument for the

Planetary CFO's approach to constructing a World Balance Sheet. This is the separate identification and ringfencing of certain capitals, and their ongoing maintenance. This is a concept that goes beyond mere depreciation.

Depreciation is a way of accounting for depletion. Many people are arguing for the recognition of this depletion in relation to the natural capital assets that produce the natural products and services that keep us all alive. However, doing this alone (without further measures) would only lead to a running down of the values of natural capital in the balance sheet. Sustainable outcomes will only be achieved if the assets are maintained at sustainable levels (or at least not allowed to fall below sustainable levels), and in order to achieve this, funds need to be established to provide for this capital maintenance activity, and amounts need to be transferred to these funds each and every year (as a deduction from, or cost set against, revenues).

Therefore, there needs to be a requirement, alongside natural capital depreciation rules, for a commitment to spend money on maintaining/restoring natural capital, as recognised by Rambaud (2016). This could be achieved using ringfencing of relevant reserves (eg natural capital maintenance funds) and equivalent cash balances held, until they are spent (on capital maintenance activities, which is when such activity becomes capital investment that restores natural capital to its full (sustainable) value in balance sheets).

Ringfencing of accounting reserves/funds in this way has been around for a long time, and forms the basis of many examples of "restricted funds" which can only be used for certain purposes. You only have to look at the charity sector for numerous examples of this. This is because the institutional providers of most grant funding to charities specify how those grants can (and cannot) be used. The charities must record this, track actual spend against those restricted reserves, and report back to the grant providers on how 'their' money was spent (and on the outcomes achieved). Although the providers' money is no longer legally 'theirs' once it has been paid over to the charity, there are usually written contracts in place to create the legal obligations concerning fund use, tracking and reporting back. If those obligations are not adhered to by the charity, the grant giver could legally require the grant to be paid back to them.

Rambaud (2016) sets out a reasoned independence between certain types of capital and the firms in which they are invested:

> "These two types of independence do not imply that there is no interaction: capital is absolutely vital for a firm and, reciprocally, firms are necessary to develop capital. However, a capital is not *defined* by its utilisation in a given firm and, reciprocally, a firm is not *defined* by the owners of the capital. This perspective allows an approach to the economic system to be based on "*unfolding processes*" (Skaggs, 2003), where "*each transaction of goods and services finds its counterpart in a flow of credit/debt instruments, and these financial flows are seen to be integrated (circular): each flow comes from somewhere and goes somewhere. Hence it is possible to represent the economy in a balance sheet manner [...]*" (Bezemer, 2010). It means that the economic system can be seen as a hydraulic system where motion is made

possible by the injection of water (capital), but where this [capital] and the different mechanisms (firms for instance) have their own substances."

Extending Rambaud's ideas a little further, what if we were to ask a new shareholder (e.g. on a new share issue raising new funds) what type of capital they are intending to invest in an entity? We could give them the choices of the capital types (one of which is natural capital). In the first instance, the key distinction would be between types of capital that are substitutable and those that are not. So that would be, for example, between natural capital and other types of capital. In this way, the new capital could be ringfenced, at the point it comes into the entity, and this would enable the non-substitutability to take effect from that earliest point. The ring-fenced capital could not be converted into unringfenced capital and this would help to ensure that the natural capital assets (and potentially the human capital assets) representing ringfenced capital were maintained sustainably.

One of the methods of maintaining natural capital assets is to identify the resource required to do so, and this can be represented by an amount of capital maintenance charge. As Rambaud states:

"Maintaining the capital means guaranteeing the integrity of the capital, which implies the necessity of finding specific ways to counterbalance … degradations."

He goes on to point out that the resources for such maintenance must be real (realised) resources, not unrealised ones:

"Because this maintenance must be effective because of the intrinsic reality of the capital, these revenues must also be actual: if we record unrealised gains, we simply jeopardise the integrity of the capital."

There are consequences of this type of approach. For example, profit (i.e. surplus) must be reconceived as comprising a sum arrived at after securing the ongoing sustainability of the natural capital and human capital (through capital maintenance). Rambaud puts it quite succinctly thus:

"In these conditions, income [profit, at a net level] is the measure of the sustainable surplus, generated by a firm"

It follows from this that, as Rambaud puts it, "the rate of return for owners is a residual concept, a mere consequence of this activity [of maintaining the natural capital and human capital assets sustainably]."

Rambaud highlights that these conceptions of capital were prevalent in early traditional accounting thinking and practices, but that in modern times such thinking has been usurped in the mainstream by practitioners preferring not to ring-fence capitals. The prevalent practice, therefore, is to see capitals as completely substitutable and convertible, so that a piece of natural capital asset today can be sold and converted into a piece of produced capital (e.g. by buying a new industrial factory with the proceeds) tomorrow. The current practice is therefore wrong and is one of the reasons why natural capital is being depleted (and/or converted) at frightening rates.

For some readers, the above might have leapt forward past something they are concerned about, which is in some ways the very first step which we have skipped glibly over, ie the difficult challenge of deciding whether it is right (and/or instrumental) to even be working with the concept of "natural capital" at all.

The natural capital concept – some theoretical foundations

There are at least a couple of very different schools of thought on this subject. One insists that it's both impossible and immoral to put a value on nature. The other suggests that **not** putting any value at all on nature is actually worse because it facilitates nature's destruction.

Let's briefly look at some examples from each of these perspectives.

At one extreme are those who suggest, for example as Murison Smith (2020) does, that the term "natural capital" is, in effect, an oxymoron, because:

> "A capital asset is not … self-regenerating. It must either be regenerated … through maintenance by people, or replaced … In this sense, it is fundamentally different from productive assets employing the [self-regeneration] of living things, such as farmland."

Even if one accepts a recognition that a natural asset can be considered as a capital asset, putting a value on that asset is problematic to some. Read (2014), for example, essentially takes the view that putting any value on natural capital at all is inconsistent with non-substitutability of natural capital, because the placing of a value on it strongly implies that an exchange involving conversion into another type of capital is possible, even if that exchange doesn't actually happen.

However, many others take a very different view to the above perspectives, and see a proper accounting for natural capital as essential to its preservation, adequate maintenance, enhancement and stewardship. Typical of this part of the spectrum of views is Helm (2015):

> "… a price has to be put on nature … where there is no price, and hence no cost to the users of these natural resources, there is no incentive to conserve them. That is why they are over-exploited and, as a result, degraded."

Many people are somewhere between the two extremes.

Stiglitz et al (2018) is typical of the school of thought that suggests we should be pragmatic, and that, in fact, we don't need to use market prices (with all their unhelpful associations), as illustrated by their description of how to value capitals, including natural capital, as part of managing the sustainability of balance sheets:

> "Measuring sustainability from a capital approach focuses on the net change in the volumes of the stocks of various assets, weighed [ie weighted, ie multiplied] by their "shadow prices" (i.e. a monetary value reflecting the true opportunity costs of all activities, taking into account all externalities and public goods generated by them); these shadow prices will in general differ from market prices, and depend on all other types of capital, technology and societal preferences. Shadow prices should also reflect future actions and their discounted consequences to make net changes in overall capital a true indicator of sustainability (for a full discussion of the theoretical issues associated with the capital approach, see Fleurbaey and Blanchet, 2013)."

The main significance of identifying natural capital and valuing it is that this approach lends itself to influencing behaviours that are driven by financial considerations. Such behaviours might be relating to capital asset management, measuring return on that capital, creation or conversion of capital, drawdown of capital (ie conversion of capital into income) or simply to track depletion and damage to that capital over time from whatever cause. These are all legitimate methods used in relation to capital that could be extremely useful in tracking what is happening to natural capital that would otherwise be more difficult to track if we reject the notion of natural capital at the outset.

Even if accounting for natural capital becomes the accepted norm, it's by no means a foregone conclusion that it will be properly protected and maintained at sustainable levels. Pressures to convert natural capital into other forms of capital, or into income, are severe in many developing countries which have a large amount of the former and insufficient of the latter. Even World Bank (2018) recognises these pressures, and, indeed, encourages such countries to develop their other capitals:

> "For resource-rich low- and middle-income countries that have linked their development aspirations to natural resources, current market signals have been discouraging. The vulnerability of these countries to commodity price shocks underscores the need to diversify their asset base, and specifically to invest in human and produced capital beyond a traditional reliance on natural capital."

One temptation for developing countries is to look at what they do have in abundance (natural capital) and use it (potentially overuse it) to make up for deficiencies in other forms of capital wealth.

In the next chapter, I develop the arguments around natural capital, its valuation and its relationship to "land" in more depth, working it into a more or less developed theory of value for natural capital.

Chapter 7

A theory of value for natural capital

"While there may be no "right" way to value a forest, a river, or a child, the wrong way is to give it no value at all."

(Hawken et al, 2010)

"Buy land – they're not making it any more"

(Mark Twain)

A number of motivations exist for the valuation of ecosystem services and ecosystem assets, based on the purpose of analysis and the context for the use of valuations in monetary terms. The different motivations point to different requirements in terms of concepts, methods and assumptions. Often, valuation is dismissed or utilized without careful consideration of the relationship between the purpose of analysis and the choice of valuation concepts and methods.
(SEEA - EEA - United Nations, New York, 2014)

An excerpt from Foster (1997) introduces this topic very nicely:

> "How do we value nature? How do we, and how should we, express our sense of the worth and practical importance of our natural environment, and the significance of our relations with other living things? How do we include such values within the processes of social decision-making? How, in particular, do we integrate them with the economic considerations which feature so prominently in those processes? … Does the currently favoured discourse of sustainability and natural capital … constitute a further, more insidious stage in its progressive *devaluing* – a new eco-friendly jargon for licensing our aspirations to technological management and control of nature?"

These are some of the questions Foster concerned himself with, and they are quite fundamental to any acceptance of the meaningfulness and usefulness of any values used for natural capital within a world balance sheet approach.

I will follow the attitude (expressed by Hawken, above) that it is better to use a roughly right value that is useful in policy making than to use an exactly wrong value of zero, the latter of which is the current default position in many parts of the world for many types of natural assets. Let's not forget that placing a value on something is not the same thing as creating a market price for it, or even encouraging such a market to exist. One of the fears is exactly that – of a natural asset being made more vulnerable to being exploited for profit in a marketplace by having a value placed on it. But valuation can, by contrast, be used to help asset stewardship, for example by highlighting the importance of its protection, maintenance and enhancement, and to discourage the drawdown and conversion of capital assets into other assets or consumables.

As within SEEA (covered in more detail in chapter 9) the focus in this chapter is on valuation of natural and ecosystem assets that are:

(i)   not exchanged in markets or

(ii)   are exchanged in markets that are believed to be highly distorted.

Attempting to calculate any value for nature is not without significant challenges. We already saw in chapter 3 that, when we used a simple discounted net present value calculation of all the future benefits to humans provided by nature, there was a wide range of values we could use for those benefits. This, and the challenge of finding an appropriate discount rate, are reflective of the fact that the measurement and valuation of nature is not a settled issue among economists, ecologists and others.

In addition to Foster (1997), Anderson (2018) is another example of an important text describing numerous challenges in this aspect of valuation of natural assets, including questions of whether it is considered appropriate and morally defensible to place any value on it at all.

As Costanza et al (2014) suggest, this is a controversial topic, but one in which there are advantages in valuing nature that are difficult to ignore:

> "There has been an on-going debate about what some see as the "commodification" of nature that this approach [valuation of ecosystem services] supposedly implies (Costanza, 2006; McCauley, 2006) and what others see as the flawed methods and questionable wisdom of aggregating ecosystem services values to larger scales (Chaisson, 2002) ... Some have argued that estimating the global value of ecosystem services is meaningless, because if we lost all ecosystem services human life would end, so their value must be infinite ...   We think that these critiques are largely misplaced once one understands the context and multiple potential uses of ecosystem services valuation ..."

However, let's start by looking at the Planetary CFO's theory of value, and then we'll move on to relevant definitions of land, and see where that leads us in terms of balance sheet valuations of both land and natural capital. Then we'll come back to some of the controversies.

Valuation of assets – some theory

Having been trained as an Accountant, and having enjoyed the challenges and experiences of applying my financial qualification and skills in many different operational contexts over the years, I do find myself sometimes drawing on financial approaches to human organisations and seeing if they can be applied, as a thought exercise, to the natural world. I know there are potential pitfalls in doing this, because there has been a very lively debate about this type of approach over the decades.

However, supposing for now that we wish to value a natural asset, we only have to visit some fundamentals of accounting and economics and we will find that there are numerous ways of valuing something, so in fact we are spoilt for choice on how to proceed with our first step – identifying a definition of "value".

There is a long tradition of people thinking about value. An early example is Ricardo (1821) in which he states:

> "It has been observed by Adam Smith, that
>
>> "… the word Value has two different meanings, and sometimes expresses the utility of some particular object, and sometimes the power of purchasing other goods which the possession of that object conveys. The one may be called *value in use;* the other *value in exchange.* The things which have the greatest value in use, have frequently little or no value in exchange; and, on the contrary, those which have the greatest value in exchange, have little or no value in use. Water and air are abundantly useful; they are indeed indispensable to existence, yet, under ordinary circumstances, nothing can be obtained in exchange for them. Gold, on the contrary, though of little use compared with air or water, will exchange for a great quantity of other goods."

Since then, numerous people have explored value and discovered a plethora of further meanings.

As just one example, in Daly (1991):

> "If we adopt a historical cost convention then the price of [natural] resources *in situ* is zero. If we adopt a replacement cost definition then the price is high."

When we say we value something today, it might mean we'd rather not lose it, or lose the access to it or the ability to experience it. Or perhaps we gain something from being able to use it, and we lose something if we lose the use of it. And the more difficult it is to restore it or replace it, the higher the value we would place on it, perhaps.

This multiplicity of meanings/perspectives gives rise to a variety of ways of placing a value on an object. For example, a monetary amount we ascribe to an object (what we call its "value") might represent:

1. The original cost of producing it, if we made it ourselves – including amounts for our time and effort as well as all the raw materials, energy and other inputs to the processes used (historic cost)

2. The amount we paid for it if we bought it rather than making it ourselves (purchase cost)

3. The cost of replacing it if it is lost or destroyed (replacement cost)

4. The cost of alternative means of satisfying the same need or desire that it fulfils (a substitution value)

5. The money that could be obtained by preparing it for sale and then selling it (realisable value)

6. The price at which it can be bought or sold in its current state in a perfect market (market value)

7. The amount we could claim from an insurance company if it was lost in an incident covered by insurance (insured value)

8. The total of all the future discounted cash in-flows and out-flows generated by the expected future use of the object until it reaches the end of its useful life (the Net Present Value, or economic value)

9. The total negative impact on the planetary biosphere from the removal or conversion of the object from its current position, condition or role (what we might call "deprival value").

10. A value or price set by policy to achieve a particular policy objective, eg in order to manage demand, or to incentivise a desirable change of land use

Meanings 2, 5 and 6 are probably the closest ones to modern everyday use of the term "value" (eg a market-based approach) and are all quite close to the meanings expressed by Adam Smith all those years ago, as quoted by Ricardo above. It immediately becomes apparent, as set out by Adam Smith in the quote, why these values can be very different for different objects, and can be very different for the same object depending on the context and the reasons for ascribing it a value.

I want to mention "least cost alternative" here. This is a concept from economics. It stems from a type of analysis that attempts to answer the question "if we didn't have this asset, what would be the least cost alternative means of producing the benefits (goods or services) the asset currently produces and would continue to produce (perhaps forever) if it continued to exist".

In terms of valuing natural capital, the least cost alternative is somewhat of a red herring. This is because we cannot assume that there will always be the ability to substitute alternative forms of capital for natural capital. In fact, from a strong sustainability perspective, we should not allow any substitutability at all, in order to preserve natural capital even at its currently depleted amount and condition.

Once a principle is chosen to reflect the characteristics of the object, its context and the motive for the valuation, calculating an actual value is the next step. The data that is needed will obviously follow from the choice that was made. For example, historic cost requires information to be gathered about those past costs. Future discounted cash flow, on the other hand, involves a more complex calculation that requires a forecast to be made of changes in future income and/or costs associated with the decision to either keep possession of the object to be valued or to transfer/sell it to someone else. It also requires a discount rate to be selected for the calculation.

It is allowable in accountancy to use estimates, when applying any of the above principles to calculations. The one caveat I would put on that statement is to bear in mind that the accuracy of any estimates used will need to be considered when using the calculated values for decision-making. Often, calculated results are more sensitive to inaccuracies in some variables used than others. This can be explored by using mathematical or statistical techniques such as sensitivity analyses. This book is not intended to be a mathematical or statistical treatise, and so I won't go into the details of such techniques here. There are many excellent textbooks that can do a much better job than I ever could at explaining what they are, how they work and how to use them in real-world calculations.

Of course, in most circumstances, all of the above approaches would result in a different value being calculated. The method we select for a particular situation, especially a novel one, therefore becomes very context-dependent.

In a sustainability context, the most concerning disjoint between such valuations would occur when someone owning or controlling a part of the natural capital places the wrong kind of value on it. For example, rainforest that has taken millennia to evolve and achieve a balanced and healthy ecosystem state should arguably be valued at replacement cost, which is very high because of the immense amount of time and effort that would be required to replicate the patient construction of the ecosystem by nature. The realisable value or market value might be much, much lower because there is much less effort and time required to cut down the trees and sell the wood to someone than there is to grow a healthy ecosystem.

Therefore, the method of valuation chosen very much depends on the purpose for which it is being done. There is a big difference between current approaches and those appropriate for maintaining natural assets within healthy ecosystems, within a sustainable custodianship role.

One valid approach, for example, would be to value natural assets at what might be called "natural replacement cost" while they remain in their natural state, and valuing them at a conversion cost if they are removed from that ecosystem (e.g. by being cut down and converted into raw materials). Their value after conversion would be a lot lower than their value in the natural state, which would then provide an important signal of the loss in value caused by removing them from their natural state and converting them into raw materials.

This might help prevent the Tragedy of the Commons, by ensuring that, as essential natural assets become scarcer, they become more and more highly valued in their natural state for the purposes of conservation, even though they also become more and more valuable (through scarcity effects) for their potential to be converted for alternative use outside the ecosystem. That duality of perspectives on the same object is a necessary step in order to reconcile the need for sustainable conservation alongside the need for sustainable harvesting and use of resources in sustainable ways for humanity to co-exist successfully with natural ecosystems in perpetuity. For effective conservation, as the level of natural assets approached the sustainable limit, the difference between the replacement cost and the conversion cost would have to continue to increase in order to reduce demand and protect the natural assets from overexploitation beyond sustainable levels. Whether this would happen naturally through the economists' calculations, or whether a global custodian would have to use interventions to manage those value differentials, is not yet clear.

The role of a global custodian could certainly legitimately include levying taxes or fines comprising (at least) the difference between the natural replacement value and the converted material value (as described above). A proviso on this is that there needs to be the means to apply the revenue from such taxes or fines to undertake the necessary replacement activity, with the intention of maintaining the natural assets at a sustainable level. The success of this approach depends on adequate prevention, detection and policing of acts giving rise to such taxes or fines. The sizes of the taxes or fines could be set at levels that provide deterrence, or simply demand management, sufficient to prevent exploitation of the natural assets beyond sustainable levels.

Another possibility is to put a value on natural assets as carbon sinks, and you'll see this method features quite strongly in the detailed workings supporting the numbers used in the Planetary CFO's world balance sheet.

There are some people, including some ardent environmentalists, who resist or even reject altogether any attempts to put a value on nature, in the way that the concept of natural capital demands.

This reluctance to place values on natural assets (or some aspects of ecosystem services) is a tradition that goes back quite a long time. For example, Schumacher (1973) states:

> "To press non-economic values into the framework of the economic calculus, economists use the method of cost/benefit analysis. This is generally thought to be an enlightened and progressive development, as it is at least an attempt to take account of costs and benefits which might otherwise be disregarded altogether. In fact, however, it is a procedure by which the higher is reduced to the level of the lower and the priceless is given a price. It can therefore never serve to clarify the situation and lead to an enlightened decision. All it can do is lead to self-deception or the deception of others; for to undertake to measure the immeasurable is absurd and constitutes but an elaborate method of moving from preconceived notions to foregone conclusions; all one has to do to obtain the desired results is to impute suitable values to the immeasurable costs and benefits. The logical absurdity, however, is not the greatest fault of the undertaking: what is worse, and destructive of civilisation, is the pretence that everything has a price or, in other words, that money is the highest of all values."

Although there are a multitude of approaches to valuation, reaching a value for natural capital, and ensuring it is maintained at an appropriate level of functionality, is, in the view of the Planetary CFO, the key to a sustainable future.

Helm (2015) makes this point very clearly:

> "Valued assets are worth looking after … Refusing to price or place an economic value on nature risks environmental breakdown …The issue is not what something is ultimately 'worth', but rather how much should be spent to preserve and enhance it."

Of course, there are many other views, and the thorny topic of placing a value on nature is explored quite thoroughly in, for example, Anderson (2018), who says:

> "The concepts we use to describe the world are not neutral. They have their own implications, histories, and often supporters and critics. The concept of "natural capital" is one such contested concept, playing a key role in current debates about the future of the natural world. For some, it is seen as a means of protecting the planet, whilst others see it as a threat to lives and livelihoods."

A good representation of the reluctance to put a value on nature is shown by the views of George Monbiot, the famous environmental campaigner. In 2014, I addressed my own response to those objections in a blog post under my online alter-ego, the Planetary CFO (Chief Financial Officer) as follows:

Blog post copy --------------------------------

(Open response from the Planetary CFO to Monbiot article in the Guardian July 2014)

Put a price on nature? We must do this to enable us to achieve One Planet Living

Author: Planetary Chief Financial Officer

(27 July 2014)

As self-appointed Planetary Chief Financial Officer ("CFO") I feel it is incumbent on me to respond to several points George Monbiot makes in the above-mentioned article.

He claims that valuation of natural assets is being done to make them more marketable by capitalists, for example as assets providing ecosystem services. My own concept is that all assets on the planet should be valued, but within various asset classes. One asset class would be Global Commons and this class would contain assets for which asset rights are carefully defined and protected. Assets within this class could not be put into any market, and the purposes of valuing them would be to provide a means to identify the relative sufficiency or deficit of such assets in relation to the liabilities to provide for the global human population alongside appropriate planetary biodiversity. These assets and liabilities would be reported each decade in a World Balance Sheet.

Monbiot criticises early attempts and methods to value natural assets. This is a legitimate concern, but not a good reason to stop trying to find better valuation methods. They will be found – we can be confident of that. That's part of the role of the Planetary CFO.

Monbiot points out the perverse incentives regarding land use – the example he quoted is of a farmer having a financial incentive to have a small number of Ospreys on his land rather than sheep, because of the huge revenues from visitors wanting to see Ospreys. If the World Balance Sheet comes into being, the scenario Monbiot painted would only exist for land which was not in the Global Commons asset class. In these other asset classes, trading would be encouraged and could take place without compromising the Global Commons.

Monbiot criticises Dieter Helm's comments about green growth being good for the economy. Here, I think I disagree with both of them, to some degree, and would like to set out an alternative frame of reference to resolve and unify what I believe are the ultimate aims of both of them in looking at natural assets. Monbiot's main point seems to be that economic growth, even if green, causes damage to the environment (i.e. the natural capital). However, within the World Balance Sheet approach, green growth is good if (and only if) it leads to a good balance between the amounts (at an appropriate value) of assets in the Global Commons asset class, compared with the liabilities to provide for the global population (see above).

Monbiot criticises valuation of (UK) natural assets, on the premise that this would hand over stewardship of them to the City of London. Within the World Balance Sheet approach, stewardship of the assets would fall to a Global Governance Body ("GGB") which doesn't yet exist except within my imagination. This also addresses Monbiot's concerns about power, if the GGB was to be set up with sufficient power to undertake its mission and role. Its mission would be:

"One Planet Living, for Humanity, Forever"

Monbiot criticises cost-benefit analyses, for their part in creating perverse incentives to convert natural assets to commercial assets, for example turning ancient woodlands into motorway service stations (another example might be railway lines such as HS2). Under the World Balance Sheet approach, the answer to this is to ensure that assets in the Global Commons asset class could not be turned into assets in another asset class. In effect, certain asset classes would be ring-fenced. Within each asset class, some conversion of assets would be allowed. Within the Global Commons asset class, however, this would be determined largely by natural processes, and any man-made asset conversions would be carefully monitored.

Finally, Monbiot quotes values as a reason not to value natural assets, on the basis that financialisation of assets is a capitalist's value not an environmentalist's one. He is right to point out that this is a fundamental issue. I'd say that it is at the core of the dilemma facing humanity at the current historical crossroads – the values of consumerist capitalism and the values of sustainability (paraphrased as One Planet Living) appear on the surface to be diametrically opposed to each other. However, as Planetary CFO, I believe that the way forward lies in finding a middle way – the way that enables these very different camps to have a meaningful dialogue for peace and reconciliation. We must find the win-wins. I think the World Balance Sheet provides a way to do this. It means we can provide capitalists with asset classes they can base a real and thriving market-based economy on. It also means the Global Commons asset class, or asset classes, can be used to drive towards One Planet Living, in aggregate, for the whole of humanity.

Blog post copy ends --------------------------------

As mentioned in an earlier chapter, Costanza et al (2014) is an example of an academic text providing support to the use of appropriate valuations of natural capital.

So far in the current chapter I have delved into the mire of value theory, with a particular focus on natural capital.

Before moving on to particular applications of the theory to land and natural capital assets in the world balance sheet, I'll let Helm have the final word on optimal value, as he is such an influential leader in the realm of natural capital and has written several respected books on the subject. He rounds squarely on the mistake of relying on GDP measures, and points us clearly in the direction of valuing natural capital within a balance sheet approach. From Helm (2015):

"By focussing on GDP, the way economic growth is measured neglects *all* assets, not just natural assets. Remarkably, there is no proper balance sheet, and the future consequences of depleting natural capital are simply ignored. Indeed, depleting natural assets typically leads to an *increase* in GDP growth. … Worse still, the renewables – natural assets such as fish stocks, the rainforests and the soils that can go on producing their services forever – have little or no value in these accounts, precisely because they are free. Accounting for nature is not therefore just some arcane and academic exercise, but rather it is vital to turning the tide on nature's destruction. It shines a torch on what is going on, and tells us what level of consumption can be sustained over time … the optimal level of natural capital is almost certainly much higher than the current depleted state of nature … the natural capital balance sheet has to start being constructed. It helps in trying to see if the aggregate of natural capital is going up or down …"

Because of the intimate relationships between land and natural capital, I'll now spend some time examining them in more detail. This is particularly important as a building block to accounting for natural capital in the world balance sheet.

Definitions of Land

There is a high degree of consensus, in language dictionaries, on the definition of land, as shown by the following two examples:

"The surface of the earth that is not covered by water" (Cambridge English Dictionary)

"The part of the earth's surface that is not covered by water" (Oxford English Dictionary)

Although quite simple, these definitions are helpful in some ways, but unhelpful in others.

Defining land by what it is **not** (not covered by water) helps to some extent with a 'first approximation' when assessing a part of the earth's surface. We can ask "is it covered by water?" If the answer is "no" then it is, by definition, land.

On the other hand, how far does the "land" extend below the surface (down through the soil and rock) or, for that matter, above the surface (up through the atmosphere and into space)? And does it include the living organisms that inhabit the land, the soil, the water and the air?

Wikipedia gives us a rather more descriptive (if more wordy) definition, based on economics, and some inkling of key challenges surrounding ownership:

"In economics, **land** comprises all naturally occurring resources as well as geographic land. Examples include particular geographical locations, mineral deposits, forests, fish stocks, atmospheric quality, geostationary orbits, and portions of the electromagnetic spectrum. Supply of these resources is fixed ... Because no man created the land, it does not have a definite original proprietor, owner or user.

> "No man made the land. It is the original inheritance of the whole species." (*John Stuart Mill*)

As a consequence, conflicting claims on geographic locations and mineral deposits have historically led to disputes over their economic rent and contributed to many civil wars and revolutions."

Continuing in an economics context, Ryan-Collins et al (2017) describe it as follows:

> "... **land** is not simply soil, and its economic uses are not simply agricultural. In fact, land is better understood as *space* and the occupation of that space over time."

It can easily be seen from the above definition of land, and the earlier definition of natural capital in chapter 6, that the concepts of land and natural capital are in some ways similar, are intimately connected, and that changes in each of these categories of assets also impacts the other.

The interplay between geospatial units of land, ecosystems and natural capital is well covered in SEEA (for which there are many sources included in the References section at the end of this book, and which is discussed in some detail below).

Accounting Guidance

The International Financial Reporting Standards ("IFRS"), and the International Accounting Standards ("IAS") set the international frameworks guiding all accountants around the world in what is deemed to be acceptable ways of accounting for everything that appears in a balance sheet or a profit and loss statement. An example is the way assets are valued and reported. There are a number of accepted ways of attributing, or calculating, a value for an asset, including "land". In accounting guidance, land is included in "property, plant and equipment", being a particular type of "property".

Excerpt from IAS 16 ----------------------------

Property, plant and equipment are tangible items that:

> (a) are held for use in the production or supply of goods or services, for rental to others, or for administrative purposes; and

> (b) are expected to be used during more than one period.

The cost of an item of property, plant and equipment shall be recognised as an asset if, and only if:

> (a) it is probable that future economic benefits associated with the item will flow to the entity; and

> (b) the cost of the item can be measured reliably.

If the cost of land includes the costs of site dismantlement, removal and restoration, that portion of the land asset is depreciated over the period of benefits obtained by incurring those costs.

Excerpts end ---------------------

From the excerpts above, we can build on what I have said about the obligation to maintain land (at least that part of it falling within the definition of natural capital) to fulfil its role as part of a sustainable living biosphere. All that is required is to establish, and enforce, the principle of holding owners of land to account for maintaining the land sustainably. This needs to be backed up by national and international governance mechanisms (eg national and international laws and environmental regulations). When those governance measures are in place, then the asset value of any piece of land an owner wants to hold will reflect that sustainability obligation on the current owner.

If the land's current state is a long way below that which would be considered biospherically sustainable, then the value of the land might even be negative, because although the owner has an asset that will produce some positive economic value, for example from agricultural produce generated from it, there could exist a large obligation (liability) to set against that, representing the amount the current owner needs to spend to restore the land to a biospherically sustainable state. If the liability is larger than the value of the economic productivity of the land, then the land (asset) net value will be negative.

It follows that the market price of any piece of land an owner wants to sell will reflect that sustainability obligation on the current owner and also the same obligation on the new owner.

It is probably quite clear that, in the paragraphs above, I've base my arguments on a definition of strong sustainability when using the terms "sustainable" and "sustainability" etc.

Excerpts from:

https://www.ifrsbox.com/ias-16-property-plant-and-equipment/

Initial costs

Some items of property, plant and equipment might be necessary to acquire for safety or environmental reasons.

Although they do not directly increase the future economic benefits, they might be inevitable to obtain future economic benefits from other assets and therefore, should be recognized as an asset.

For example, water cleaning station might be necessary in order to proceed with some chemical processes within chemical manufacturer.

Initial Measurement

An item of property, plant and equipment that qualifies for recognition as an asset shall be measured at its *cost.*

The cost of an item of property, plant and equipment comprises:

1. its *purchase price* including import duties, non-refundable purchase taxes, after deducting trade discounts and rebates
2. any *costs directly attributable* to bringing the asset to the location and condition necessary for it to be capable of operating in the manner intended by management. Examples of these costs are: costs of site preparation, professional fees, initial delivery and handling, installation and assembly, etc.,
3. the initial estimate of *the costs of dismantling and removing the item and restoring the site* on which it is located.

Subsequent Measurement

An entity may choose 2 accounting models for its property plant and equipment:

1. *Cost model:* An entity shall carry an asset at its *cost less any accumulated depreciation and any accumulated impairment losses.*
2. *Revaluation model:*An entity shall carry an asset at a *revalued amount.* Revalued amount is its fair value at the date of the revaluation less any subsequent accumulated depreciation and subsequent accumulated impairment losses.

An entity shall revalue its assets with sufficient regularity so that the carrying amount does not differ materially from its fair value at the end of the reporting period. If an item of property, plant and equipment is revalued, the entire class of property, plant and equipment to which that asset belongs shall be revalued.

Excerpts end --------

Excerpts from:

https://www.iasplus.com/en/meeting-notes/ifrs-ic/2012/ifrs-ic-march-2012/ias-16-property-plant-and-equipment-ias-38-intangible-assets-and-ias-17-leases-2014-purchase-of-right-to-use-land

IAS 16, IAS 38 and IAS 17 — Purchase of right to use land

The Committee (the IFRS Interpretations Committee) received a request from Indonesia to clarify whether the purchase of a right to land should be accounted for as a purchase of property, plant and equipment, a purchase of an intangible asset or as a lease of land.

In Indonesia, the local laws do not permit entities to own title to land, rather only individuals may own land. To facilitate entities acquiring rights to use land, the government can grant either rights to exploit or cultivate the land (agricultural usage) or rights to build upon the land (commercial usage). The initial transfer occurs between an individual and the entity through the government while extension and renewals occur directly between the entity and the government. Once the entity purchases the usage rights, the individual does not retain any rights over the land and the entity has to return the land only if the government revokes the entity's right on the group [grounds?] of public interest or if there is a change in the allocation of use of the land. The Indonesian standard setter noted that different interpretations have developed in their jurisdiction as a result of this issue.

During the March 2012 meeting, the Committee discussed a request from a specific jurisdiction [Indonesia] for clarification on the purchase of a right to use land and whether it should be accounted for as a purchase of property, plant and equipment, a purchase of an intangible asset or a lease of land. In this jurisdiction, entities are not allowed to own freehold title to land but instead purchase the right to exploit or build on the land.

--- excerpts end --

UK Blue Book and SNA

The following definitions for "land" are from the 2017 amendments to the UK National Accounts Blue Book (which is the general rule book for UK national accounting):

1. Land is defined as the ground itself, including soil covering and associated surface water; the associated surface water includes any inland waters (reservoirs, lakes, rivers) over which economic ownership rights can be exercised and from which economic benefits can be derived by their owners.

2. The enforcement of ownership rights is an important characteristic of land as an asset. The SNA 2008 and ESA 2010 distinguish ownership into legal and economic; the legal owner is the unit entitled in law to the benefits of possession. However, a legal owner can contract with another unit for the latter to accept the risks and rewards of using the entity in production, in return for an agreed payment. The nature of the agreement is a financial lease, where the payments reflect only the placing of the asset at the disposal of the borrower by the provider[3]. The economic owner of entities, such as goods and services, natural resources, financial assets and liabilities, is the institutional unit entitled to claim the benefits associated with the use of the entity in question in the course of an economic activity by virtue of accepting the associated risks. In this article "ownership rights" refers to economic ownership rights.

3. Institutional units are defined as the elementary economic decision-making centre characterised by uniformity of behaviour and decision-making autonomy in the exercise of its principal function; examples of these are financial corporations, private non-financial corporations, public corporations and households.

4. The value of land will be shown under natural resources in the balance sheet; this excludes the value of improvements, the value of buildings on the land and transfer costs, which are all shown separately under fixed assets.

5. Land will appear on the non-financial balance sheet and will be valued at its current market price; this current market price excludes the costs of ownership transfer, which are treated, by convention, as gross fixed capital formation (GFCF) and of land improvements, and are subject to consumption of fixed capital.

Figure 29 – OECD classifications of land

Source: Organisation for Economic Co-operation and Development (OECD) - Eurostat compilation guide on land estimation 2015. ("n.e.c." is not elsewhere classified):

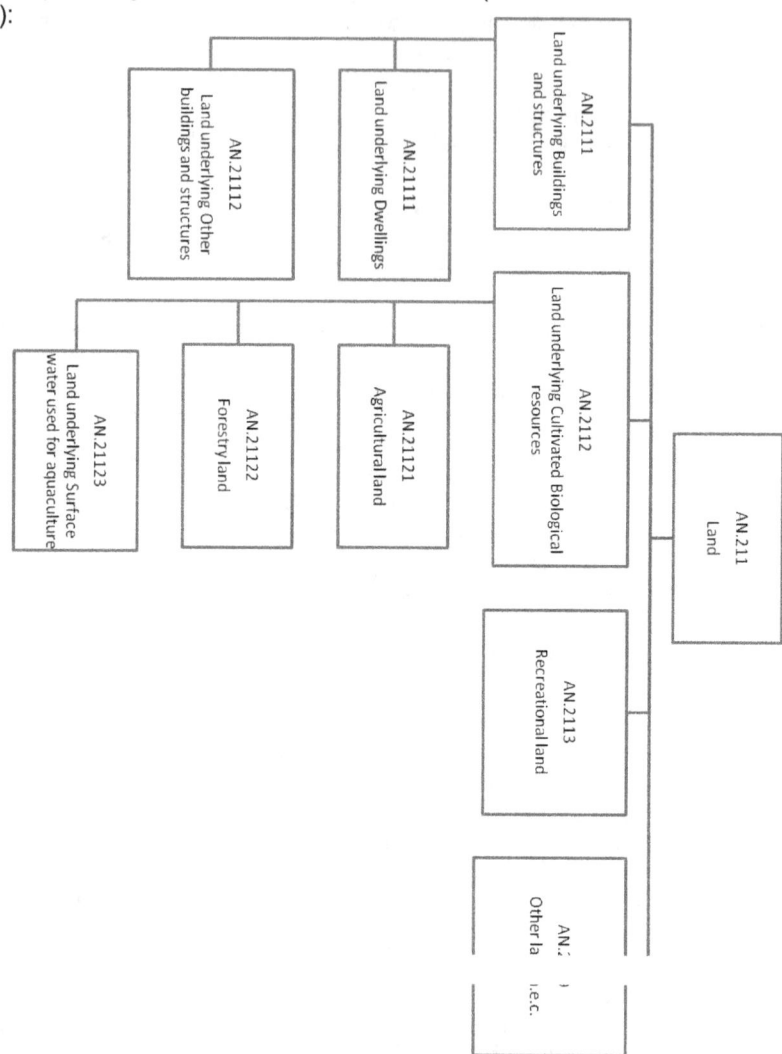

Accounting for Land in the World Balance Sheet

Let's be clear that frameworks such as SNA don't yet provide the answers we need in order to compile an adequate world balance sheet.

The following is from the UN - SEEA – EEA (2014) which recognises this:

> "Non-market valuation strategies are also needed in cases where comparison with, or augmentation of, standard national accounting estimates is the motivation for valuation. In this case, an important first step is to recognize that the SNA does not record externalities that arise through economic or other human activity, whether they are positive externalities (e.g., the ecosystem service of flood protection) or negative externalities (e.g., the degradation of river systems through pollution). The focus of valuation is thus on the estimation of nonmarket values for ecosystem services and ecosystem assets that are not recorded in the SNA, and the alignment of these estimates with valuations already recorded in the SNA ... Work on adjusting or extending SNA income accounts and balance sheets must be considered within the context of the objectives, concepts and measurement challenges outlined in chapters I to V of this publication. Three considerations in particular must be highlighted: adjustment requires assessment of ecosystems in physical terms; adjustment or extension requires the use of valuation techniques to enable derivation of estimates in monetary terms; and adjustment requires aggregated measures of ecosystem services and ecosystem assets."

There is also a basic conflict between the ways mainstream economics treats land (a specific example of natural capital) and the ways it needs to be valued in the world balance sheet. This comes down, largely, to basic definitions. In economics, land is valued for its economic outputs, ie the future streams of economic products and services, for example wood from felled trees growing on the land or manufactured products rolling out of a factory built on the land. This is explained more fully in chapter 8.

In the world balance sheet, however, the Planetary CFO wants to value land as an asset in its proper state as a sustainable part of the whole biosphere. This includes ensuring it is in a fit state to yield products and services, in sustainable ways, to support the global human population in perpetuity. This is not restricted to purely providing economic benefits to humans. It needs to include the value of the natural capital as a functioning part of a larger system of systems.

A significant part of this larger value is not recognised by mainstream economics. This is a problem, because, as well as any value of the land to the biosphere, any deterioration in that value is also not recognised by mainstream economics.

There are a couple of measures that work mutually to address these problems (lack of capture of land value by the state and lack of recognition of value in mainstream economics). These are:

1)   to roll out Natural Capital Accounting (to include land) across all nations, and include natural capital values in a world balance sheet

2)   to place obligations on landowners, and other stewards of natural capital, to reinforce expectations about their stewardship of the land, which include undertaking sufficient work to regenerate and restore the characteristics of the land that contribute towards regaining (strong) sustainability within the biosphere.

Returning to valuation controversies surrounding the natural capital concept

We saw in chapter 3 and earlier in the current chapter that valuation methods for nature, and even the act of placing any value at all on it, is controversial.

Most of the objections to valuing nature are dealt with in modern ecological economics by considering the value to be a sum of a number of additive values, mostly found through personal preferences or "willingness to pay". For example, in Tietenberg (2018):

> "… the total willingness to pay (TWP):

> TWP = Use Value + Option Value + Nonuse Value"

> *Use value* reflects the direct use of the environmental resource. Examples include fish harvested from the sea, timber harvested from the forest, water extracted from a stream for irrigation, even the scenic beauty conferred by a natural vista.

> *Option value* reflects the value people place on a future ability to use the environment. It reflects the willingness to pay to preserve the option to use the environment in the future even if one is not currently using it.

> *[Nonuse], Passive-use* or *nonconsumptive use values* arise when the resource is not actually consumed in the process of experiencing it. These types of values reflect the common observation that people are more than willing to pay for improving or preserving resources that they will never use."

While this doesn't get us all the way to an adequate answer, it *starts* to address (albeit inadequately) the concerns of deep ecologists such as Arne Naess, who suggest that it is immoral to place a value on nature because it facilitates its monetisation, commoditisation and exploitation.

One valid criticism of economic valuation approaches is where they are based on willingness-to-pay (to acquire the asset not currently owned) or willingness-to-accept (to accept compensation for the loss of the asset currently owned). In many cases, and especially in relation to valuing nature, there is likely to be an element of hypothetical bias in people's answers to surveys of their willingness-to-pay or willingness-to-accept preferences.

Hypothetical bias can enter the picture because the respondent is being confronted by a contrived, rather than an actual, set of choices. Since he or she will not actually have to pay the estimated value, and has potentially very little understanding of the significance of the hypothetical scenario underlying the question, the respondent may treat the survey casually, providing ill-considered answers.

A particular case of this is where the respondent is being asked about the value of a natural asset (eg natural capital comprising part of the global commons), when it is currently valued at zero and the respondent (via the global industrial supply chains) is currently not paying anything for the use (or abuse and exploitation) of that asset.

These sorts of valuation methods can also be undermined by the personal circumstances of the respondent. A respondent with very small amounts of financial resources (eg income) is likely to give much smaller willingness-to-pay answers than one with much larger financial resources.

Let me paint a hypothetical scenario to illustrate this. For those of you who have heard of the Biosphere 2 experiment in the 1990s, imagine a re-run of that 2-year experiment. For those unfamiliar with it, Biosphere 2 was a project where 7 volunteers lived inside a closed set of connecting bio-domes containing air, water, soil, plants etc with no inputs or outputs (wastes) allowed to enter or leave the domes, except for the sunlight falling on them and the energy 'leakage' out through the glass walls at night. Everything was recycled that possibly could be.

In the imaginary re-run, which I'll call Biosphere 3, because of the strict limits on availability of such materials, suppose that each inhabitant had a daily budget of financial resource, and each of the main materials required for survival was made exclusive to each "consumer" (eg with breathable air provided via breathing apparatus and personal cylinders, and exhaled air collected in similar cylinders for recycling, water provided in personalised bottles, food in personalised containers) But suppose further that this was all provided as a public good for the first six months, on a strictly need-to-consume-for-survival basis. Suppose also that some inhabitants had financial resources very different from others – say, some had $100 per day while others had $100,000 per day.

In this scenario, what would willingness-to-pay or willingness-to-receive questioning and valuation methods reveal about the values of the various survival essentials? I would guess that the answers would be very different between participants with different financial resources, and they would also be very different with passage of time.

On day one, probably everyone would be willing to pay almost all, if not actually 100%, of their 'budget' for breathable air (even if they don't actually have to pay for it), on the basis that none of them could survive the day without breathable air, whereas everyone could survive without water or food for one day. The trouble with that is that it gives a value for breathable air of $100 for some respondents, $100,000 for other respondents. As long as this doesn't affect the actual amounts of air, water and food provided (because they are being provided as a public good, not as a market-traded exchange) there is no problem with continuing provision.

The situation would get more complicated some days later, because after some days without water, survival would become a matter of securing water as well as air, and after an important threshold of deprival, no amount of air (or money) would compensate for lack of water, without which death would follow. Therefore, everyone would be prepared to pay something for some water, even if all the rest of their budget would be allocated to breathable air in their willingness-to-pay answers. So, perhaps their willingness-to-pay valuations would represent 90% of their "budget" for air and 10% for water each day, in order to survive until the next day. Some time after that point, edible food would have to be part of their answers, to avoid theoretical death, on the basis that no amount of money, air and water can stop someone dying if they don't have food. So perhaps their valuations of willingness-to-pay would represent 90% of the budget allocated to air, 7% to water and 3% to food each day, in order to survive to the next day. And so on. Perhaps this situation and the associated willingness-to-pay values would reach some form of stable equilibrium after, say, six months.

It can easily be seen that the "values" of each of the necessities, as measured by willingness-to-pay, would vary considerably between participants, and would vary considerably over time during those first six months.

Now consider the scenario that the actual costs of providing all those necessities each and every day in Biosphere 3 was a lot higher than any of the personal financial resources of the 'poorest' of the individual participants, but not beyond the financial resources of the 'richest' participants. Assume, for example, that the cost of breathable air was $50,000 per day per person, water was $30,000 and food was $10,000.

Further, assume that the "provider" after the first six months changed, and was then a computer or Artificial Intelligence operating on market exchange principles (a complete contrast from providing essentials as a public good), and was unwilling (or unable) to compromise and incur a 'loss' on provision (eg the provider was not going to accept a lower price than the actual cost of provision). It will be clear that this is a very different state of affairs compared with the first six months of public good service provision.

The willingness-to-pay answers for the poorest participants under this new model for 'traded' provision would now be, in fact, an irrelevant and gross under-estimate of the value of the provision, for any answers they give, even if they answer 100% of their personal budget (ie $100 per day) as the willingness-to-pay value for any one of the essentials. They simply won't survive day one, because they don't have sufficient financial resources to pay for the true cost of the provision of the essentials for life. Their survival during the first six months was dependant on the provider subsidising the true 'cost of living' (ie incurring the cost of the public goods themselves and not passing them on to the consumer).

At least some of the "richer" participants might well survive the new regime for provision, but even though some of them might be able to cover the average actual costs of provision, they might not all survive the whole 2 years.

For example, if there is a bidding war, and if the Artificial Intelligence has profit maximisation as its aim, its optimum market strategy might be to use its monopoly power to manipulate prices to extract the maximum revenue, even if this means only very few participants surviving to the very end of the 2 years.

This might seem a very extreme scenario, contrived in order to challenge the validity and accuracy of willingness-to-pay or willingness-to-receive valuation methods. However, if you consider for a moment the overall insights derived from Kenneth Boulding's "Spaceship Earth" conceptual writings, it doesn't take a huge leap of the imagination to see how the whole of the Earth can be thought of as a larger version of Biosphere 3. In fact, the reason the 1990's dome experiment was called Biosphere 2 was because it's designers considered the Earth to be "Biosphere 1".

So, Biosphere 1 (the current Earth we live on) has some similarities with Biosphere 3. The Earth is a finite, closed system, except for the sunlight falling on it (and the solar energy escaping through the atmosphere into space). The main differences between the Earth (Biosphere 1) and my hypothetical, imaginary Biosphere 3 are matters of scale, the key ones being the overall size of the Earth and its biological and chemical systems, and the size of the global human population.

With this perspective in mind, my "Biosphere 3" thought experiment can be seen to challenge the willingness-to-pay and willingness-to-receive valuation methods used in Biosphere 1 (the Earth we live in).

The Biosphere 3 scenario highlights the downsides of a marginalist approach to valuation. Willingness-to-pay and willingness-to-receive approaches are difficult to apply without the respondents falling into a marginalist perspective. That is, they are very likely (even if subconsciously) to consider a price or value in a way that is heavily influenced by their current circumstances and by the existing state (and prices / values) of the objects in the existing systems of supply (whether market-based or public goods provision). Many of these existing prices / values are effectively zero or heavily subsidised in current global supply chains, so this is likely to give a very strong bias towards very low valuations resulting from these methods of valuation.

Summary of chapter 7

There are difficulties in placing values on nature, and the topic is far from settled, within individual academic disciplines let alone in a multidisciplinary sense. It would be easy to bend under the weight of valuation controversies and take extreme positions such as placing no value on nature, or insisting on infinite value for nature. But this would be a mistake. At one of those extremes, it would result in insufficient challenge to the overexploitation of nature and insufficient recognition of externalities in economic analyses. At the other extreme it would result in irreconcilable positions between those who would recognise our need for an economics of nature's benefits and those who would exclude nature from economic analyses and protect it instead by alternative regulatory measures (eg legal environmental protection based on a deep ecology perspective).

This type of discussion, for example in relation to land and natural capital, is of immense importance, because if we get the stewardship of them wrong and let the world's land and natural capital continue to be degraded at the rate currently occurring, these immeasurably useful assets will be lost not just to us but to all future generations.

If, on the other hand, we achieve good stewardship, then there is a bright future where land and natural capital will form the core of the thriving of all future generations for as long as that stewardship is maintained.

Chapter 8

Economic perspectives on land and natural capital

"Economics cannot function as a reliable guide until natural capital is placed on the balance sheets of companies, countries, and the world."

(Hawken et al, 2010)

"Economics has a theory that explains income … and one that explains the prices of assets (though not entirely, as the "price" of entrepreneurship is a residual) but no theory at all to explain the distribution of wealth among individuals. It is the historical result of whose ancestors got there first, of marriage, of inheritance, plus individual ability and effort, and just plain luck."

(Daly, 2011)

Land (and the natural capital associated with it) has been given relatively little attention in economics in recent times. In fact, its significance has, for a long time, been largely absent from mainstream discourse, despite its impacts on behaviours at all levels of analysis from the individual level to the global level.

As a backdrop, Appendix 1 shows a representation of the various schools of thought in economics and their historical roots. I won't go into great detail regarding how each strand treats land and natural capital. Suffice to say that treatments vary quite considerably, from ignoring them, treating them as part of general capital or treating them as a special category of capital assets requiring their own ringfencing, maintenance and protection. This latter treatment harks back to the very early days of the discipline of economics. As Ryan-Collins et al (2017) point out, in early classical economics, land was treated separately from other asset classes, because of its distinct characteristics. This difference was fundamental to their approaches, as land was actually treated as one of the three separately identified and managed factors of production, the other two being labour and capital. These three factors were considered mostly complementary at that time, rather than as potential and (in many instances, actual) substitutes (the latter being the dominant economic approach today).

In this chapter, I will talk quite a lot about Steady State Economy ("SSE") which is a non-mainstream approach to economics (although it is becoming more mainstream all the time). I review and comment on the work of Brian Czech, who is Director of CASSE (the Centre for the Advancement of Steady State Economy). I suggest that SSE, while not representing a silver bullet for reaching sustainability, is a very useful concept and an approach that might be part of the public policy toolkit to help us squeeze through the coming bottleneck. More about the bottleneck later in the chapter. In the meantime, let's look in more detail at land.

Appendix 2 comprises an article by Chen (2020) expressing a typical current mainstream "economic" view on land and how it is treated in most economic calculations. I would take strong exception to Chen's statement that "we may consider land as a resource with no cost of production". This treatment of land would be to grossly abuse it and under-value it, both in pure economic terms but also (more importantly) in terms of encouraging accelerating environmental degradation. In direct contrast to Chen's description of land's role in production, I (and many non-mainstream economists such as Daly), would argue that land needs to be restored and maintained in a sustainable state that not only supports any economic production that relies upon it, but also so that the land performs, in perpetuity, its proper role as part of earth's living biosphere.

Ryan-Collins et al (2017) give an extensive account of how land was, through twentieth century history, subsumed into general capital in mainstream economics, giving a false impression of its characteristics. This also means that the mechanisms by which it impacts on wealth distribution and "rentier" behaviour have become obscured.

While their arguments explaining why land results in "rentier" behaviour sound logical, I'm not totally convinced by some of the conclusions from Ryan-Collins et al. They dismiss the ability of markets to adjust prices of land, and their position on that subject seems to be a strong part of their argument for economic rents to exist in the first place. However, there is, as we know, a market in land, being an important element of the purchase price of a property which comprises buildings and land to be marketed as freehold property. An obvious example is that a buyer can choose between similar properties (or plots of land without buildings) for sale in different cities, and this market competition will impact on prices and could, potentially, compete out the economic rent, to some extent. It is still true that the effectiveness of this market mechanism depends on there being enough owners willing to sell property (including land) at any point in time, and enough buyers looking to buy.

Ryan-Collins et al go on to talk about a related topic - the positional value of land, being the fact that land can often increase in value because of developments around and near that land that were not a result of any actions taken by the land owner. They argue that this element in the increase in land value is "unearned" and should, arguably be nationalised by government bodies. This ignores the fact that there is a risk associated with owning land and the positional value of land can go down as well as up. If the neighbourhood suffers negative developments rather than positive ones, the positional value of the land owned by the landowner could well decline. If it was going to be seen as fair to nationalise increases in positional value of land, surely it would also only be fair for the government to compensate landowners for decreases in the positional value of land when neighbourhoods suffer deterioration. I very much doubt that most of those advocating for the nationalisation of increases in positional value of land would also advocate for this fair compensation if positional value decreases.

The multiple uses of land make reflecting it in economics more complicated than other types of capital assets.

Ryan-Collins et al argue for measures such as land value tax to enable the public sector to capture some of the economic rents from landowners. What is required, in my view, is a balance, at equilibrium, in a sharing of land-based economic rents (including positional value changes, either positive or negative) between public sector bodies and private sector landowners.

That is an attempt to tackle some of the inequalities Ryan-Collins et al argue are connected with land ownership. However, there are other problems associated with land. One of them is the lack of stewardship recognised and implemented by many landowners. This is a strong contributor to our current unsustainability. It is aided and abetted by a lack of recognition, in mainstream economics, of the "externalities" generated by how land is maintained and used, and its place in environmental degradation.

Steady State Economics, and other non-mainstream perspectives, especially on natural capital and planetary boundaries

I'd like to talk about Steady State Economics ("SSE"), and some other non-mainstream branches of economic thinking, as I think these have an enormous amount to offer in guiding us to a better future.

SSE sits alongside a growing number of different ways of looking at the economy. It draws on a diverse range of new ways of looking at things, including the advent of Stock Flow Consistent ("SFC") methods of modelling the economy.

The origins of the SFC modelling approach go back to the late 1960s and 1970s. The two main figures in those early years were Wynne Godley at the University of Cambridge and James Tobin at Yale University.

SFC models have a post-Keynesian closure, in the sense that demand matters and full employment is not considered to be the general state of the economy. Moreover, and based on the early insights of Godley and Tobin, there is a thorough modelling of the real and the financial sides of the economy and of their *interdependencies*.

The emphasis on careful accounting within the SFC approach reveals the intellectual kinship of the SFC approach to national accounts–based macroeconomic models, first introduced by Richard Stone (e.g. in Stone and Brown, 1962) as part of his wider pioneering work on national accounts.

Lavoie (2012) traces the history of SFC models, which resulted in models by Godley and Lavoie, and also Jackson et al, that can be used to provide a coherent framework for SSE scenarios:

> "Various important surveys of flow-of-funds analysis and a stock-flow consistent approach to macroeconomics can be found, among others in Bain (1973), Davis (1987), Patterson and Stephenson (1988), and Dawson (1996).

Such an integration of financial transactions with real transactions, within an appropriate set of sectors, was also advocated by Gurley and Shaw (1960: ch. 2) in their well-known book, as it was by a number of other authors, inspired by the work of Copeland, argued very early on that Minsky's views on the fragility of the financial system could be examined with the help of a model relying on financial flows and national balance sheets."

I say more about this in my previous book "People or Planet: Towards a regenerative economy", including reviewing some recent modelling of the Canadian economy, by Jackson and Victor in 2019, projecting forward using SSE assumptions, to see how feasible such an economic approach might be.

Steady State Economics might not be the best answer to current and future sustainability challenges. It might not even be sufficient as a solution, in its current form, as advocated by CASSE (The Centre for Advancement of Steady State Economics).

It might, however, be a useful stepping stone to better solutions we don't yet know about, let alone express in economic terms. Some of the work of Brian Czech, Director of CASSE, and other authors in "Best of the Daly News" (ie Czech, 2020) is examined further below. And it might be a whole lot better than the current way economies are managed (or left to markets) in most parts of the world today.

However, before getting into some more detail on SSE, I'll set some wider context first, which will help to explain why this, and other new forms of economic thinking, are a necessary field of thought and practice to address our current predicament.

The Bottleneck humanity hopes to pass through

"The Precipice" by Toby Ord (ie Ord, 2020) resonates with my own perspectives on the long-term development of humanity and the risks it currently faces.

Ord points out that humanity is at a critical crossroads, where its power has outstripped its wisdom, resulting in several serious existential risks (including unsustainability of our impacts on nature, rogue AI (Artificial Intelligence), engineered biological agents and conflicts that might, potentially, involve nuclear weapons).

The finite planetary limits of the biosphere that supports us are like a bottle containing a model ship in the classic "ship in a bottle". Our population and civilisation are like the ship. The human ecological footprint has been growing as we have developed (the ship has been growing in size and complexity inside the bottle). But we are realising that the finite bounds of the biosphere, and the damage caused by our overshooting sustainable thresholds, is reducing the size of the biosphere and its capacity to support us (the neck of the bottle has been narrowing, as a result of our actions) and the rate of that depletion in biospherical capacity is accelerating.

We want humanity to progress further, because our future potential is immense if we can more effectively harness the energy from the sun (the only input from outside the bottle) and if we can access materials from outside the earth system, for example by mining materials on the moon, from asteroids or find even more distant exploitable resources. After all, the universe outside the bottle is potentially infinite in materials, energy and evolutionary progress for living beings.

Our challenge is to pass through the neck of the bottle, and to pull what we can of the ship, through with us, without destroying the bottle that is humanity's birthplace.

It becomes obvious there are two main options for doing this, which are not mutually exclusive.

Firstly, we can modify our impacts on the natural biosphere, to reduce (and eventually reverse) the rate of degradation of the biosphere's capacity to support us (slow down, and then reverse, the rate at which the neck of the bottle is shrinking).

Secondly, we can alter our civilisation and the way it draws resources from the biosphere and uses them, for example adopting circular systems of material and energy flow, such as those advocated in circular economy, or even implementing something along the lines of a steady state economy, a GDP-growth-agnostic economy or something similar (remodel the ship so it will more easily pass through the neck).

If we can do these things, a bright future awaits and the innumerable future generations of humanity will thank us for our efforts.

If we fail, however, our failure will go down in history as the biggest failure of any known life reaching a state of advanced intelligence and civilisation.

We should use the sense of responsibility this imparts as a spur to action.

The bottleneck analogy is used also, extensively, in White and Hagens (2020) "The Bottlenecks of the 21st Century".

More detail about steady state economics

Brian Czech and Herman Daly are two of the most prominent advocates of steady state economy.

From Daly (2005) "Economics in a Full World":

> "Even trying to define sustainability in terms of constant GDP is problematic because GDP conflates qualitative improvement (development) with quantitative increase (growth). **The sustainable economy must at some point stop growing [in physical terms], but it need not stop developing**. There is no reason to limit the qualitative improvement in design of products, which can increase GDP [and also other measures, eg measures of wellbeing, I would add] without increasing the amount of resources used. The

main idea behind sustainability is to shift the path of progress from growth, which is not sustainable, toward development, which presumably is… Natural resources … can be measured and bequeathed. In particular, people can measure their throughput, or the rate at which the economy uses them, taking them from low-entropy sources in the ecosystem, transforming them into useful products, and ultimately dumping them back into the environment as high-entropy wastes. Sustainability can be defined in terms of throughput by determining the environment's capacity for supplying each raw resource and for absorbing the end waste products… Most ecological economists, myself included, believe that natural and man-made capital are more often complements than substitutes and that natural capital should be maintained on its own, because it has become the limiting factor. That goal is called strong sustainability."

In "Supply Shock" (2013) Czech talks about technology as having an impact, setting it up as a straw man which he later shoots down:

"Technological progress allows the same amount of natural capital to produce a greater amount (or value) of goods and services. With technological progress, apparently, economic production may increase without a growing ecological footprint. In other words, real GDP may increase without a growing ecological footprint. Theoretically, we could reconcile the conflict between economic growth and environmental protection with technological progress. So, let's just keep progressing technologically and we can continue to grow the economy, with no additional environmental impact."

He first pours water on the straw man of technology as follows:

"… technological progress is limited by the laws of thermodynamics … If technological progress rained down like manna from heaven, it could disrupt the relationship between real GDP and the ecological footprint. However, technological progress does not really rain down"

Czech states that there is "… conflict between economic growth and environmental protection in the absence of technological progress." And this is a statement that most environmentalists (and many mainstream economists) would agree with. However, at the core of Czech's challenge against the ability of technological advances to come to our rescue is an appeal to the discrediting of the environmental Kuznets curve ("EKC"):

"… finding ultimately that there is not only a basic conflict, but a *fundamental* conflict between economic growth and environmental protection… There is no evidence for a macroeconomic environmental Kuznets curve. Many sector- or industry-specific environmental problems have been created and exacerbated as a function of economic growth; few have exhibited a Kuznets curve."

(Here, he references Stern (2004) "The Rise and Fall of the Environmental Kuznets Curve.")

Again, this point about the EKC is something that many economists agree with. It is not, in itself, a strong justification for steady state economy.

The empirical evidence about the EKC is not evidence that material decoupling (driven by technology advances and other drivers of decoupling of economic growth from material throughput and therefore impacts on the environment) is *impossible* – it is only evidence that it has *not been achieved substantially yet*.

It is also evidence that *affluence* conspires against sustainability. Again, it is *not* proof that, with changes in social and political policy, we could never facilitate a sustainable economy which had, in aggregate, sufficiently stretched out the links between (financial) economic activity and material throughput. All the evidence above shows is that increasing *affluence* does not drive such changes, and might impede them to some extent.

Czech appears to recognise the fallacy of the EKC and the potential for technological advancement to represent at least a partial reconciliation between economic growth and protection of nature (the underlining in the following excerpts is mine):

> "The only hope for reconciling economic growth with species conservation and environmental protection lies squarely with technological progress, not some fallacious environmental Kuznets curve … Yet we cannot quite conclude that end-use innovation cannot *possibly* reconcile the conflict between economic growth and environmental protection, because there is a great deal of nuance in the market that negates the phrase "all else equal." (In economics jargon, *ceteris paribus* means all else equal.) … *Theoretically, the economy may grow somewhat, with somewhat less natural capital reallocated from the economy of nature to the human economy* … *The only solid conclusion to be drawn thus far is that, in theory, the possibility of reconciling economic growth with environmental protection via technological progress, at least temporarily, cannot be denied*. However, it is not occurring and does not appear likely, partly because much innovation is not end-use but rather explorative and extractive, both of which increase the reallocation of natural capital to the human economy. Even end-use innovation does not appear to offer a **sure** prospect for reconciling substantial rates of economic growth with environmental protection, although it does appear to offer a clear prospect of lessening the impact of economic growth (at any rate), and **perhaps a lesser prospect of reconciling modest rates of economic growth with some aspects of environmental protection… Any of these prospects are eventually limited by the entropy law, which establishes limits to productive efficiency.**"

I agree with all of these statements, and would like to point out that nobody yet has a very clear view of how much "headroom" there might be to engage in some economic growth, and at the same time decouple/ dematerialise the economy, before the entropy law limits (aka "thermodynamic limits") are reached. This potential, plus the more effective use of nearly free energy from the sun, *might* be enough for us to pass through the bottleneck. We just don't know enough yet to be confident of this. Two things will help us address these issues. The use of World Balance Sheets, and the precautionary principle.

Working out how much headroom we do or don't have is one of the reasons it's so important to do our stock checks and compile World Balance Sheets. By doing this, it will make comparisons between human systems and natural ones more possible, at global scale, to enable us to have a better idea about the remaining headroom at any particular balance sheet date. The precautionary principle would then help us in our assessments of what the World Balance Sheets tell us about the state of the planet and the headroom available for our human economies.

A word about physical economy as distinct from financially measured economy – each offers a different kind of growth

It's not "economic growth" per se that is the thing that risks breaching sustainability thresholds. Instead, it's the absolute size of the economy, in terms of physical throughput, that has this risk associated with it. That is what must be compared with planetary and biospherical limits. This draws inspiration from the work of Fraser Murison Smith (2020) - ("A Planetary Economy"). Growth (or shrinkage) is only a direction of travel. And the direction of travel of financial measures of the economy, while associated with the direction of travel of the physical economy, are **not** so inextricably linked that one follows the other in lockstep. Despite the protestations of "steady-staters", technical advances do happen, efficiency does improve, and Jevons' Paradox (aka "the rebound effect") doesn't always totally counteract those efficiencies. This is what gives many the hope that we will be able to pull ourselves (and each other) through the bottleneck before the neck of the bottle becomes too small or closes altogether.

The financial measurement (rather than just physical measurement) of such an economy is another matter, and the two (physical measurement and financial measurement) must not be confused when working out whether the aggregate global economy at a particular point in time "fits" within planetary (ecological) limits. If ithe physical economy fits, then the financial valuation of the economy also fits. The corollary of this ("if the financial economy fits, then the physical one does") is clearly **not** true.

If there is a difference between the limits and the existing aggregate physical economy, then there is headroom for physical growth. Whether this translates into financial economic growth or not is a separate and distinct question.

If, on the other hand, there isn't any headroom for physical growth, then the physical economy has reached the limits and there must not be any further physical growth. Whether this translates into a limit on financial growth or not is another matter. This is one of the most important questions regarding the extent of the allowable material throughput of the economy, over and above the physical aspects of the economy tied in a very intimate way as necessities for human existence, such as the basic provision of food, water, shelter, clothing, medicines.

In "Prospects for Reconciling the Conflict between Economic Growth and Biodiversity Conservation with Technological Progress" (2008), Czech argues that it is not possible to reconcile economic growth and biodiversity loss, because:

a) The level of human economic activity determines how much natural capital is available for biodiversity
b) The mechanism for resolution [of the conflict] depends on use of economic surpluses arising from existing economies (which are reducing biodiversity) to fund research that would solve that problem.

This is an interesting argument, and has its merits. It's the same as saying there is not enough headroom, already, for us to use technological advancement to pull ourselves through the neck of the bottle – that it is already too late for that and we should not put any further economic resources into that technological effort.

However, in practical terms it has limited application, since the existing economy cannot be halted overnight, nor replaced quickly with something else, which means that we are faced with a dilemma similar to that with climate change and carbon emissions. We know we cannot eliminate carbon emissions instantaneously. Instead, we seek international agreements on reduction timescales that balance a number of factors that are set alongside the global temperature rise that will be caused by existing cumulative emissions **PLUS** the emissions we are yet to make before that timescale is reached.

From the same paper by Czech:

> "Economic growth is an increase in the production and consumption of goods and services, and it occurs with increasing population or increasing per capita production and consumption. An increasing gross domestic product (GDP) indicates a growing economy. Gross domestic product is a measure of the production of goods and services, income derived from that production, and expenditure thereon (Abel & Bernanke 2003). Increasing real GDP (i.e., adjusted for inflation) is sometimes considered synonymous with economic growth (Goodwin et al. 2007)."

Here, we see that Czech uses "economic growth" as being synonymous with material throughput growth, and so conflates the effects of price/value changes and volume changes, which is one of the well-recognised weakness of the GDP measure when assessing sustainability.

In applying his "trophic theory of nature" to the link between human economy growth and species loss, Czech dismisses the potential impacts of, for example, technical progress reducing the amount of natural material used to sustain each person, or to provide goods and services to each person. He uses empirical evidence well, but does not address (or rebut) a hypothesis I now put forward that technical progress _might_ provide enough improvement to see humanity "pass through the neck of the bottle".

Czech's arguments rely on his "trophic theory of money", as well as his trophic theory of nature, and on his view that information services and other potentially dematerialised services are not capable of being sustainable services in the long-term. From "Supply Shock":

> "In short, because of the trophic structure of the human economy, GDP provides a reliable indicator of the ecological footprint. To some degree, the relationship between GDP and the ecological footprint can be muddied by inflation, technological progress and "animal spirits." However, inflation is easily accounted for, so that the relationship between _real_ GDP and the ecological footprint may be muddied only by technological progress and animal spirits."

His argument overlooks at least one mechanism for investing in technology - the ability to use credit, rather than surplus - and thereby to reduce impacts of the economy on nature, at least at sufficient levels to let us pass through the neck of the bottle.

Czech argues, for example, that information services are not benign in their impacts on nature because:

> "The information is typically purchased to increase production in those sectors [ie agricultural, extractive, manufacturing and capital-intensive sectors], resulting in more drawdown of natural capital (Ruttan 2001)."

Perhaps some information is used in that way, but it doesn't have to be so forever – information services can have a very light footprint on the biosphere, and can have a positive impact depending on how the information is used.

Of biodiversity loss, and the potential for research, innovation and investment to help address this challenge, he says:

> "… an extinct species cannot be resurrected to function with ecological and evolutionary integrity regardless of how much money is expended."

This is clearly true currently (although DNA mapping, cataloguing and storage technologies might eventually address this).

However, there have always been extinctions. We know the rate of extinctions is very high currently. We can't stop them immediately, so the question becomes one of deciding what level of species extinctions we can reconcile with the amount of economic activity we need to see us develop through the bottleneck. A deep ecology argument for stopping all damage to the biosphere and all species might be tempting in response, but this approach might be the enemy of making it through the bottleneck if it stifles development (including technology development) that could be essential to making that journey possible.

Czech admits to the possibility of technology improvements reducing the impact on nature:

> "Dietz et al. (2007) estimated "an annual growth rate in the global footprint of 2.12% per year" and surmised that "the requisite technological improvement needs to exceed 2% per year" for environmental protection. Annual productivity gains exceeding 2% typified the "advanced capitalist economies" during the third quarter of the 20th century (Maddison 1987), but gains falling well below 2% have befuddled growth theorists and national income accountants ever since. In countries with less-advanced economies, much of the recent economic growth has resulted from increases in factor inputs (land, labor, and capital), not from the efficiency with which those factors were used (Oguchi 2005)."

In Czech (2019) he claims that most of the 'low hanging fruit' in terms of technical efficiencies have already been obtained:

> "R&D is inching to the limits of its capacity to produce new technologies that increase productivity, not for any lack of human imagination, but rather for lack of the real resources required for economic growth. ... As total factor productivity reaches its limits, so too will the effects of R&D on GDP and real money supplies."

This is, in effect, observing a 'law of diminishing returns' (in technology investments). But that doesn't prove there will never be any significant breakthroughs, leapfrogging our abilities to get more from less. He offers no substantive proof for his suggested reasons for R&D "reaching the limits of its capacity".

He also points to empirical evidence of, in effect, the Jevons Paradox (the rebound effect). But that **doesn't** mean that technological advances are always destined to be counteracted by the Jevons effect.

In his own words (from Czech, 2008):

> "The only solid conclusion to be drawn from this section … is that, in theory, the possibility of reconciling economic growth with biodiversity conservation via technological progress cannot be ruled out … The argument then is that the basic conflict between economic growth and biodiversity conservation may be lessened with technological progress. The phrase *may be lessened*, as opposed to *is lessened*, is also more appropriate because of the preponderance of R&D devoted not to conservation purposes but rather to increasing profits and economic growth… Economic growth will continue to cause environmental problems, including biodiversity loss, whereas a stabilized or steady state economy may be reconciled with environmental protection and biodiversity conservation."

This last statement is true, but there is not yet a proof that a steady state economy is **necessary** in order to pass through the bottleneck, nor that it is the only way to do so. This particular question has not been addressed by Czech (or by anyone else, as far as I'm aware). I think most of Czech's work appears to be premised on an assumption that we **never** pass through the bottleneck and are stuck inside the bottle forever. If this assumption came to pass, then the steady state economy would indeed be a very good and valid thing to propose as one way to build towards sustainability (but potentially not the only way, and perhaps not even a sufficient way in itself without other measures)

From Ruttan et al (2011):

> "The demonstration that technical change can be treated as largely endogenous to the development process does not imply that the progress of either agricultural or industrial technology can be left to an "invisible hand" that drives technology along an "efficient" path determined by relative resource endowments."

This gives us hope that public policy, acting on and through institutions, rather than relying on market mechanisms, can potentially redirect research and development in ways that are more likely to be planet-positive, which could ultimately help us to squeeze through the neck of the bottle.

Institutional change might be part of this pathway. From the same source:

> "There is general agreement that institutional change has evolved and continues to evolve in response to long-term changes in resource endowments such as the pressure of population against land resources or a rise in the price of labor relative to capital."

Let's look for a moment at the role of money in all of this

In "Supply Shock" (2013) Czech argues:

> "In summary, … money is a function of agricultural surplus. It truly *originates* from agricultural surplus, in the sense that matters most at this point in history. Agricultural surplus is what "generates" money; not tourism, not even ecotourism and certainly not the bank. Therefore, money supplies indicate the amount of agricultural surplus, and in turn the ecological footprint. Lots of agricultural surplus generates lots of money. No agricultural surplus generates no money. Limits to agricultural surplus means limits to money.
> *Real* money, that is."

He claims that, because money originally arose from agricultural surpluses (which is probably true) then (with the "therefore" in the excerpt above) there is a basic (almost inherent?) unsustainability of money created in other ways (eg by banks). He backs this up through his "trophic theory of money", in which he criticises the money circulating as a result of goods or services which are "dematerialised" ie which do not have an impact on the real economy or on nature:

"… expenditures might go toward non-material, unreal things, but only for short unsustainable periods of time."

No substantive proof or evidence for the above statement is given in the book, except to make the general observation that (among other things):

"… [in 2008] Markets crashed, back down to Earth, back down to the real economy of goods and services, produced and consumed by real people with common sense."

However, he says more about this subject in Czech (2019) "The trophic theory of money: principles, corollaries, and policy implications".

"If the origins of money are in agricultural surplus pursuant to the trophic theory of money, then it is not far-fetched to hypothesise that the quantity of money — and/or the level of GDP — is proportional to agricultural surplus."

This hypothesis is in danger of confusing correlation with causality. So what evidence is there? Yes, there is some evidence in early civilisations of such a proportional relationship, but in most modern economies that relationship no longer holds. Money has become so much more than its origins, and that has brought good as well as bad impacts on nature. Money expansion, and its ability to facilitate innovation, investment, efficiency and progress has reduced the per-capita impacts on nature. But it has also brought speculation, instability and over-exploitation of nature.

Czech says:

"The shekel, for example, originated as literally 180 grains (or "she") of barley (Acton and Goldblatt 2010). One can hardly find a better example of money supplies tracking with agricultural surplus! (Barley reserved for exchange, and therefore not consumed as food, represents a surplus.) The salient point, though, is that the grain of barley could have instead been a gram of silver, nickel, or lead. Although each of these metals was also useful as a commodity, none would have been useful as money per se if the barley (and other food) surplus hadn't allowed for the division of labour and the subsequent exchange of goods and services."

That is, indeed, a good example of the story of money's history, but a really important point is that it does not determine the future history of money – that is for modern humans to decide, for good or for bad.

Even the vaguely hinted implication of a corollary - that an alternative money (eg a gram of silver, nickel, or lead) somehow could not exist without an agricultural surplus going forward in time - does not bear up under closer examination. Money stores, eg in metal coin - could be used, after a lack of agricultural surpluses, eg to buy the services of labour to restore degraded agricultural land, if the degradation of land was what caused the lack of agricultural surpluses.

Czech posits that:

> "Pursuant to the trophic theory of money, the human economy — the size of which is measured by GDP — proliferates in proportion to agricultural surplus."

This is clearly not the case in modern times, where money supply has far outstripped agricultural surpluses. The debate is therefore not about whether the human economy is in proportion to the agricultural economy, but what the implications, risks and opportunities are in relation to the lack of proportionality between the two in modern societies.

To Czech, the 'extra' money circulating as a result of these activities is somehow inflation-generating because:

> "The key point, vis-à-vis the trophic theory of money, is that none of the brokers, agents or bankers would be operating in the absence of agricultural surplus. Their income required [requires?] real surplus at the trophic base of the economy [otherwise their activities are inflationary?]."

His final conclusion includes the statement that:

> "Limits to agricultural production, therefore, mean limits to real money and real GDP."

His hypothesis - that money arising without being generated by agricultural surpluses is inherently inflationary - is not proven within his work. I try to address this in more detail in a specific section below about money and inflation.

Before I move on to that section, I'd like to make a point on economic thinking. The issues surrounding the above discussions are similar to those around the economic concept of the "production boundary" – the definition of what constitutes productive activity (and therefore what does not). Many early economists considered that only agriculture was "inside the production boundary". In most modern economics, many more things, including many banking and financial services, are considered inside the production boundary. Although this has contributed to many problems, including accelerating rates of environmental degradation, placing such activities inside the production boundary did not inevitably lead to inflation, as would be implied by Czech's trophic theory of money. It does raise a question about whether there are some limits (and over what timeframes) on the proportional sizes of the various sectors within the production boundary, in physical throughput terms and (if relevant) in financial terms.

Is inflation an inevitable consequence of dematerialised services, as seems to be suggested by Czech?

Is inflation a symptom of an economy overreaching its productive base, ie beyond the "trophic limits" of the "real economy"?

In "Supply Shock (2013), Czech states that:

> "Inflation is precisely what happens when a monetary authority (such as the Federal Reserve System in the United States) increases the money supply faster than the real economy can grow …

> For our immediate purposes it is necessary to acknowledge the simple fact that inflation can cloud the tight relationship between real GDP and the ecological footprint. However, the cloud is quickly lifted when we specify that we are talking about "real GDP," or GDP adjusted for inflation."

Czech appears to draw his views about inflation by focussing on the "real economy" and posits that the "real" economy only comprises activities with an ecological footprint, and everything else is not part of the "real" economy, is explained by "animal spirits" and is therefore inflationary if it is involved in the circulation of money:

> "… 'real' expenditures go toward real things — real goods and services — that have real ecological footprints. Real expenditures do not go toward non-material things with no ecological footprints."

Czech admits that he is playing a bit footloose and fancy free with some of the language here:

> "I am taking a bit of rhetorical license here, because "animal spirits" was coined by Keynes to describe the emotions or attitudes of consumers. Here I am adapting the term to describe not only the "propensity to consume," as Keynes called it, but the propensity to *use money* in order to consume. Even in the most modern of monetary economies, the use of money is not necessarily required for consuming things we find valuable such as friendliness or compassion. It is our common sense or "animal spirits" that tell us when it is appropriate to use money for procuring satisfaction."

I say more about economics and natural capital in chapters 17 and 21 in my previous book "People or Planet: Towards a Regenerative Economics" (2020).

For now, suffice it to say that natural capital features much more strongly in some approaches to economics than in others. The more ecologically-oriented approaches place natural capital at the centre and emphasise that placing appropriate values on it will help us protect, maintain and enhance the biosphere on which we all depend. This is also one of the key reasons I've started working on compiling World Balance Sheets – ie to see how central and important natural capital turns out to be in financial as well as ecological terms.

The World Balance Sheet will not only be useful as support for ecological economists and "heterodox" economists, however. It will also be useful for classical and neo-classical mainstream economists, by helping to show how all the various strands of economics are impacting the amounts and proportions of natural capital that exist over time.

Chapter 9

Methodology for drawing up the WBS

"It is remarkable that until recently, and still today, many nations of the world have not had adequate balance sheets of the stock of assets that would be expected of any corporation. Flows of gross domestic product are widely reported … but the state of the asset base that can produce annual income is frequently overlooked."
(Cohen et al, 2018)

Chapter summary

- Should everything be monetised or is there room for non-financial measurement of economic throughput?
- What should a proper methodology look like – what are the main elements?
- Where does planetary governance fit in?
- What has already been covered earlier in the book?
- What is missing from the methodology?
- How are the gaps going to be filled?
- Would it be useful to run volumetric measurements (suggested by Murison Smith) *alongside* financial ones in the world balance sheet, in meaningful ways?
- Accounting frameworks - IFRS (International Financial Reporting Standards) compared with SNA (System of National Accounts)
- Fundamental accounting principles
- Discount rates

How will future world balance sheets be produced, shared and discussed? By whom will they be updated? How will stocktakes be undertaken, to establish counts (and general condition) of capital assets, including natural capital assets? How frequently should such stocktakes be done? Who will approve data updates, and ensure adequate sufficiency, quality and accuracy of the data used for them?

These are some of the important questions to be answered in order for a World Balance Sheet approach to be developed and embedded to support how we operate sustainable management of our impacts on this planet's biosphere. I won't attempt to answer all these questions in this tome. Any answers I do try to address will only be very provisional ones, subject to improvement by others. This is the nature of explorations at this time, when the whole concept of a World Balance Sheet is so young. It is just emerging and will take some time to come to fruition.

The World Balance Sheet is, by its own nature, a global phenomenon and it therefore lends itself to a global maintenance and updating approach. However, global governance systems are currently underdeveloped and under-resourced. Systems such as the United Nations were born out of times of great global military conflict and mass death and destruction. They are not best suited to the more invisible and insidious 'boiling frog' types of risks such as climate change and biodiversity and habitat loss/ degradation.

Murison Smith (2020) provides some excellent descriptions of a form of planetary governance that would provide the necessary framework for all of the activity required to maintain World Balance Sheets. But there are also other authors and other examples of globalised governance. One of the most obvious existing examples is the United Nations which, through its UNEP (United Nations Environment Programme) division, already compiles and shares much useful data in the public domain. Given the mixed record of the UN in delivering real-world impact on the environment, it's at the very least debatable whether it can provide the sort of global governance required to underpin the further development and ongoing maintenance of the World Balance Sheet.

Many people have already considered these matters. I think it's fair to say that most have come to the conclusion that this is not going to be an easy thing to get up and running on an ongoing basis.

For example, Stiglitz et al (2018) summarise it thus:

> "For these [environmental] assets, physical as well as monetary asset accounts can, in principle, be compiled to describe the opening and closing stocks as well as the changes in these assets. In practice, many conceptual and data problems limit our ability to both quantify several of these assets in physical terms and to value them in monetary terms."

Murison Smith (2020) puts an interesting point of view – that terms such as "sustainability" have been politically co-opted, and that monetising natural capital (or what he calls "natural capacity") is not the best way to achieve a "stable" economy in the long-term as part of a "planetary economy". He points out that any valuation given to nature is going to be wrong to some degree, and could therefore be misleading.

He prefers, instead, to focus on quantities of material throughput and energy transfers between the global economy and the natural world, as a means of assessing whether the global human economy can be brought into balance with planetary natural systems, for long-term stability.

It could be argued that this is just semantics and he might be describing sustainability but just using different language. However, there is validity in his critique of the downsides of trying to place financial values on natural systems.

What is critical, he argues, is that the throughputs impacting nature (by drawing materials from it and emitting wastes back to it) must be in balance with nature if the human population and its civilisations are to survive and thrive in the very long term.

Assessments of this, and measurements of it in planetary balance sheets, can take into account physical measurements of amounts of throughput and this can provide useful information about how ell we are doing in transitioning from the current state of affairs to the ideal planetary state of "stability".

There is potential for a beneficial synergy between the physical quantity approach Murison Smith advocates and the financial approach I have been advocating in this book. They're not mutually exclusive approaches. In fact, they are mostly complementary. There's no reason, given sufficient administrative resources, that it would not be possible to draw up world balance sheets that give information about the state of the world's assets not just in financial terms but also in physical ones. This could provide additional sense-checking.

A simple example is one from earlier in this book, in relation to forest cover. Adequacy of forest cover can be assessed both in financial terms (eg the sum of future discounted cash flows from all the sustainably harvested forest products) and also in non-financial terms, for example in absolute and relative amount of forest land cover on the earth. All of these measures have something to offer. The financial measure can tell us something about livelihoods and human wellbeing derived from use of harvested forest products. The forest land cover measure can tell us something about the stability of the quantities of standing forest and (potentially) how close that quantity might be getting to some sustainability threshold as studied by ecologists.

By having both financial and non-financial measures calculated and reported on world balance sheets, we can get a better, more informative picture of the state of assets than by using just one type of measure on its own.

As mentioned already, the World Balance Sheets presented in this book are just the start of a whole new endeavour to improve the visibility of meaningful information for ensuring future sustainability. I'm not the only author looking at this topic and considering how different frameworks for gathering and presenting balance sheet information can help in this quest. The notable economist Joseph Stiglitz, in Stiglitz et al (2018) points out:

> "A full balance sheet approach to economic sustainability would also imply a more nuanced approach to sustainability, one that is not likely to rely on a "single number" [such as GDP]. This makes it more difficult to decide, to take a pertinent example, when it is appropriate to engage in fiscal stimulus. In this context, a complete [national] balance sheet would have several important characteristics:
>
> - Private wealth should be considered alongside the assets and liabilities of the public sector, as private liabilities may be converted into public liabilities if particular agents fail (due to bank bailouts, for example). In addition, the tax base upon which the government can draw for meeting its liabilities depends on the net wealth of the private sector. In both of these respects, some sort of distributional information is important since aggregation may mask the fact that, for many agents, debt is not covered by assets. The share of households (or firms or

banks) with negative net worth may be a useful indicator. There is also value in considering the transmission of wealth between generations through examining data on inheritance of assets more closely.

- A better [national] balance sheet would also take into account the fact that, even though the value of an asset (e.g. land) has increased, and overall measures of wealth have gone up, this is not the same as an increase in the volume of productive assets.

- More detailed [national] balance sheets of financial corporations and other institutional sectors are critical to understand[ing] risks and vulnerabilities. The G20 Data Gaps Initiative (DGI) recommends producing quarterly institutional sector accounts. We should also recognise that, when risk is not properly measured, we may underestimate the fragility of firms, households, and other institutions in the face of financial stress. [national] Balance sheets should be more detailed, both in terms of showing more granular sub-sectors (to illuminate differences in vulnerabilities as measured, for example, by debt-to-income ratios) and more detailed data for each of those sub-sectors, while taking into account the costs and benefits of collecting and analysing more detailed data. More detailed [national] balance sheets within a sub-sector would allow for a better analysis of risk through examining inter-connectedness by having breakdowns by counterparty sector, or breakdowns of debt by maturity and currency.

- All relevant types of pension liabilities need to be included."

Although many of Stiglitz's comments are about national balance sheets, they are equally valid if applied to world balance sheets.

He goes on to summarise that, while a lot of work has already been done, for example on Natural Capital Accounting, there is a long way to go and some significant barriers to overcome:

"The need to measure environmental assets and, in particular, ecosystems and planetary boundaries is now being recognised. Lots of research over the last 50 years has gone into measuring these assets and into developing valuation techniques that would allow monetary values to be estimated for them. However, the most critical measurement issues have still not been resolved... measuring sustainability, in the narrow sense of keeping the total monetary value of the stock of natural capital constant, is plagued with uncertainties that result from a combination of difficulties to find price estimates in the absence of markets; difficulties to predict future demand; uncertainties about system behaviour including lack of knowledge about the inter-dependence of different systems; and so on. A more comprehensive approach should aim to develop an information system that enhances our knowledge about all components of natural capital, including subsoil assets, land and the way it is used, and ecosystems. This is the ambition of the systems approach... "

How good (or how limiting) are existing accounting frameworks as support for the World Balance Sheet?

With apologies in advance, some of the following material is copied from my previous book "People or Planet: Towards a Regenerative Economics" (2020).

Section summary:

- What should an accounting framework provide?
- System of National Accounts ("SNA")
- International Financial Reporting Standards ("IFRS")
- System of (Integrated) Environmental and Economic Accounts ("SEEA"):
- Comparisons between SNA and SEEA
- Comparisons between SNA and IFRS
- Conclusions

An accounting framework should provide:

- Useful guidance on methods, for example for compiling accounts
- Consistency of practice across a variety of entities and geographies (and, ideally, across all entities across the whole globe)
- The basis for meaningful comparisons between all sets of accounts that are compliant with the framework
- The basis for consolidation of accounts (from any or all entities) when all of those accounts to be consolidated are compliant with the framework

SNA

The System of National Accounts ("SNA") is an internationally recognised framework for governments to account for the assets, liabilities and activities in the countries they govern. Most countries comply with it, to some extent, although not all countries do so extensively, completely or consistently.

One of its main deficiencies is that not all of the natural world is considered as an environmental asset for accounting purposes under SNA, and even those that are considered are included in the "non-financial balance sheet" of a country. The only natural assets or flows of benefits that are considered for SNA accounting are the ones where there is a direct economic consequence for people. These are defined as being within what is described as the "production boundary" ie benefits produced by economic units (ie "the various establishments, enterprises, government and household entities about which economic data are collected").

Despite the inadequacy of definitions and boundaries in SNA, which has no doubt been arrived at for convenience in assessment and calculation, the inclusion of any environmental assets (which were, for many years, omitted completely) is a very positive step forward in a discipline that is not renowned for its speed of innovation.

Valuation in SNA is of some significance in debates about how it sits with other frameworks such as SEEA (which I discuss in some detail in the next section). The basis of valuation in SNA is the use of **exchange value**, and this applies to capital items (such as natural capital) as well as to income or expenditure.

As Dasgupta (2007) points out, "economists observe that to say someone is accumulating capital is to suggest that they are sacrificing something now for future benefit." This implies a form of **intertemporal exchange or exchange through time**. An exchange through time might sound complicated, but any time one forgoes consumption in the present for future benefit, that is an exchange between present and future versions of one's self.

It's important, through whatever valuation method we choose, to impute values for non-marketed assets – otherwise, we would have no value at all for them to use in any balance sheets.

To many environmentalists, exchange value doesn't sit comfortably with them. This is because of the implication of the possibility of exchange, for example involving the substitution of natural capital for other types of capital such as produced capital, or, indeed, the exchange of natural capital for cash. Either of these things implies exploitation and conversion of the natural capital "if the price is right". However, just because a theoretical exchange value is calculated doesn't mean that the object being valued will actually be exchanged. In many cases, for items of natural capital, there is no market in which such exchanges could happen, and in some instances government regulation prevents exchange (for example in the case of national parks and other protected areas).

However, as UN (2019) points out, exchange value in SNA can be reconciled with ecological economics and environmentalism:

> "Nordhaus (2006) emphasizes that credible national accounts need to include 'a full set of current and capital accounts along with the accounts linking the current and capital accounts.' In the SEEA context, these linking accounts are likely [to include] extent, capacity, or condition "accounts." These are important for assets not exchanged in markets, because the assumption in a market is that prices reflect condition or capacity. Therefore, this additional information is needed to impute prices for non-marketed assets.

It will be useful, at this point to briefly make the distinction between price and value, even if both are imputed for non-marketed assets. Price is the value attributed to a small change in the amount of the asset, usually in relation to an actual or imputed exchange transaction.

From UN (2019):

> "Formally then, the price of an asset is the marginal (or incremental) value associated with a change in the underlying stock (extent, capacity, or condition), often experienced along with a change in time."

Value can be ascribed per unit of the asset, and can be multiplied up to provide a figure for the entire stock of the asset (or vice-versa, by division).

UN (2019) indicates caution in using this way of thinking about value:

> "The closest thing to total value is the change in value associated with moving from the current stock to a level of the stock equal to zero. For many forms of natural and ecosystem assets this is not a useful thought experiment."

The subjects of value and price are sometimes highly charged ones in some discussions between accountants and environmentalists. This can often be alleviated by pointing out that any value we place on assets, including natural capital, can be seen in the context of the purposes for the valuation. If the purpose is not to facilitate exchange of the asset, but to help understand the current and future welfare benefits flowing to humanity from the asset in its standing condition and amount, then calculating value can provide a basis on which to have a more objective comparison than might otherwise be possible. For example, in many cases, it can be demonstrated that the value of a standing asset is greater than the value of converting it into (ie exchanging it for) barren land, by cutting down all the trees for wood.

However, there is an area of accounting in SNA which is useful for world balance sheet considerations. SNA does recognise actual and contingent liabilities, and included in the latter are:

- Failure of the banking system which requires support beyond government insurance

- Environmental recovery, disaster relief

As well as these explicit examples of contingent liabilities, another similar example (which is used as a key feature in the Planetary CFO's world balance sheet) is an amount which is titled "human welfare commitment". This item is described more fully elsewhere in the book, but it can be seen that it is quite consistent with examples of other types of liabilities already included in SNA.

There is an increasing interest in academic circles in the theory and (emerging) practice of accounting for Natural Capital within (or as an extension to) SNA. This is seen as complementing SNA rather than providing an alternative to SNA.

For example, La Notte and Rhodes (2019) examine current trends in experimental methods for accounting for Natural Capital in national accounts. They set this within a described set of international standards called the Experimental Ecosystem Accounts ("EEA") of the System of (Integrated) Environmental and Economic Accounts ("SEEA"):

"In the traditional national economic accounts, based on the System of National Accounts (SNA), no consideration was given either to environmental damage or to ecosystem assets and services. In the early 1990s the United Nations Statistics Division (UNSD) proposed a System for Integrated Environmental and Economic Accounting (SEEA) (Bartelmus et al., 1991) to fill the information gap in the SNA core accounts with a series of satellite accounts to record environmental data in a consistent way. [in] SEEA (ref. paragraph 1.23 in UNSD et al., 2003) natural capital is defined as including three basic categories:

> • resource functions which cover natural resources extracted and converted into goods and services (e.g., timber from natural forests, subsoil deposits);

> • sink functions which absorb pollution and wastes generated by production and consumption activities (e.g., air emissions, wastewater, solid waste);

> • service functions which guarantee habitat for all living beings (e.g., air, water, amenity functions).

SEEA is such an important topic that I'll now spend some time explaining what it is and exploring some of its uses (and challenges).

"SEEA" (System of Environmental and Economic Accounts)

Also known as "SEEA – CF" (for Central Framework) or

"SEEA EEA" (System of Environmental and Economic Accounting Experimental Ecosystem Accounts)

SEEA has informed and influenced the Planetary CFO's methodology for natural capital valuations in the Planetary CFO's world balance sheets, so it's worth taking some time to look at this emerging standard for accounting for nature.

> Environmental assets are addressed and accounted as individual components that make up the environment, mass and biomass, that can be harvested, extracted, or otherwise taken for direct use in economic production, consumption, or (owned) stock accumulation. Environmental assets are accounted as raw stocks of natural resources and not as media for ecological health and growth. In asset accounts an addition to a stock of resources (e.g., growth in stock and discoveries) is contrasted with a reduction in stock (e.g., extraction, natural and catastrophic losses) in order to calculate how much a total stock has changed at the end of an accounting period (usually one year). This kind of information is useful to check whether any resource is managed sustainably, i.e., whether periodic removal of biological resources exceeds natural rates of growth and replenishment."

According to Wikipedia:

> "The **System of Environmental-Economic Accounting (SEEA)** contains the internationally agreed standard concepts, definitions, classifications, accounting rules and tables for producing internationally comparable statistics on the environment and its relationship with the economy. The SEEA is a flexible system in the sense that its implementation can be adapted to countries' specific situations and priorities. Coordination of the implementation of the SEEA and on-going work on new methodological developments is managed and supervised by the UN Committee of Experts on Environmental-Economic Accounting (UNCEEA). The final, official version of the SEEA Central Framework ("SEEA CF") was published in February 2014."

The following is from The London Group (2018), which gives some more description of how this accounting framework is being supported and expanded in practice around the world (in which I have emboldened a key statistic):

> "The SEEA EEA [System for Integrated Environmental and Economic Accounting Experimental Ecosystem Accounts] was formally published in 2014 as a joint publication of the United Nations, European Commission, Food and Agriculture Organization of the United Nations, Organisation for Economic Co-operation and Development and the World Bank. While the ecosystem accounting system described in SEEA EEA was novel, it reflected the integration of many existing strands of expertise including statistics and

national accounting, ecology and natural science, geography and geo-spatial measurement. By providing a platform by which these disciplines could exchange and share ideas, there has been rapid growth in the development and testing of ecosystem accounting. **From a zero base in 2012, there are currently over 40 countries with ecosystem accounting programs of some type underway and there are applications in, and participation from, all sectors – public, private, academia and civil society.**"

The SEEA (**System of Environmental-Economic Accounting**) Central Framework ("SEEA CF") was adopted by the United Nations Statistical Commission as the first international standard for environmental-economic accounting in 2012. It was produced and released under the auspices of the United Nations, the European Commission, the Food and Agriculture Organization of the United Nations, the Organisation for Economic Co-operation and Development, the International Monetary Fund and the World Bank Group.

The SEEA CF covers measurement in three main areas:

1. **Environmental flows.** The flows of natural inputs, products and residuals between the environment and the economy, and within the economy, both in physical and monetary terms.
2. **Stocks of environmental assets.** The stocks of individual assets, such as water or energy assets, and how they change over an accounting period due to economic activity and natural processes, both in physical and monetary terms.
3. **Economic activity related to the environment.** Monetary flows associated with economic activities related to the environment, including spending on environmental protection and resource management, and the production of 'environmental goods and services'.

As an aside here, UN (2014) makes what I think is an unhelpful distinction between "SNA and non-SNA benefits", which it says "facilitates coherence and alignment with standard national accounting measures". The distinction is based on the current production boundary defined in SNA.

While this coherence might be good in the short-term, surely the hope must be that the SNA develops to encompass all natural benefits and assets in due course. That being the case, the real distinction is between assets and benefits that are either inside the *production boundary* or outside it. This explicitly recognises that the production boundary might change in future, as a normal process of improvement and alignment to current and future realities. This might only appear to be a subtle change of language. However, it makes more sense to me to express things in ways that are more future-proofed than the existing wordings in UN (2014).

By convention, the measurement scope of non-SNA benefits for ecosystem accounting purposes is limited to the flow of ecosystem services with an identifiable link to human well-being. This means that many ecosystem services are excluded from SEEA (for example those that support other species or other ecosystems, even if the essential supporting benefits that humans receive could not be produced without them). This has implications for the incompleteness of SEEA accounting, even if it is more comprehensive than either SNA or IFRS.

At a global level, in 2020, the first global consultation on individual chapters of the revised SEEA EEA was launched starting with Chapters 3-5 on ecosystem units, ecosystem extent and ecosystem condition. The 2020 revision to the SEEA EEA, undertaken under the guidance of the UN Committee of Experts on Environmental Economic Accounting, has the aspiration of:

> "providing an agreed statistical framework for ecosystem accounting, including agreed terminology, concepts, definitions and classifications for ecosystem assets and services in both physical and monetary terms using an accounting approach".

The revision will bring together work on four sub-topics that have been the subjects of various working groups over recent years:

- spatial areas
- ecosystem condition
- ecosystem services
- valuation

King et al (2019) set the background by summarising the benefits of the use of Natural Capital approach with a useful diagram:

Figure 30 (their figure 3), adapted by them from SEEA EEA (UN et al., 2014):

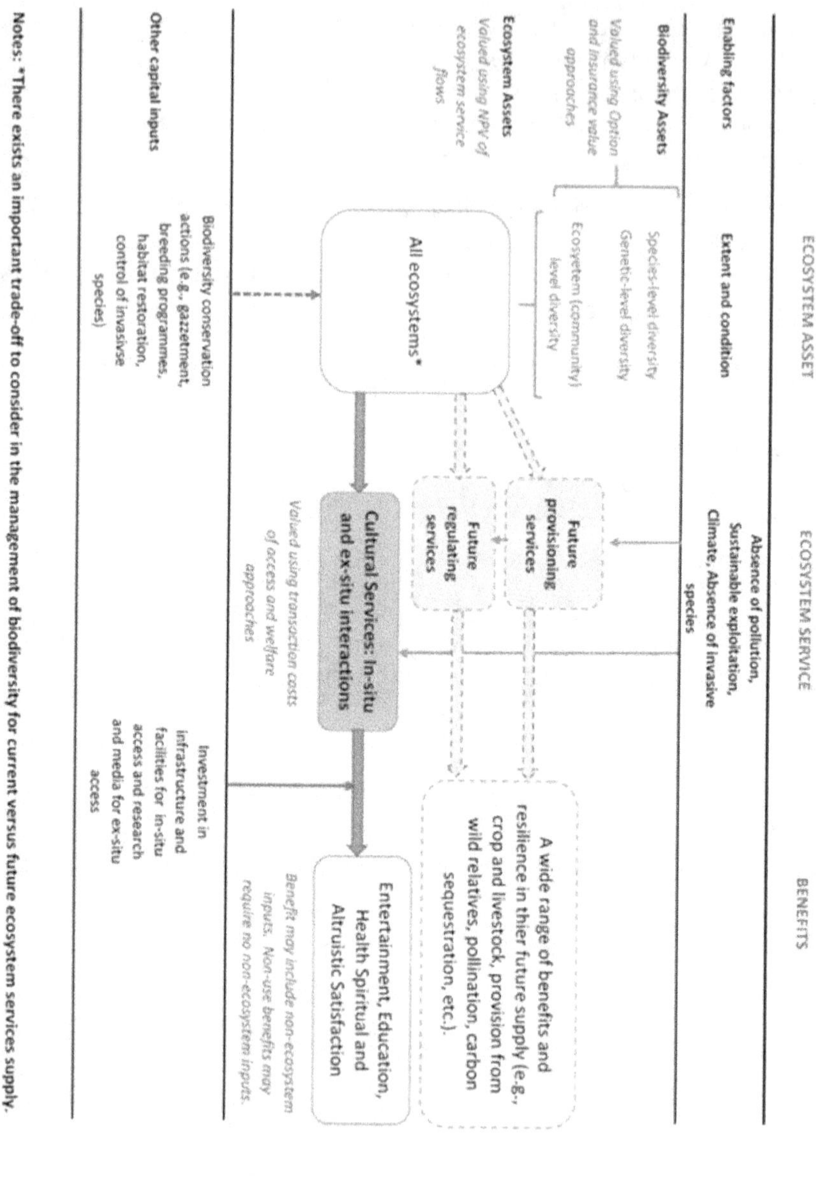

Figure 3: Logic chain for biodiversity as an asset that maintains capacity for future ecosystem-service delivery.

Notes: *There exists an important trade-off to consider in the management of biodiversity for current versus future ecosystem services supply.

King et al (2019) go on to highlight some of the work going on to produce recommendations for the 2020 revision of the SEEA EEA.

As an example, they give some recommended areas for further development of valuation methods:

"Additional measurement approaches suggested in the meeting for habitat and biodiversity related ecosystem services, that could be evaluated further, included:

- Use of nature conservation volunteering time as a measure of the bequest value;

- Using reserve / protected area planning models (e.g., Marxan) to identify the minimum costs of protecting a set of species and habitats;

- Use of marginal values for flagship species derived from collective conservation actions (a related approach is presented in this paper with respect to Orangutan reintroduction);

- Use of compliance costs (or opportunity costs of land) associated with implementing a country's biodiversity policies and any associated subsidies."

They conclude that environmental accounting is an area of continuing research and development, encompassing the disciplines of accounting, economics and ecology:

"Overall there is clearly need for further research with respect to the links between thematic biodiversity accounts (for measuring and valuing biodiversity as an asset) and ecosystem service accounts and the valuation of ecosystem assets based on Net Present Values of these services. Whilst a focus on final ecosystems services is clearly needed to avoid double counting of benefits, accounting approaches or auxiliary accounting tools need to be developed that either communicate the dependencies and trade-offs between the use of ecosystem services and the depreciation of the biodiversity asset base, or integrate such depreciation into ecosystem service values.
Making the links between the SEEA-EEA and decision support should also be a key research area for the environmental accounting community. Admiraal et al. (2013) proposes an interesting approach using portfolio theory (which seeks to maximise returns whilst minimising risk) that could be explored in an accounting context. This would be achieved by using information on biodiversity to guide investment in a portfolio of ecosystem assets to generate policy acceptable returns on investment (determined from monetary ecosystem services account), whilst managing risk and reducing volatility in services supply (by maintaining a suitable portfolio of biodiversity)."

In the referenced work, Admiraal et al (2013) expand a little on the portfolio, risk and resilience techniques mentioned:

"We expand on earlier research by arguing that these three lines of research can be combined to put total economic value in a framework that would foster sustainable use of ecosystems. The concepts of insurance value and resilience stock are part of resilience thinking, which is a perspective for a sustainability analysis of systems, whereas economic valuation is a method for optimization. This distinction suggests that the two apply to different stages in a process and can therefore complement each other (Fischer et al., 2009). We present portfolio theory as a framework in which investment in total economic value can be combined with investment in ecological resilience."

The three lines of research referred to above are:

- limits of optimization of the economic value of ecosystem services
- ecosystem resilience
- portfolio theory applied to investment in total economic value and investment in ecological resilience

It's good to see the combination of accounting, economic and ecological language being used in such modern research. Not many years ago, this would be very rare, and almost exclusively would occur pejoratively. Now, the dialogue between the various disciplines is much more explorative and constructive.

Having said the above, there is ongoing debate on the availability of widely accepted economic theories and the practicalities of including natural asset values derived from those theories in national accounting. For example, King et al (2019) say:

"Valuation
Capturing the full range of values that biodiversity embodies in the accounting framework is likely to be difficult due to [a] number of reasons. Natural science knowledge as well as economic theory that would help to value the role biodiversity plays in underpinning ecosystem services and in supporting ecological redundancy is lacking. Some valuation knowledge and practice are available for estimating the (mostly non-use) values associated with important habitats and charismatic species, particularly using stated preference valuation techniques. These methods are thought to be the only economic valuation techniques capable of measuring non-use values. Since these are based on a welfare value concept, however, including such values in SEEA would not be consistent with other (transaction) values in the accounts. An alternative solution for inclusion of these values in the SEEA would be via Satellite wealth-based accounts, which would also be highly useful for informing public policy (Badura et al 2017 EU INCA report). The nature-based recreation paper also discusses the use of simulated exchange values to purge consumer surplus from welfare values."

One way forward to try to resolve difficulties of theorising and putting theory into practice is to undertake pilot projects. One such initiative is the NCAVES project.

Natural Capital Accounting and Valuation of Ecosystem Services ("NCAVES") Project

The United Nations Statistics Division, the United Nations Environment Programme, the Secretariat of the Convention on Biological Diversity, and the European Union launched the project in 2017. It aims to assist the five participating partner countries, namely Brazil, China, India, Mexico and South Africa, to advance the knowledge agenda on environmental-economic accounting, in particular ecosystem accounting. It will initiate pilot testing of SEEA Experimental Ecosystem Accounting (SEEA EEA) with a view to:

- Improving the measurement of ecosystems and their services (both in physical and monetary terms) at the (sub)national level;
- Mainstreaming biodiversity and ecosystems at (sub)national level policy planning and implementation;
- Contribute to the development of internationally agreed methodology and its use in partner countries.

NCAVES Workstreams

The project is organized along several workstreams.

- **Compiling ecosystem accounts**: A range of ecosystem accounts will be piloted in the five project countries (see below for description each country). These accounts will be in physical and monetary terms. The accounts will be subsequently applied in scenario analysis based on national policy priorities.

- **Guidelines and methodology**: the country pilots will feed into the revision of the SEEA EEA and guidelines (on biophysical modelling, valuation, and scenario analysis) that will contribute to national and global implementation of NCA [Natural Capital Accounting];

- **Indicators**: Development and testing of a set of indicators in the context of the post 2020 Biodiversity Agenda and other international initiatives

- **Business accounts**: Contribute to the alignment between SEEA and corporate sustainability reporting

- **Communications**: increase awareness of natural capital accounting both in project countries and beyond through developing a range of products

- **Enhanced capacity building and knowledge sharing**: enlarging the community of practitioners on natural capital accounting by e-Learnings and training workshops (in country and regional).

In parallel, within the project countries inter-institutional mechanisms around NCA (Natural Capital Accounting) will be established or strengthened, through a country assessment feeding into developing a national roadmap.

NCAVES Pilot Countries

Brazil

Pilot in Rio Grande river basin, specifically in the states of Maranhao-Tocantins-Piaui-Bahia (MATOPIBA) focusing on hydrological services as well as soil related services.

China

Support ongoing pilots in the provinces of Guangxi Autonomous Region and Guizhou. At the national level support will be provided to develop natural resource balance sheets.

India

A suite of ecosystem accounts will be assessed in a pilot for the State of Karnataka. Several ecosystem services will be assessed at the national scale.

Mexico

Building on earlier pilot accounts for the state of Aguascalientes, ecosystem extent, condition and services accounts will be compiled at the state and national level.

South Africa

Various types of ecosystem accounts will be compiled, including ecosystem services accounts for KwaZulu-Natal (KZN) province, and ecosystem extent accounts at the national level.

As well as the United Nations, other international organisations are working to further the inclusion of Natural Capital in systems of national accounts and in economic thinking.

For example, the "London Group" (under the auspices of the United Nations) is an informal group of experts primarily from national statistical agencies but also international organizations. The London Group generally meets annually, and the meetings provide a forum for review, comparison and discussion of work underway by participants towards development of environmental accounts.

La Notte and Rhodes (2019) point out that the EU is active in this space:

> "In Europe the 7th Environment Action Program (EU, 2013) and the EU Biodiversity Strategy (EC, 2011) include objectives to develop natural capital accounting (NCA) in the EU; specifically, the Knowledge Innovation Project for Integrated Natural Capital Accounting (KIP INCA) tackles ecosystem and ecosystem services accounts."

For example, this is from EU KIP INCA (2015):

> "Establishing a sound method of natural capital accounting with a strong focus on ecosystems and their services is a key objective of the 7th Environment Action Programme (EAP) and of the EU Biodiversity Strategy. It will help understand better how job creation, economic growth and well-being rely on natural capital and will support a number of key strategic EU policies, such as the Europe 2020 strategy … the KIP aims to design and implement an integrated accounting system for ecosystems and their services in the EU, and thereby provides an EU contribution to testing the SEEA EEA and could feed into international initiatives, such as the Sustainable Development Goals."

Transitional Arrangements for inclusion of Natural Capital in national balance sheets

If a whole class of assets (in this case Natural Capital) is to be added to national balance sheets, how is that to be done (technically) without creating unintended consequences, for example (potentially) the following?

- Creating inconsistency of data sets pre- and post- the change of approach
- Opening up opportunities for uncertainties and lost public confidence in the national finances
- Introducing volatility of balance sheet values, for example for gross and net worth, from one year to the next, for reasons outside human control (eg. natural disasters)
- Introducing measurement errors with material policy consequences (for example on national policies for taxation, inflation, austerity and quantitative easing)

These are common problems with many new accounting concepts. However, none of them is insurmountable, as there is much experience of transitional situations in the accountancy profession and elsewhere. Consider the change, in 1971, from pre-decimal to decimal currency in the UK, the adoption of the Euro as a currency across much of Europe in 1992, or the "Millennium Bug" debacle of 2000. Each of these events gave rise to significant risks and concerns similar to the ones above. But all were successful transitions.

SEEA EEA is undoubtedly an important set of standards supporting the development, measurement and use of Natural Capital accounting.

However, this is a topic in which there is a large amount of interest, and a growing number of international initiatives aiming to contribute to what is still an emerging and developing field.

These initiatives are not restricted to seeking values for natural capital, but are also looking at the role of natural assets in maintaining biodiversity, which could provide another layer of (additive) value.

La Notte and Rhodes (2019) highlight that:

> "Other theoretical frameworks [than SEEA EEA] have been developed, and are referred to by researchers and practitioners working on natural capital and ecosystem services. The very popular frame reported in the Millennium Ecosystem Assessment (MA, 2005) has fed numerous initiatives, among which we mention The Economics of Ecosystems and Biodiversity (TEEB)."

A point to note here is that ecosystems, and the natural living things (eg trees) within them, can have multiple values (that could add together) in connection with their role in maintaining biodiversity as well as the natural products that can be harvested from them, as well as the carbon sequestration they provide (in the biomass they comprise and the soils they enrich).

As noted by King et al (2019), in relation to biodiversity:

> "People value biodiversity in many different ways, and a plethora of conceptual frameworks, classifications and typologies have been proposed over the past two decades, in an attempt to make better sense of this complexity ... A forest, for example, qualifies as habitat only in the sense that it provides suitable conditions for particular organisms to live - i.e. it supports the existence and persistence of biodiversity. We therefore regard the role that this same forest might play in, for example, sequestering carbon as a function of the overall biomass and/or functioning of this ecosystem as, again, falling outside the scope of 'habitat and biodiversity related ecosystem services' "

This is to say that carbon sequestration provided by forests is a distinct, additional value-add to the value of the existence of biodiversity in that forest.

Demonstrating this additive characteristic of natural assets and biodiversity is an ongoing challenge.

It's one thing to value a natural asset. But how do we reflect the fact that many natural assets have been degraded or damaged by human activities?

Valuing the degradation of natural capital assets is also a challenging topic, as it can be done in at least two different ways, as explained in UN (2014):

".. whether the valuation of ecosystem degradation should be based on analysing forgone income due to the reductions in the current and future flows of ecosystem services, or if valuation of ecosystem degradation should be based on the costs of restoring the ecosystem to a previous state.

I'll not look at TEEB and biodiversity in any more detail in this current book – there are plenty of sources of additional information elsewhere – I've simply included a brief reference to it here for completeness.

Even with these advances in recognition of environmental assets, they are generally only shown so far in satellite statements, not in national balance sheets, and they are generally shown as experimental numbers. Also, these numbers often reflect flows, rather than stocks, of natural products and services.

There are some exceptions emerging to take this accounting further. Examples of countries that are doing this are the UK and Finland.

However, I've drawn inspiration from methods and frameworks such a SEEA in the Planetary CFO's theory of value (chapter 7) and the Planetary CFO's methodology for the world balance sheet (chapter 9).

Land and SNA

Because land is such an important element of recognising and valuing natural capital, it's worth digging a little deeper to try to understand what the SNA says about it.

The following definitions for "land" are from the 2017 amendments to the UK National Accounts Blue Book (which is the general rule book for UK national accounting, which should be compliant with SNA):

1. Land is defined as the ground itself, including soil covering and associated surface water; the associated surface water includes any inland waters (reservoirs, lakes, rivers) over which economic ownership rights can be exercised and from which economic benefits can be derived by their owners.

2. The enforcement of ownership rights is an important characteristic of land as an asset. The SNA 2008 and ESA 2010 distinguish ownership into legal and economic; the legal owner is the unit entitled in law to the benefits of possession. However, a legal owner can contract with another unit for the

latter to accept the risks and rewards of using the entity in production, in return for an agreed payment. The nature of the agreement is a financial lease, where the payments reflect only the placing of the asset at the disposal of the borrower by the provider[3]. The economic owner of entities, such as goods and services, natural resources, financial assets and liabilities, is the institutional unit entitled to claim the benefits associated with the use of the entity in question in the course of an economic activity by virtue of accepting the associated risks. In this article "ownership rights" refers to economic ownership rights.

3. Institutional units are defined as the elementary economic decision-making centre characterised by uniformity of behaviour and decision-making autonomy in the exercise of its principal function; examples of these are financial corporations, private non-financial corporations, public corporations and households.

4. The value of land will be shown under natural resources in the balance sheet; this excludes the value of improvements, the value of buildings on the land and transfer costs, which are all shown separately under fixed assets.

5. Land will appear on the non-financial balance sheet and will be valued at its current market price; this current market price excludes the costs of ownership transfer, which are treated, by convention, as gross fixed capital formation (GFCF) and of land improvements, and are subject to consumption of fixed capital.

Of particular note in the context of the main discussions in this book is the use, in the above instructions, of market price for land valuation for inclusion in the balance sheet, and that the land is included in the **<u>non-financial</u>** balance sheet in SNA.

SNA reports two balance sheets – a financial one and a "non-financial" one. The financial balance sheet reports financial assets and liabilities. The 'non-financial' balance sheet reports assets and liabilities that are not financial but which have a financial effect. They are shown at an appropriate financial value. The distinction between the two balance sheets is rather anomalous, as every organisation other than nations does not make this distinction – they simply report all financial and 'non-financial' assets and liabilities in a single balance sheet for the organisation.

It's clear from the above discussion that, at least in the UK, Natural Capital is largely excluded from the national balance sheets, but at least the inclusion of natural products and services in the Environmental Accounts (a set of satellite statements), albeit only as an annual flow so far, is a step in the right direction.

This is a rapidly developing topic, and the UK Office of National Statsistics ("ONS") does explain that this is an area of UK national accounting that is subject to experimentation. For example, from the Office of National Statistics (2019b):

"The methodology used to develop these estimates remains under development; the estimates reported in UK Natural Capital Accounts (2019) are experimental and should be interpreted in this context. Experimental Statistics are those that are in the testing phase, are not yet fully developed and have not been submitted for assessment to the UK Statistics Authority. Experimental Statistics are published to involve customers and stakeholders in their development and as a means of building in quality at an early stage."

Other countries are undertaking similar experiments in national accounting, for example in the NCAVES project.

IFRS (International Financial Reporting Standards)

The International Financial Reporting Standards ("IFRS"), and the International Accounting Standards ("IAS") set the international frameworks guiding all accountants around the world in what is deemed to be acceptable ways of accounting for everything that appears in a balance sheet or a profit and loss statement. An example is the way assets are valued and reported. There are a number of accepted ways of attributing, or calculating, a value for an asset. In chapter 7, I take a deeper dive into IFRS/IAS in relation to land valuation.

What are the main differences between IFRS and SNA?

The following is from Cullen et al (2017), in which I've emboldened some particularly important text:

> "Recently, international accounting standards have become increasingly important in commercial and public sector accounting. The International Accounting Standards Board (IASB) and the International Public Sector Accounting Standards Board (IPSASB) have developed several standards in this respect, the former relating to commercial accounting and the latter to public sector accounting. In these international accounting standards, the boards prescribe how corporations and government bodies should record various transactions and positions, and how they should address specific reporting issues, to arrive at transparent and comparable information in financial statements. The standards that are developed by the IASB are called International Financial Reporting Standards (IFRS) which are applied by many large private companies, especially multinationals, in more than 100 countries. The standards that are developed by the IPSASB are known as International Public Sector Accounting Standards (IPSAS) and these are increasingly adopted by many governments around the world.

> The principles underlying these international accounting standards are broadly in line with the principles of the 2008 SNA. Both try to arrive at standards that are correct from a conceptual point of view, but that are also feasible to apply from a practical point of view. As they share the same underlying principles, the guidance from international accounting standards is generally in line with 2008 SNA guidance. This is important as company and government accounts are relevant inputs in the compilation process of the national accounts. The closer the alignment between the two, the easier it will be to obtain the correct input data, which will improve the quality of the national accounts, while at the same time will reduce the reporting burden on corporations and government entities.

> However, even though there is a general alignment between the accounting standards and the 2008 SNA, there are some specific differences. One important difference is the treatment of holding gains and losses. Whereas in the 2008 SNA these are treated as revaluations, they are recorded, at least partly, as income according to the accounting standards. Another significant

difference relates to the boundaries for the recognition of non-financial assets. **Generally, one can state that the asset boundary of the 2008 SNA is larger than the one applied in business accounting**. This mainly concerns the recognition of intellectual property products, such as those resulting from research and development, as assets in 2008 SNA. The accounting standards also apply different rules with regard to contingent liabilities and provisions, in that they generally recommend including the expected value related to these two items on the balance sheet, whereas they will only be included in the central framework of the national accounts once they become explicit liabilities (except for standardised guarantees).

Moreover, international accounting standards may be applied to entities that do not qualify as statistical units as distinguished in the 2008 SNA. This will mainly be the case for multinational corporations. Whereas in the national accounts information is needed on the national parts of these corporations, international accounting standards may only be applied to create accounts for the multinational group as a whole, consolidating relationships between the entities located in different countries. In that case, the applied standards may still be the same, but additional work is needed to break down the relevant amounts into their national components. In most cases, such information is often available, if only because of reporting requirements to national tax authorities.

Because of the importance of correspondence between accounting standards and statistical requirements, a close co-operation between the standard setters and national accountants is very important. For that reason, recent years have seen an increased co-operation between the accounting world and the statistical world in further aligning existing accounting rules and in developing new standards."

The significance of the bold text is that it signifies that SNA is likely to include a rather larger set of asset types within its scope than the IFRS does. On the flip side, the SNA is not likely to include some liabilities recorded under IFRS as contingent liabilities (as an expected value), until they become explicit liabilities. There are therefore some liabilities that appear on the balance sheet under IFRS rules that would not appear under SNA. So, by comparison with IFRS, SNA is likely to show fewer assets, but also some fewer liabilities.

Despite recording more asset types than IFRS, the same book suggests that balance sheets drawn up under SNA are still likely to be omitting many important non-financial assets:

"Balance sheets are not complete without an appropriate inclusion of stocks of non-financial assets. Notwithstanding their importance for policy analysis and research, the adequate measurement and valuation of non-financial assets poses many problems, and most countries do not yet have a full set of balance sheets in terms of non-financial assets. Many gaps exist, in particular when it comes to the recording of non-produced non-financial assets [for example, natural assets]. However, in recent years much progress has been achieved, and future improvements are expected."

Fundamental accounting principles

The following is from Steven Bragg, CPA, at AccountingTools, Inc.

"A number of basic accounting principles have been developed through common usage. They form the basis upon which the complete suite of accounting standards have been built. The best-known of these principles are as follows:

- *Accrual principle*. This is the concept that accounting transactions should be recorded in the accounting periods when they actually occur, rather than in the periods when there are cash flows associated with them. This is the foundation of the accrual basis of accounting. It is important for the construction of financial statements that show what actually happened in an accounting period, rather than being artificially delayed or accelerated by the associated cash flows. For example, if you ignored the accrual principle, you would record an expense only when you paid for it, which might incorporate a lengthy delay caused by the payment terms for the associated supplier invoice.
- *Conservatism principle*. This is the concept that you should record expenses and liabilities as soon as possible, but to record revenues and assets only when you are sure that they will occur. This introduces a conservative slant to the financial statements that may yield lower reported profits, since revenue and asset recognition may be delayed for some time. Conversely, this principle tends to encourage the [recording] of losses earlier, rather than later. This concept can be taken too far, where a business persistently misstates its results to be worse than is realistically the case.
- *Consistency principle*. This is the concept that, once you adopt an accounting principle or method, you should continue to use it until a demonstrably better principle or method comes along. Not following the consistency principle means that a business could continually jump between different accounting treatments of its transactions that makes its long-term financial results extremely difficult to discern.
- *Cost principle*. This is the concept that a business should only record its assets, liabilities, and equity investments at their original purchase costs. This principle is becoming less valid, as a host of accounting standards are heading in the direction of adjusting assets and liabilities to their fair values.
- *Economic entity principle*. This is the concept that the transactions of a business should be kept separate from those of its owners and other businesses. This prevents intermingling of assets and liabilities among multiple entities, which can cause considerable difficulties when the financial statements of a fledgling business are first audited.
- *Full disclosure principle*. This is the concept that you should include in or alongside the financial statements of a business all of the information that may impact a reader's understanding of those statements. The accounting standards have greatly amplified upon this

concept in specifying an enormous number of informational disclosures.

- *Going concern principle.* This is the concept that a business will remain in operation for the foreseeable future. This means that you would be justified in deferring the recognition of some expenses, such as depreciation, until later periods. Otherwise, you would have to recognize all expenses at once and not defer any of them.
- *Matching principle.* This is the concept that, when you record revenue, you should record all related expenses at the same time. Thus, you charge inventory to the cost of goods sold at the same time that you record revenue from the sale of those inventory items. This is a cornerstone of the accrual basis of accounting. The cash basis of accounting does not use the matching principle.
- *Materiality principle.* This is the concept that you should record a transaction in the accounting records if not doing so might have altered the decision making process of someone reading the company's financial statements. This is quite a vague concept that is difficult to quantify, which has led some of the more picayune [ie petty] controllers to record even the smallest transactions.
- *Monetary unit principle.* This is the concept that a business should only record transactions that can be stated in terms of a unit of currency. Thus, it is easy enough to record the purchase of a fixed asset, since it was bought for a specific price, whereas the value of the quality control system of a business is not recorded. This concept keeps a business from engaging in an excessive level of estimation in deriving the value of its assets and liabilities.
- *Reliability principle.* This is the concept that only those transactions that can be proven should be recorded. For example, a supplier invoice is solid evidence that an expense has been recorded. This concept is of prime interest to auditors, who are constantly in search of the evidence supporting transactions.
- *Revenue recognition principle.* This is the concept that you should only recognize revenue when the business has substantially completed the earnings process. So many people have skirted around the fringes of this concept to commit reporting fraud that a variety of standard-setting bodies have developed a massive amount of information about what constitutes proper revenue recognition.
- *Time period principle.* This is the concept that a business should report the results of its operations over a standard period of time. This may qualify as the most glaringly obvious of all accounting principles, but is intended to create a standard set of comparable periods, which is useful for trend analysis.

These principles are incorporated into a number of accounting frameworks, from which accounting standards govern the treatment and reporting of business transactions."

Discounting

As I use discounting in a number of places in this book, it's worth spending a short time explaining it and giving a simple formula for calculating its effects on a flow of value into the future forever (ie in perpetuity).

Discounting is a method of multiplying each future payment by a reduction factor to represent the fact that it is to be made at some point in the future. A future payment is worth slightly less than one today, based on the idea that money that will be received or paid at some time in the future has less value, looking at it today (because of some uncertainties attached to it), than an equal amount collected or paid today (which then has no uncertainty attached to it). The future payment has a risk associated with it (it might never have to be paid, or might be reduced by the time it comes to making the actual payment). Mathematically, because of this discounting, even though the payments might carry on forever, the total of the discounted payments does not become infinity but instead sums to a finite number. This makes it possible to have a finite number in the assets or liabilities in the balance sheet that represents the total of all those (discounted) payments or receipts going on forever.

This "exponential discounting" method is supported in UN (2019):

> "Overall, the use of exponential discount rates, which is consistent with the advice in the SEEA Central Framework, is likely a reasonable starting place for the purpose of national accounting for natural or ecosystem assets."

Fortunately, there is a simple formula for calculating the total value (V) in perpetuity of a continuous flow of values each year, discounted at discount rate r%. With r expressed as a fraction (eg 2% as 0.02), then the total value is

$V = 1/r$

There are a number of challenges with selecting and using discount rates. These stem from the contextual nature of the rate. For example, Kant (1999), argued that:

(i) an individual may have different rates of time preference for different objects of his/her utility bundle;

(ii) the rate of time preference for an object will depend upon the role of the object in the economic and other necessities of the individual; and

(iii) the influence of the individual's personal factors on the rate of time preference will be object and context specific.

One source of general but relevant information is a discussion of "Declining Discount Rates" ("DDR") as per Groom and Hepburn (2017), from which I note that they say that UK Green Book discount rates, once as high as 6% on a flat rate basis, have fallen to about 4% for discounting of near-term future timelines, reducing to a lower rate than that for long-term future timelines, partly informed by concerns to accurately reflect long-term projects such as public investments in flood defences, nuclear power, and to reflect the social cost of carbon and transport. Groom and Hepburn suggest that the same might also apply to public investments in "nature based solutions" (ie Natural Capital). Here are some key excerpts from their paper, describing the main changes to the UK Green Book and the academic sources of the ideas involved:

> "… changes to official guidance for discounting in project and policy appraisal in the United Kingdom (HMT, 2003), France (Lebègue, 2005) and Norway (Hagen et al, 2012), among others. In these countries, the discount rate applied to costs and benefits in the distant future is lower than the discount rate applied today; a declining discount rate (DDR) is employed. These policy changes have had real-world consequences… These developments follow advances in the theory of discounting (e.g. Gollier, 1997, 2002a,b, 2004; Weitzman, 1998) that had previously remained largely untouched since the initial formalisations of Samuelson (1937) and Koopmans (1960; 1972). Over the past couple of decades, new ideas in discounting have been developed, deployed and diffused unlike ever before. The all-too-frequent gap between the "supply" of ideas from academics and the "demand" for those ideas by the policymakers appeared to close, at least momentarily … Gollier's research was triggered by a request from the French government to evaluate public investments in Nuclear Power. With decommissioning horizons of 150 to 1000 years, a precise theory of the appropriate social discount rate was necessary. While considerably more technical than Weitzman (1998), Gollier's two papers also strongly influenced the 2003 update to the UK Green Book."

The UK Green Book now uses step-wise reductions in discounting rates for long-term projects:

> "In 2003, HMT implemented two major changes in discounting guidance for government departments in the updated "Green Book". First, the headline discount rate was reduced from 6% to 3.5%. Second, DDRs were introduced, declining step-wise to 1% (forward rate) for horizons of 300 years or more... The full schedule: for horizons: H [years into the future] =[30, 75, 125, 200, 300] the period to period discount rate is [3%, 2.5%, 2%, 1.5%, 1%]."

The 2003 Green Book changes regarding DDR have stood the test of time. A review in 2013 (ten years after their introduction), concluded that they had been successful. This was highlighted by Groom and Hepburn:

> "In 2013, HMT held a workshop in which evidence on discounting from the previous decade was presented to representatives from various [UK] government departments. Academics, including Christian Gollier, presented

research corroborating previous results. This strengthened the position taken in the existing guidance and lead to DDRs being retained in the Green Book."

Through relatively recent modern history, discount rates widely deployed across the world have been reasonably modest at about 4% or lower in the long-run (see Deutsch, 2020, who also referenced World Bank data for this estimate), being about the same as the average return on capital.

Recent **interest rates** in the UK, for comparison, have been about 2% or less, with the bank base rate dropping as low as 0.25% in the UK, and these are historically very low. It would be foolhardy to assume that they will stay that low in the long-term. I say more about the relationship between discount rates and interest rates in the section below.

The work on DDR, combined with the comparison with interest rates and the long-term characteristics of the timelines relating to sustainability horizons, is why I have generally used a discount rate of 2% on some asset classes, as a simplification of the UK Green Book step-wise DDR rates through timelines of 30, 75, 125, 200 and 300+ years, and wherever I have used a different rate from this, I've explained why I have done so.

As another example, in the USA, where the changes to the UK Green Book regarding the use of DDRs, while not fully persuasive, were highly influential and continue to generate debate. According to Groom and Hepburn:

> "The new guidance ultimately specified that "intergenerational projects" should be subjected to a flat discount rate of 2.5% for their duration (IAWG 2010; Sunstein 2014). By comparison, general guidance on regulatory analysis is to employ a flat discount rate of 7% (for projects displacing private capital) or 3% (if displacing consumption), as set by Office of Management and Budgets Circular A-4 (OMB 2003)... Discounting guidance [in the USA] remained unchanged, despite the RFF workshop and compelling expert opinion. While the [UK] Green Book is cited, our interviewees noted the British and French precedent was not decisive in making the argument for DDRs in the US. So, the supply and demand sides have, thus far, been left wanting by the apparent difficulty of broking the US ideas market and its large transactions costs. Nevertheless, the [US] National Academy of Sciences committee on the SCC reported in January of 2017 and raised the issues of DDRs once again (NAS 2017, CH6). So DDRs remain live and policy relevant... "

Meanwhile, regarding the Netherlands, from the same report:

> "Nevertheless, DDRs were not recommended by the Ministry of Finance, because the real interest rate was already 0% and a decline to negative risk free rates was considered problematic. With a time invariant risk premium of 3%, a discount rate of 3% was recommended for the appraisal of all government projects. CPB (2015) asserted that there is insufficient information available to determine the term structure of the risk premium, and there are too many difficulties in establishing project-specific discount rates.

So, a flat term structure of 3% was recommended. DDRs were not adopted in practice."

I recognise that my choice of a flat discount rate of 2%, resulting from my simplification of the UK Green Book DDR step-wise structure, is somewhat arbitrary. I hope it will turn out to be a sensible choice.

One question that naturally arises is whether it's valid to use different discount rates on different asset classes, in the way I've done in my calculations and world balance sheets (where entries are drawn from, or derived from, a variety of sources).

The discount rates I have deployed have been used in calculations in relation to natural capital, as this was an identified area of deficiency in, for example, SNA accounting. Other types of capital have, generally, been left without amendment, and mostly the original sources of information about them used 4% discount rates, being somewhat of an industry standard in most circles.

I think, where there is going to be little (if any) substitutability between natural capital and other types of capital, then the use of different discount rates in relation to different types of capital is going to have little impact in practice.

Interplay of discounting rates and (compounding) interest rates

Interest rates and discount rates are, in one sense, the opposite of each other. Compound interest, if it applies to an outstanding loan balance, tends to increase the amounts of future financial commitments from year to year, whereas discount rates tend to reduce them (because the discount rate is reflecting that money flows in the future are not worth as much as they are today).

Brealey et al (1995) base their notion of discounting for net present value calculations on an opportunity cost of money/capital:

> "discount rate: Interest rate used to compute present values of future cash flows … Money can be invested to earn interest. If you are offered the choice between $x now and $x at the end of the year, you naturally take the money now and get a year's interest [by lending it to someone else at the prevailing interest rate]."

Other authors make the same argument in relation to discounting rates and cost of capital rather than discounting rates and interest rates.

However, the fundamental link means that if interest rates and discount rates are nearly the same, they have a general effect of cancelling each other out. During times when this is the case, economists could be justified in either largely ignoring both interest rates and discount rates, or in building in only minor net effects of either (or both).

Average interest rates in the last 30 years have varied, but have generally dropped from above 4% to below 4%. Discount rates vary considerably, depending on the views of the person undertaking the calculations and the purposes for which they are doing them.

Although discounting is normally applied to future income and outgoings, for example in calculations of Net Present Value, some similar principles could be applied to the future utility of assets held at the current time (including money or other financial assets). In the same way that there is a risk of future financial flows not occurring because future circumstances are unpredictable, something else that is unpredictable is the future ability of an owner of an asset (eg cash) to be able to enjoy or utilise that asset in the ways they might want to in the future. It's worth remembering that a money asset does not have any intrinsic value in itself. It's only worth something as a means of exchanging it into something that is actually useful in the real world or real economy.

Therefore, in the same way that some people argue that future money flows should be discounted to the current point in time, it could be argued that the future ability to utilise the current value of the net flows should also be discounted back to the current time. If the discount rate was the same for both these calculations, the net effect would be cancel out all the discounting altogether.

Conclusions on chapter 9

The main conclusion from the above analysis is that organisations using IFRS are likely to be showing fewer assets than those using SNA. Furthermore, those using SNA are likely to be showing fewer assets than actually exist (especially natural capital, as previously noted) because it only records assets with a direct economic benefit to people.

Market prices (or some type of proxy for market prices) are most often used to value assets under both standards. For natural capital, this is highly likely to grossly undervalue the assets (which often have a thin or non-existent market, resulting in them being given a very unhelpful value – often zero, in fact).

Any World Balance Sheet that we produce using data based on either of these standards is likely to be incomplete and many of the most important assets that are included would be under-valued, if they appear at all.

Because of these deficiencies in the major international accounting standards, they can only be used as a starting point for the World Balance Sheet. Items will then have to be revalued to better reflect the purposes of tracking the extent of progress towards sustainability.

SEEA is an experimental system of accounting standards which attempts to fill in some of the gaps left by IFRS and SNA. I've referenced SEEA in some of my calculations. However, SEEA is a young and emerging framework, and as such it suffers from numerous deficiencies and challenges. This is to be expected, as its practitioners must find out what works and what doesn't, in a very complex field of investigation and calculation. It should be kept in mind that SEEA is trying to value a huge variety of ways nature provides direct and indirect benefits to humanity from complex ecosystems comprising millions (perhaps billions) of species interacting in myriad ways across habitats, localities and regions in ways that don't respect articial administrative borders drawn up by human societies and their governments.

Ultimately, I've used common sense to arrive at valuations that make some arguable sense if the SEEA valuations look wholly inadequate (or are unavailable) for the purposes of the world balance sheet.

It's hoped that, over time, all these accounting standards and frameworks will converge towards each other, or at least will dovetail neatly into each other at their edges, and that this will improve the usefulness of accounting rules and guidance to support sustainability ambitions worldwide.

Chapter 10

Where are we heading? Some scenarios of the future

"Occasionally, chewing over some random letter writer's dilemma, I'll find myself imagining scenarios where the problem could be sidestepped by an innocent fib or series of evasive manoeuvres. Then, I slap myself on the wrist."
(Lynn Coady)

In this chapter, I take a tentative peek into the future. I apologise in advance that some of the techniques I use are quite technical. They necessitate quite a lot of "math", graphs and quite a few illustrative world balance sheets at various points in the future, for various scenarios. If this sort of technical wizardry makes your veins run cold, you might want to skip ahead to the commentaries for each of the three scenarios, to see the gist of the results described quite succinctly in words.

My main tool is scenario analysis, which is a well-known method and framework for such deliberations.

My second tool is a spreadsheet containing the Planetary CFO's 2020 World Balance Sheet. I take this as a baseline and then model the various scenarios for the likely calculated World Balance Sheets through to 2050, 2100 and beyond, that are based on assumptions which, once calculated, bear (I hope) some common-sense resemblance to the scenario situations described over those timescales.

My third tool is a personal synthesis from reading a wide range of works from other authors on human civilisational history of emergence, growth, maturity and decline, one of the most obvious examples being "Collapse" by Jared Diamond. There is much research describing evidence of this pattern of growth and decline in many human civilisations through history. This constitutes a rich catalogue of success followed by failure. Care needs to be taken in interpreting such growth and collapse when looking forwards rather than backwards. Looking back, all past civilisations other than our current one collapsed. But there are two equally valid ways of projecting that information forward.

One way of looking forward would be to say that history provides evidence that all civilisations ultimately collapse – its just that our civilisation hasn't reached that point of collapse yet. A problem with this attitude is that the future is unknowable, and that conditions and events in future do not necessarily follow the precedents of the past, especially when it comes to sustainability on a finite planet. Covid-19 has been a recent example of an unprecedented event. We cannot necessarily say that, because all past civilisations have collapsed, all future ones will suffer the same fate.

Another way of looking forward would be to say that the same history provides evidence that our current civilisation has successfully addressed and solved the problems that caused all previous civilisations to collapse. A problem with this attitude is that, at the time they were still thriving, the same could have been said by the peoples of all previous large-scale civilisations, in relation to the civilisations that preceded them but were no longer existent at that time, and yet they did, themselves, ultimately collapse.

Even if we were to take the view that none of the previous civilisations foresaw their eventual collapses, that might be a false statement. It could be that one or more of those civilisations could foresee what was happening, but that they didn't have the tools to overcome the problems, leading to collapse.

That teaches us that there is a risk that:

- We don't yet realise and understand the existing or future problems (yet to become apparent) that lead to our own civilisational collapse, or
- That even if we do see and understand those existing or future problems, we lack the tools to solve them and avoid civilisational collapse

So, we can easily see that predicting the future is notoriously difficult. Even attempting scenario analysis (which uses the caveat that it does not produce predictions but just impressions of some of the most likely futures) is fraught with difficulties.

Scenario analysis is not an exact science, and is not far removed from science fiction. Consider the science fiction author Isaac Asimov, who invented a fictional predictive science of "Psychohistory", which he first introduced in some short stories in 1942 – 1944 and which is described in Wikipedia as follows:

> **"Psychohistory** is a fictional science in Isaac Asimov's *Foundation* [science fiction] universe which combines history, sociology, and mathematical statistics to make general predictions about the future behavior of very large groups of people, such as the [fictional] Galactic Empire.
>
> Psychohistory depends on the idea that, while one cannot foresee the actions of a particular individual, the laws of statistics as applied to large groups of people could predict the general flow of future events. Asimov used the analogy of a gas: An observer has great difficulty in predicting the motion of a single molecule in a gas, but with the kinetic theory can predict the mass action of the gas to a high level of accuracy. Asimov applied this concept to the population of his fictional Galactic Empire, which numbered one quintillion [a very, very large number]. The [fictional] character responsible for the science's creation, Hari Seldon, established [the first] two axioms:
>
> - that the population whose behavior was modelled should be sufficiently large
> - that the population should remain in ignorance of the results of the application of psychohistorical analyses because if it is aware, the group

changes its behaviour. [so, it appears Asimov was aware of the Hawthorne Effect]

Ebling Mis [a fictional character] added these axioms:

- that there would be no fundamental change in the society [over the timeframes being analysed and forecast]
- that human reactions to stimuli would remain constant [over the timeframes being analysed and forecast]

Golan Trevize [another fictional character] in 'Foundation and Earth' added this axiom:

- that humans are the only sentient intelligence in the galaxy.

Psychohistory has one basic, underlying limitation which Asimov postulated for the first time on the last page of the final book in the *Foundation* series: psychohistory only functions in a galaxy populated only by humans. In Asimov's Foundation series, humans form the only sentient race that developed in the entire Milky Way Galaxy. Seldon developed psychohistory to predict the actions of large groups of *humans*. Even robots technically fall under the umbrella of psychohistory, because humans built them, and they thus represent more or less a human "action", or at least, possess a thought-framework similar enough to that of their human creators that psychohistory can predict their actions. However, psychohistory cannot predict the actions of a sentient alien race; their psychology may differ so much from that of humans that normal psychohistory cannot understand or predict their actions.

The end of the series [of Asimov's fictional stories] offered two possibilities:

1. sentient races actually very rarely develop, such that only humans evolved in the Milky Way Galaxy, and in most *other* galaxies, it appears probable (given this assumption) that only one sentient race would develop. However, statistically, two or more alien races might evolve in the same galaxy, leading them into inevitable conflict. The fighting in this other galaxy would only end when one race emerged the victor, and after the prolonged conflict with other races, would have developed an aggressive and expansionist mindset. In contrast, humans had never encountered another sentient species in the Milky Way Galaxy, so they [i.e. the human species] never felt greatly compelled to expand to other galaxies, but instead to fight other humans over control of the Milky Way. Eventually, such an aggressive alien race would expand from galaxy to galaxy, and try to invade the Milky Way Galaxy.
2. through genetic engineering, subsets of humanity could alter themselves so significantly from baseline humans that they could for all intents and purposes be considered "aliens". Specifically exemplifying this theory, we find Asimov's fictitious Solarians: humans evolved from an old Spacer [human] world who had genetically modified themselves into hermaphrodites with telekinetic mental powers."

Interestingly, Asimov himself seems to have been somewhat ambivalent about whether his fictional version of predicting the future is ultimately a positive or negative tool. Again, from Wikipedia:

> "On September 25, 1987, Asimov gave an interview to Terry Gross on her National Public Radio program, *Fresh Air*. In it, Gross asked him about psychohistory:
>
>> Gross: "What did you have in mind when you coined the term and the concept?"
>>
>> Asimov: "Well, I wanted to write a short story about the fall of the Galactic Empire. I had just finished reading the *Decline and Fall of the Roman Empire* [for] the second time, and I thought I might as well adapt it on a much larger scale to the Galactic Empire and get a story out of it. And my editor John Campbell was much taken with the idea, and said he didn't want it wasted on a short story. He wanted an open-ended series so it lasts forever, perhaps. And so I started doing that. In order to keep the story going from story to story, I was essentially writing future history, and I had to make it sufficiently different from modern history to give it that science fictional touch. And so I assumed that the time would come when there would be a science in which things could be predicted on a probabilistic or statistical basis."
>>
>> Gross: "Do you think that it would be good if there really was such a science?"
>>
>> Asimov: "Well, I can't help but think it would be good, except that in my stories, I always have opposing views. In other words, people argue all possible... all possible... ways of looking at psychohistory and deciding whether it is good or bad. So you can't really tell. I happen to feel sort of on the optimistic side. I think if we can somehow get across some of the problems that face us now, humanity has a glorious future, and that if we could use the tenets of psychohistory to guide ourselves we might avoid a great many troubles. But on the other hand, it might create troubles. It's impossible to tell in advance.""

Asimov might, of course, have created his concept of psychohistory in such a way that it had flaws that provided ambiguity about its ultimate usefulness, exactly because that would give him the best possible chance of providing open-ended stories that could go on forever. As with many things, if you start out with an intention to make something ambiguous, it becomes a tautology that it will become so, except by some accident that changes its direction from the intended course.

Back in the real world, there are some things we know that often frustrate efforts to predict the future of human behaviours, or affect our ability to respond to events, for example:

- the Hawthorne Effect
- unexpected events that are not within human control
- the laws of physics, especially thermodynamics and entropy
- physical limits on the planet and its biosphere
- general unpredictability of behaviours of individuals and (perhaps to a lesser extent) groups of people

However, despite these difficulties, my own view is that the scientific method implicit in real-world scenario analysis is a lot better than doing nothing. Its limitations need to be recognised, of course, and its results need to be assessed alongside less formalised sources of information and judgements about likely cause and effect relationships. All of these formal and informal methods and sources can be part of an overall picture to inform policy decisions at local, regional, national, international and global levels of decision-making. No single method of information provision should be relied upon to the exclusion of all the others.

Despite the potential objection that undertaking scenario analysis might be little better than science fiction, the alternative, of not undertaking any such analysis, leads us to being apt to sleep-walk into oblivion. Unless we make some kind of estimation of what futures might come about, then we are almost certainly condemning ourselves to an actual future which is worse than it could have been.

This is one of the enduring truths about the battle against unsustainability. We may not be able to solve all problems, but any actions we do take will almost certainly make the ultimate outcomes better than they would otherwise be. They might avoid civilisational collapse, or fend it off for numerous generations, or make the post-collapse society a better place than it would otherwise be, by leaving a better legacy of assets for the survivors to base a recovery on.

This is the prize of the optimist – to know that they are improving things anyway. The only uncertainty is by how much things will be better. By contrast, the pessimist is almost certain to be part of turning their less beneficial predictions into reality, through their lack of actions to make things better.

It's by no means certain that optimism among individuals will translate into optimism collectively or, indeed, actions that create truly sustainable outcomes at a global level. Therefore, although I'm going to include at least one optimistic scenario, I'm also going to include a pessimistic one, to serve as a warning of what might happen if we collectively sleep-walk our way into the future.

The following figure, from Friedlingstein et al (2020) illustrates very graphically the size of the challenge in tackling carbon emissions. It also shows how natural capital (including the water in the oceans and the soils on land) has been acting as a carbon sink, and how (ultimately) increasingly large amounts of carbon have been belching out into the atmosphere.

Figure 31

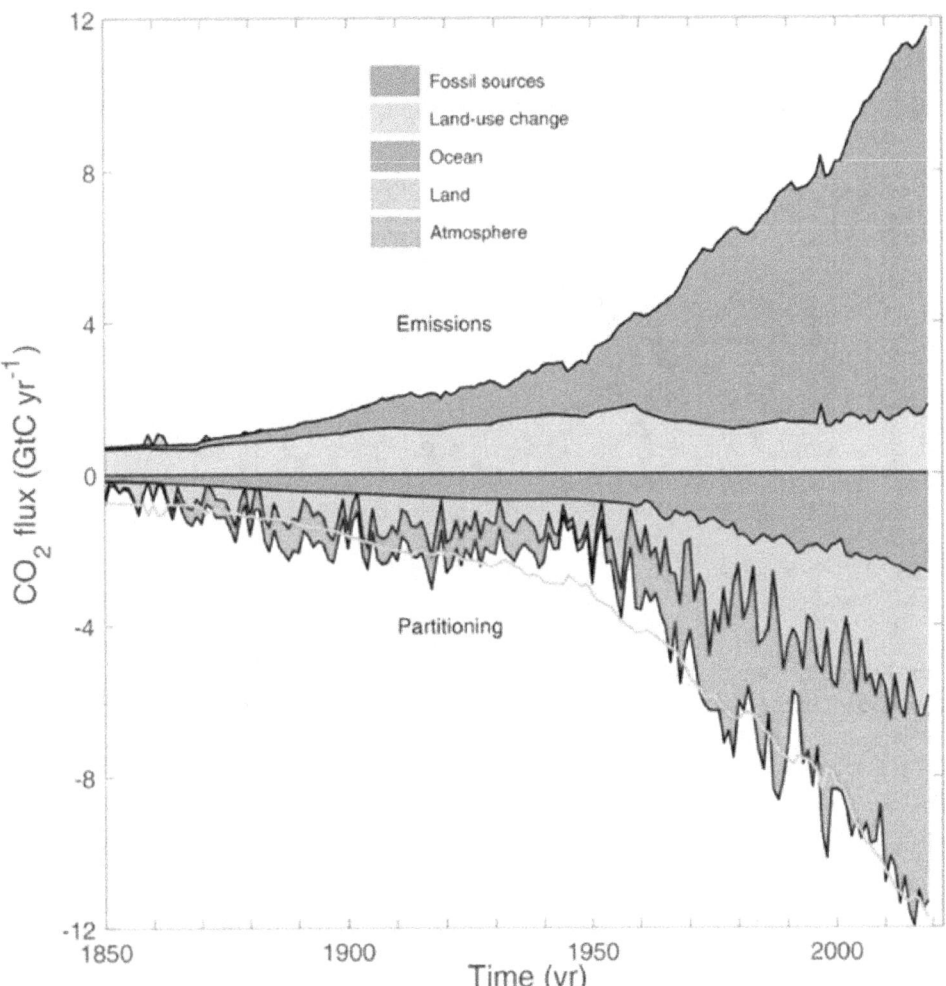

For those of you with black and white versions of this book, the data categories in the above figure are listed in the legend in the same order in which they appear in the graphic, from top to bottom.

I couldn't continue here without referencing one of the most widely reported sources of information about climate change historical data and projections into the future – the United Nations, especially the UNFCCC (United Nations Framework Convention on Climate Change). The two figures below (from UN Emissions Gap Report 2019 and IPCC 2018 Report, respectively) give some idea of the challenges in trying to construct scenarios reflecting carbon emissions, let alone any other aspects of sustainability pathways. It also gives interesting evidence of the impacts of crises such as the global financial crisis of 2008.

Figure 32

Figure 2.1. Global greenhouse gas emissions from all sources

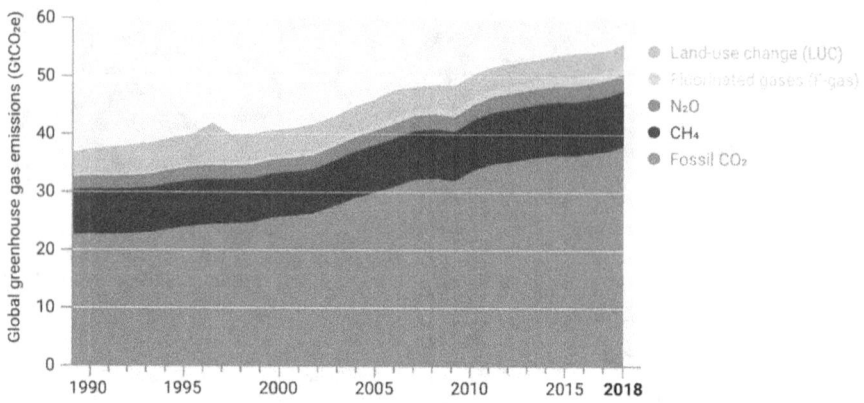

Source: Olivier and Peters (2019), Houghton and Nassikas (2017) for land-use change emissions, and Friedlingstein *et al.* (2019) for updates from 2016 to 2018

This first of the two diagrams (which is effectively a zooming in and further breakdown of the upper half of the previous figure) shows that the inertia in the system, and in its rate of growth each year, is huge. The tiny dent in the upward trajectory in about 2008 shows the impacts of the global financial crisis at that time. A blip.

Figure 33 – potential pathways for tackling that inertia and turning it round

Cumulative emissions of CO_2 and future non-CO_2 radiative forcing determine the probability of limiting warming to 1.5°C

a) Observed global temperature change and modeled
responses to stylized anthropogenic emission and forcing pathways

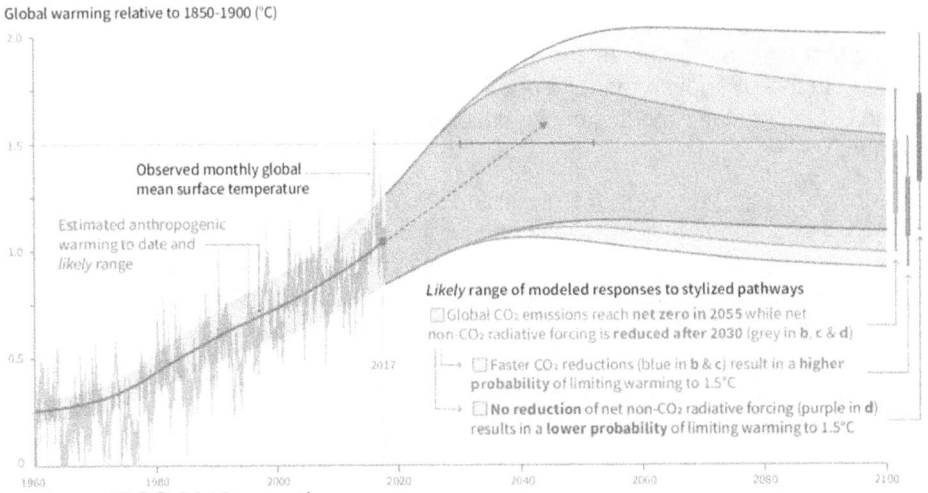

(source = IPCC 2018 report)

You can see in the second figure from the UN (above) that the impact of the tiny slowdown in emissions during the 2008 global financial crisis (visible in the previous figure) is indiscernible in this one. The global warming data (the squiggly grey line on the left half of the diagram) does not show any visible dip around 2008.

This is because it was a very small slowdown compared with the massive volumes of emissions over numerous decades, and the time-lags between raised concentrations in the atmosphere and raised global temperatures. This is one reason there is a significant difference between weather (a short-term phenomenon) and climate (a longer-term one).

It's also why many observers and researchers comment on emissions and climate change being like a supertanker that is out of control. One small push back on the bow of a supertanker is not going to slow it down perceptibly. It takes much more than that.

Climate change deniers claim this is evidence of lack of cause and effect relationship between emissions and climate change, but they are misguided, as they are making the mistake of confusing weather and climate, and focussing on too short a timescale. Enormous amounts have been written about climate change denial and climate change communication, so I'll not mention it further here.

Another challenge in achieving meaningful emissions reductions (in addition to addressing denial and time lags) is the extent of non-territorial ("consumption") emissions. These are emissions that are not generated in a country consuming goods and services ("territorial emissions"), but in countries from which those goods and services are imported (sometimes called "embedded carbon" or "embedded emissions") which were the emissions generated during the extraction and production processes in that producing/exporting country or further back in the supply chain. In most countries, these consumption emissions are not even reported. In the UK, government ministers have recently been raising the prospect that the UK might start reporting consumption emissions as well as territorial emissions.

The following figure (from Hickel and Kallis, 2019) shows the extent of the proportions of consumption emissions and territorial emissions in the highest-emitting countries over recent decades. It's notable that some countries are net 'exporters' of emissions (because they generally import goods and services with high levels of emissions in their production processes), whereas others are net 'importers' of emissions (because they generally export goods and services with high levels of emissions in their production processes).

Figure 34 (Hickel and Kallis, 2019, originally from Global Carbon Budget)

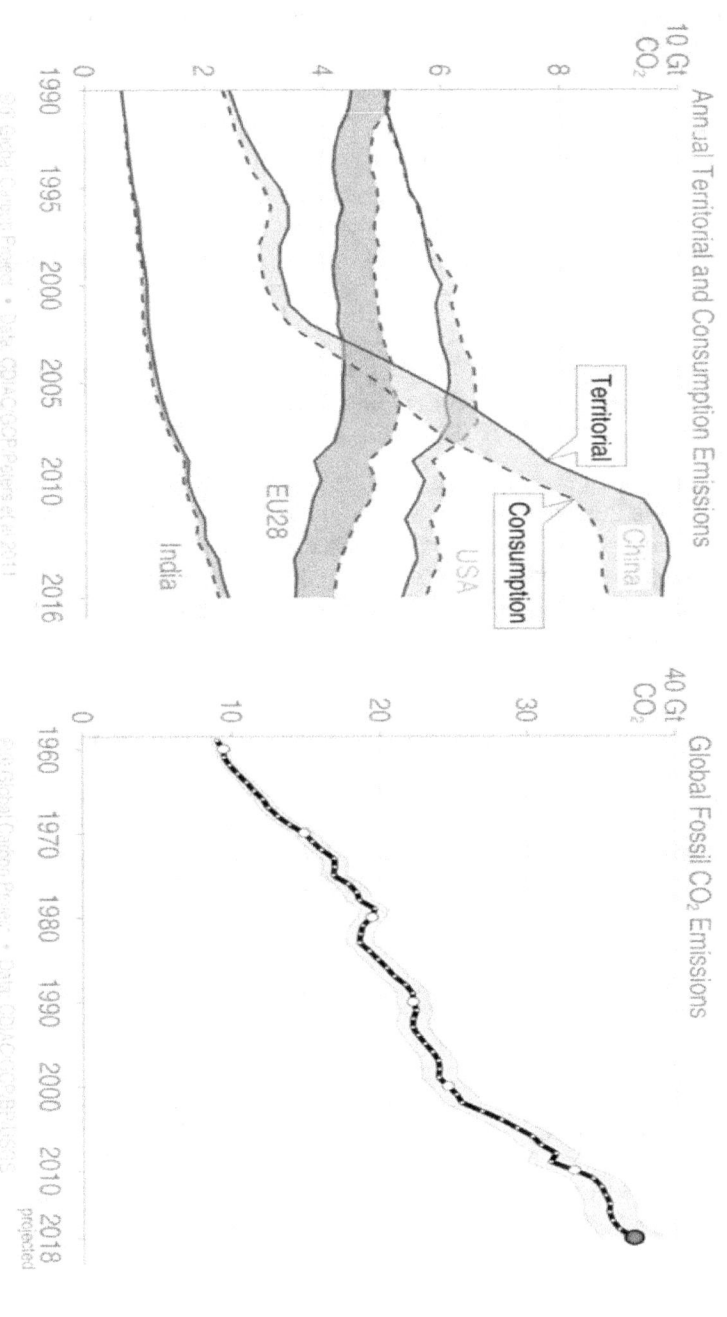

Figure 4. (a) Annual territorial and consumption CO₂ emissions for select regions, 1990–2016; (b) Global CO₂ emissions 1960–2018. Source: Global Carbon Budget (2018).

I'll draw on Mora et al (as referenced earlier) to cut through some of the complexity around climate change, for example by using their summary percentage changes in NPP (Net Primary Production) over long timescales, to project the impacts of climate change scenarios on natural capital.

As with any scenario analysis worth its salt, our first step is to define our scenarios. Traditionally, we would start with a base case that would show no change, or least change. Then, we would look to create scenarios with greater or lesser amounts of optimism or pessimism, perhaps illustrating some of the key features of either progress in a positive direction or trajectories into a set of darker places for the future of humanity.

Most of the scenarios I use are based on information set out in the (2014) Fifth Assessment Report ("AR5") of the United Nations Intergovernmental Panel on Climate Change ("IPCC") which is the most recent in a series of such reports.

There are some factors that need to be modelled in all scenarios, and so I'll briefly describe the main ones here. It will be appreciated that the extent to which these play out in each scenario will differ, depending on the values of various key causal variables over time in each scenario. However, in setting out their basic characteristics, this enables readers to more readily compare these assumptions with those made by other modellers in scenario analyses elsewhere.

Carbon concentrations, other aspects of growing conditions and plant growth

As a starting point, the scenarios represent futures in which the effects of climate change are not all negative all of the time. For example, increased amounts of carbon in the atmosphere generate more rapid growth in some plant types (even if negative on other types). This effect is well reported, although it is generally thought that these positive effects turn negative after the carbon concentrations have exceeded a certain amount.

For example, the following is from Bellassen (2014):

> "… the finding that unharvested forests, for example, are absorbing more carbon than they release, accounting for half the sink, is contrary to the tenet of ecology, known as Odum's framework, that carbon flows in natural forests should be in equilibrium. This carbon-sink behaviour of mature forests is attributed to large-scale environmental changes that violate the assumption of the steady conditions underlying Odum's framework: higher atmospheric CO_2 concentrations are accelerating tree growth worldwide and nitrogen emitted by industry, agriculture and fossil-fuel burning is increasingly fertilizing managed forest soils in Europe, China and the eastern United States… Other changing climate factors, such as temperature and rainfall, and changing forest-management strategies, such as leaving trees to grow for longer before cutting them back, seem to be of secondary importance to the global carbon budget of forests, although they may be locally important"

On the other hand, Mora et al (2015) say that deterioration in number of growing days under moderate temperature increases will more than offset the positive effects of increased carbon concentrations on some plant growth, especially in equatorial regions (eg including rainforests). The following is a summary from a 2015 article in Time Magazine (the emboldening is mine):

> "The number of days when plants can grow could decrease by 11% by 2100 assuming limited efforts to stall climate change, affecting some of the world's poorest and most vulnerable people, according to a new study in *PLOS Biology*. Climate change affects a number of variables that determine how much plants can grow. A 7% decline in the average number of freezing days will actually aid plant growth, according to the study, which relied on an analysis of satellite data and weather projections. At the same time [however], extreme temperatures, a decrease in water availability and changes to soil conditions will actually make it more difficult for plants to thrive. **Overall, climate change is expected to stunt plant growth**. 'Those that think climate change will benefit plants need to see the light, literally and figuratively,' said lead study author Camilo Mora, a professor at the University of Hawaii, in a statement. "

Here's the relevant excerpt from the original source:

> "… although the global mean number of days above freezing will increase by up to 7% by 2100 under "business as usual" (representative concentration pathway [RCP] 8.5), suitable growing days will actually decrease globally by up to 11% when other climatic variables that limit plant growth are considered (i.e., temperature, water availability, and solar radiation). Areas in Russia, China, and Canada are projected to gain suitable plant growing days, but the rest of the world will experience losses. Notably, tropical areas could lose up to 200 suitable plant growing days per year. These changes will impact most of the world's terrestrial ecosystems, potentially triggering climate feedbacks. Human populations will also be affected, with up to ~2,100 million of the poorest people in the world (~30%of the world's population) highly vulnerable to changes in the supply of plant-related goods and services. These impacts will be spatially variable, indicating regions where adaptations will be necessary. Changes in suitable plant growing days are projected to be less severe under strong and moderate mitigation scenarios (i.e., RCP 2.6 and RCP 4.5), underscoring the importance of reducing emissions to avoid such disproportionate impacts on ecosystems and people."

Comparing Net Primary Production with population projections

The main findings from Mora et al, in terms of the total impacts on plant growth (Net Primary Production) for various temperature changes, alongside projected human consumption of NPP, are shown in the figure below.

Figure 35 (Mora's figure 6)

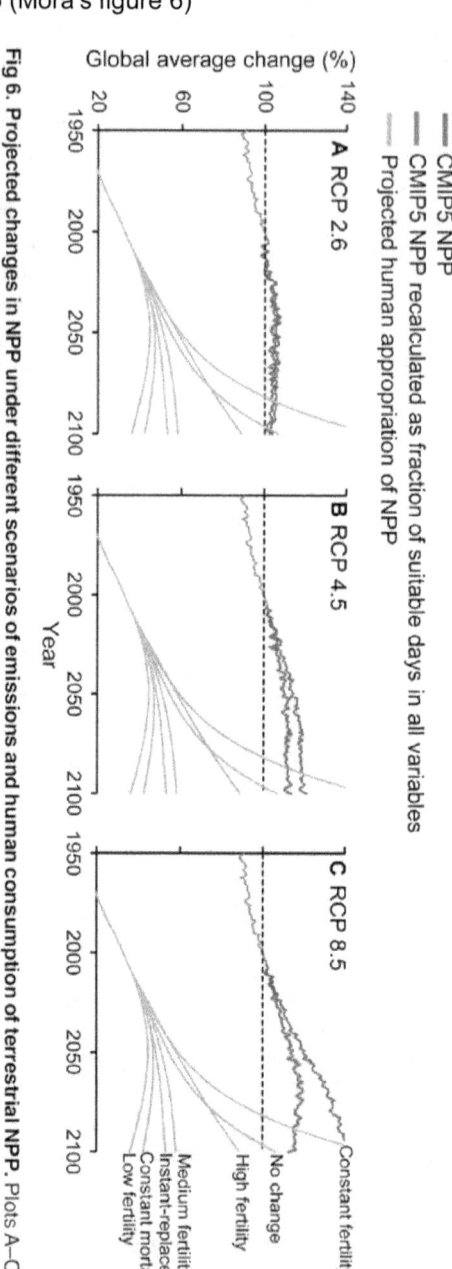

Fig 6. Projected changes in NPP under different scenarios of emissions and human consumption of terrestrial NPP. Plots A–C show the global average change in NPP under different scenarios before (blue lines) and after (red lines) accounting for unsuitable plant growing days. Grey lines indicate the projected global human appropriation of terrestrial NPP (i.e., modern per capita appropriation of NPP multiplied by human population projections under different scenarios). Additional details are shown in S4 Fig. Data are provided in S5 Data.

The results from Mora et al (in the above figure) show, for all of Mora's scenarios, higher NPP than the reference year (2005). However, it can be seen that the rate of increase in NPP is declining in all the scenarios, and indeed all of them result in declining **absolute** NPP from about 2100 onwards, if not sooner. This is particularly concerning when observed alongside projected human consumption of NPP, where only low human fertility can keep human consumption of NPP in proportion to that NPP. All other scenarios for human fertility use up increasing proportions of NPP through to 2100 and beyond.

The population projections used by Mora et al are from Gerland et al (2014), based originally on UN data, and the following is a summary:

> "There is an 80% probability that world population, now 7.2 billion, will increase to between 9.6 and 12.3 billion in 2100."

It is difficult to incorporate all the individual effects and feedback loops between carbon concentrations, other aspects of growing conditions, and tree growth. However, Mora et al appears to suggest that the effects, in aggregate, are not immaterial, and so I will try to take it into account in all my scenarios. I will also consider a few "what-ifs" for sensitivity analysis, to see if inaccuracies in the basic data or assumptions make any significant difference to end results.

What about carbon sequestration policies – can they help reduce or limit carbon emissions and concentrations (and will they)?

Carbon sequestration policies, projects and initiatives show some potential to be part of the solution, but they're not without their problems and critics.

The following is from Abenezer (2014) – a literature review on this subject:

> "Policies targeting carbon sequestration have to deal with specific design problems; additionality, permanence, and leakage. Additionality refers to the difficulty of assessing whether the project would be implemented without the policy in question. Permanence in carbon sequestration during the project period can be hampered by natural causes, such as variation in temperature and precipitation, storms and fires, but also from intentional violation of the rules of the project by, for example, harvesting before the project period expires. Leakage can occur when, for example, land conservation in one region results in forest land conversion in other regions."

The figure below (their table 1), from the same report, shows the costs per tonne of carbon for various carbon sequestration policies or initiatives, mostly relating to forests but one (Manley et al) in an agricultural context.

Figure 36

Table 1: List of survey studies, sink activities, and marginal sink enhancement cost, in 2011 prices

Survey study	Carbon sink activity and geographical scale	Marginal cost range, US/ton C
Sedjo et al., (1995)	Forest plantation and management, global	1.5 – 133
Richards and Stokes (2004)	Forest plantation and management, global	13 – 188
Van Kooten et al. (2004)	Forest plantation and agroforestry, global	4.5 – 24
Manley et al. (2005)	No-till cultivation in agriculture, global	1.5 – 443
Van Kooten et al. (2009)	Forest plantation, forest management, and agroforestry, global	0 – 60
Phan et al. (2014)	Avoidance of deforestation, developing countries	0.4 – 171

(Source = Abenezer, 2014)

Note that the above numbers are expressed in terms of marginal costs. I've explained elsewhere in the book (for example in chapter 4) why this type of cost is not necessarily a good way to arrive at a value per tonne of carbon actually sequestered, or the value of an amount of standing forest. Nevertheless, it does provide some indication that carbon sequestration costs (on marginal cost basis), might be as high as USD 443 per tonne on the basis of these studies, and in fact it might be considerably higher over the timespans covered by the scenarios.

Carbon sequestration policies and initiatives (eg REDD+, the Reducing Emissions from Deforestation and forest Degradation initiative, in addition to the examples in the above figure) are still in their early days, and it's not yet clear what contribution they will ultimately make. For the purposes of my scenarios, therefore, I do not model them specifically. Instead, I take the view that they are part of the wider series of deliberate or unintended factors that impact on carbon concentrations in the atmosphere resulting in levels of natural capital and NPP at various points in the future. The scenario characteristics are painted in such broad brushstrokes that this is an acceptable simplification.

Past trends that will be helpful in assessing the future in all scenarios

Managi and Kumar (2018) give us some broad-brush information about how the main types of capital have been changing in the last few decades:

"Has the world been preserving its wealth globally? Natural scientists have warned about global sustainability in terms of planetary boundaries (Steffen et al 2015). Since the marginal utility of consumption is different across countries, aggregating national figures to reach global Inclusive Wealth is not without problems. That said, the most straightforward approach is simply to add up total change in capital assets in dollars. Produced and human capital per capita increased 94% and 28%, respectively, while natural capital per capita declined by 34% from 1992 to 2014. Put together, wealth per capita has been slightly positive, especially over the last decade. In contrast, GDP *per capita* growth has been mostly linearly positive, except for an enormous drop in this trend in 2009 due to the Great Recession."

The following is an excerpt from the methodological annex to the same report:

"In figure 8 [my figure 29 below], we show the global trend of natural capital and CO_2 emission damages. It is clear that the damages [vertical bars and right hand scale] are increasing consistently from 1990 to 2014, while the natural capital stock [solid line and left hand scale] is sharply declining."

Figure 37

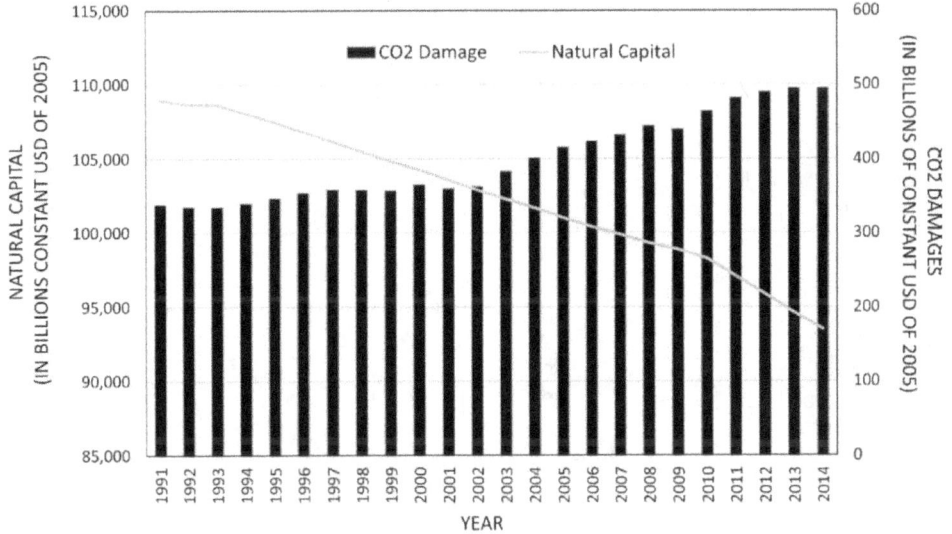

(source = Managi and Kumar, 2018)

Now, let's put some of this together into a table comparing and contrasting the value of the key variables in the scenarios I'm going to use.

Table of variables for each scenario – sequenced from most optimistic to least

variable	Scenario 1 – optimistic transition	Scenario 2 - least change (Base Case Scenario)	Scenario 3 – overload and collapse
Brief description	Mitigation and adaptation actions are prioritised and climate stability achieved by 2100, enabling sustainable thriving by 2500	Mitigation and adaptation are patchy and insufficient, always lagging behind the curves reactively, so sub-optimal	Mitigation and adaptation both fail at scale, with disastrous collapse ensuing from 2100 to 2500. Only scattered remnants of human civilisation remain. Unclear whether advanced human civilisation will ever be rebuilt in an environment permanently hostile to human existence
Warming by 2100	1.5 degrees	3 degrees	6 degrees
global population at 2050	8 billion	9 billion	15 billion
global population at 2100	9 billion (peak)	11 billion	40 billion (peak)
global population at 2500	5 billion	15 billion	4 million
NPP at 2050 (2020 = 100)	105	110	130
NPP at 2100 (2020 = 100)	110	100	110
NPP at 2500	150	50	1
Natural capital index in year 2050 (2020 = 100)	110	90	50
Natural capital index in year 2100	150	80	10
Natural capital index in year 2500	300	50	1
notes	New enlightenment brings sustainable society, far less conflict and destructiveness and biosphere in balance – new era of abundance and new potential	Sub-optimal, with unnecessary suffering and inequalities continuing – ultimate position unclear	Conflict, war-damage, disease and ever more frantic use of technologies to get maximum food calories from every piece of nature result in almost complete collapse of the biome and its biodiversity – any surviving living things are constantly on the edge of extinction

I've invented a "natural capital index" here, to represent both the quantity and health of natural assets. That would have to be a composite index of a number of factors and would need to include some factor for biodiversity.

I don't have the time or the expertise to construct such an index in detail or to calculate it from actual historical data. That is a task that could be done by other researchers. In the meantime, I take an educated guess that the relationship between the scenario conditions will result in index values as shown in the table. Because of this process, they are very approximate values. In scenario 2, the index values follow a path of steady improvement. In scenario 1, the path is one of gradual decline. In scenario 3, the decline is more rapid and leads to eventual collapse.

Things I have __not__ assumed, and __not__ relied upon, in any of my scenarios

For reasons set out earlier in the book, I've not relied upon the Hartwick Rule. In case you can't recall what that is, it is proposed by some researchers as a rule of thumb for ensuring sustainability, in perpetuity, through reinvesting rents extracted from natural capital back into capital formation or maintenance.

There are a number of areas of contention with the Hartwick Rule, and many researchers who have provided counterfactuals as well as many who have produced more generalised rules along similar lines, from which the Hartwick Rule is a specific example or case. The issues include the initial capital asset conditions (and sufficiency) and the rates of improvement in extractive and productive technologies. I'm not entirely clear, from my own readings on this topic, whether the Hartwick Rule might ultimately fall foul of the laws of thermodynamics and entropy, in which case it might only hold (if ever) over a finite range of circumstances and eras on our finite planet.

It seems that the matter of the validity and applicability of the Hartwick Rule is far from settled, and there are sufficient areas of doubt to persuade me to undertake my analyses without relying upon it.

In any case, it might not even be necessary to rely on that rule in order to achieve sustainability. For example, ultimately, sustainability is achieved if the capital assets (including natural capital) are sufficient to provide for the needs of all future generations, in perpetuity. That is the acid test, and the compilation and ongoing updating of world balance sheets (the main technique described in this book) will help us to know if we are getting nearer to that goal or further away from it.

In any case, the means to solve sustainability problems is likely, in practice, to comprise lots of actions and policies, rather than a single rule of thumb that could oversimplify policy responses.

Now, let's proceed to describe the scenarios I have actually used in my analysis, and to show the resulting future world balance sheets associated with them. I'll start with the most optimistic scenario, and work downwards to the most pessimistic one.

Scenario 1 – an optimistic sustainable future to 2050, 2100, 2500 and beyond

Steinberger et al (2020) have produced a scenario where all the global human population are provided with a decent subsistence living with a sustainable level of energy production and use:

> "It is increasingly clear that averting ecological breakdown will require drastic changes to contemporary human society and the global economy embedded within it. On the other hand, the basic material needs of billions of people across the planet remain unmet. Here, we develop a simple, bottom-up model to estimate a practical minimal threshold for the final energy consumption required to provide decent material livings to the entire global population. We find that global final energy consumption in 2050 could be reduced to the levels of the 1960s, despite a population three times larger. However, such a world requires a massive rollout of advanced technologies across all sectors, as well as radical demand-side changes to reduce consumption – regardless of income – to levels of sufficiency. Sufficiency is, however, far more materially generous in our model than what those opposed to strong reductions in consumption often assume … We find that, with a combination of the most efficient technologies available and radical demand-side transformations that reduce excess consumption to sufficiency-levels, the final energy requirements for providing decent living standards to the global population in 2050 could be over 60% lower than consumption today. In countries that are today's highest per-capita consumers, cuts of ~95% appear possible while still providing decent living standards to all."

Under this scenario, carbon emissions patterns are similar to pathway "P1" in the following two figures from the IPCC Fifth Assessment Report (IPCC 2018). They show the breakdown of the main sources of emissions. BECCS is Bioenergy with Carbon Capture and Storage (BECCS) and AFOLU is Agriculture, Forestry and Other Land Use (AFOLU).

Figure 38

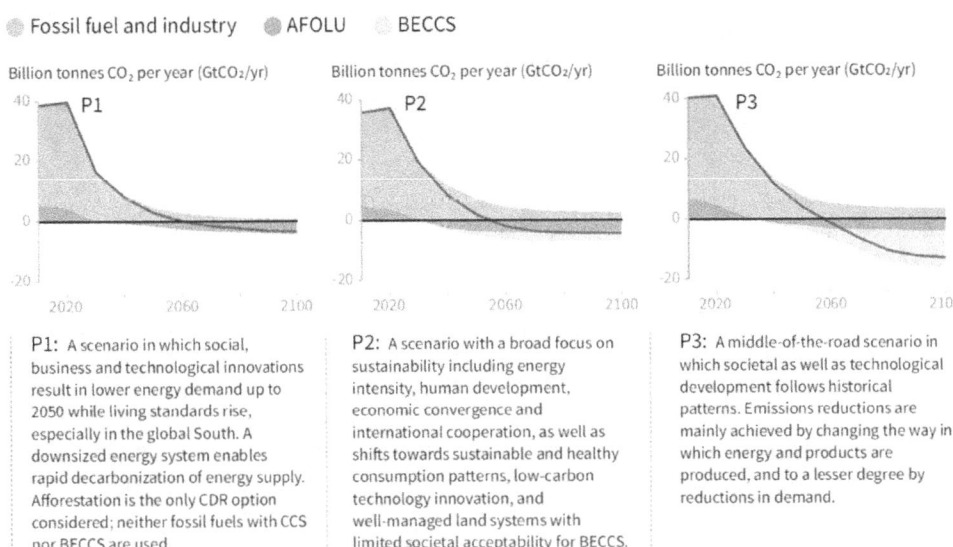

● Fossil fuel and industry ● AFOLU ● BECCS

Billion tonnes CO₂ per year (GtCO₂/yr)   Billion tonnes CO₂ per year (GtCO₂/yr)   Billion tonnes CO₂ per year (GtCO₂/yr)

P1: A scenario in which social, business and technological innovations result in lower energy demand up to 2050 while living standards rise, especially in the global South. A downsized energy system enables rapid decarbonization of energy supply. Afforestation is the only CDR option considered; neither fossil fuels with CCS nor BECCS are used.

P2: A scenario with a broad focus on sustainability including energy intensity, human development, economic convergence and international cooperation, as well as shifts towards sustainable and healthy consumption patterns, low-carbon technology innovation, and well-managed land systems with limited societal acceptability for BECCS.

P3: A middle-of-the-road scenario in which societal as well as technological development follows historical patterns. Emissions reductions are mainly achieved by changing the way in which energy and products are produced, and to a lesser degree by reductions in demand.

All these pathways to limiting warming to 1.5 degrees above pre-industrial levels use Carbon Dioxide Removal (CDR), but the amount varies across pathways, as do the relative contributions of Bioenergy with Carbon Capture and Storage (BECCS) and removals in the Agriculture, Forestry and Other Land Use (AFOLU) sector.

Figure 39

Global total net CO₂ emissions

Billion tonnes of CO₂/yr

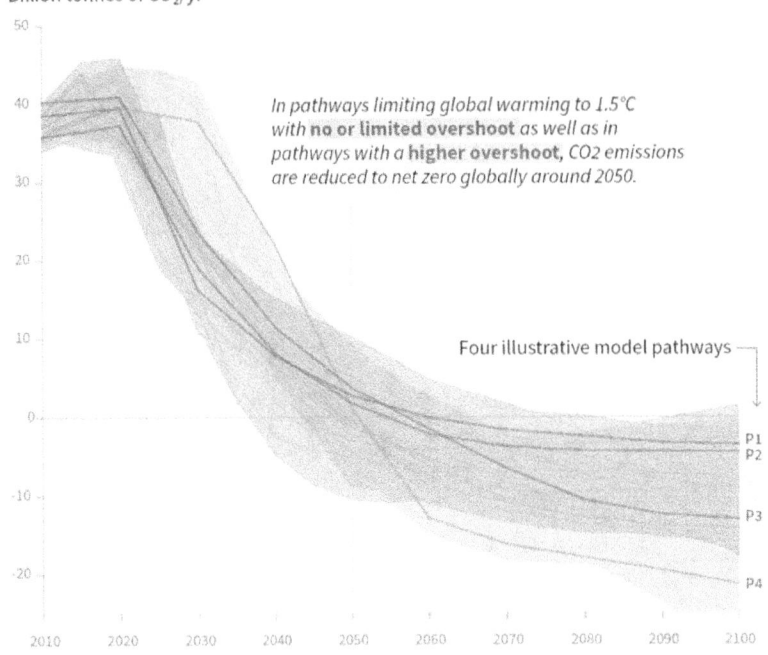

*In pathways limiting global warming to 1.5°C with **no or limited overshoot** as well as in pathways with a **higher overshoot**, CO2 emissions are reduced to net zero globally around 2050.*

Four illustrative model pathways

P1
P2
P3
P4

To put this in some practical context, the levels of emissions reductions required, on average, each and every year from 2021 to 2050 are similar to the levels of reductions that occurred in 2020 as a result of massive lockdowns around the world during 2020 in response to the covid-19 pandemic.

The figure below (from the same report) comprises some illustrative pathways representative of this optimistic scenario. These show relationships between global net zero emissions being achieved in 2055 versus 2040 and the equivalent cumulative levels of carbon in the atmosphere at stabilisation (which then carries on as stable long-term concentration and therefore stable level of temperature and stability of climate) corresponding to each of these two pathways. Note that this will not represent a return to previous normality – it will just be the case that the temperature and climate will not be getting any worse from that point of stability onwards (around 2040 to 2055). This comparison is provided as an example of the sensitivity analyses that are possible around the scenario presented.

Figure 40

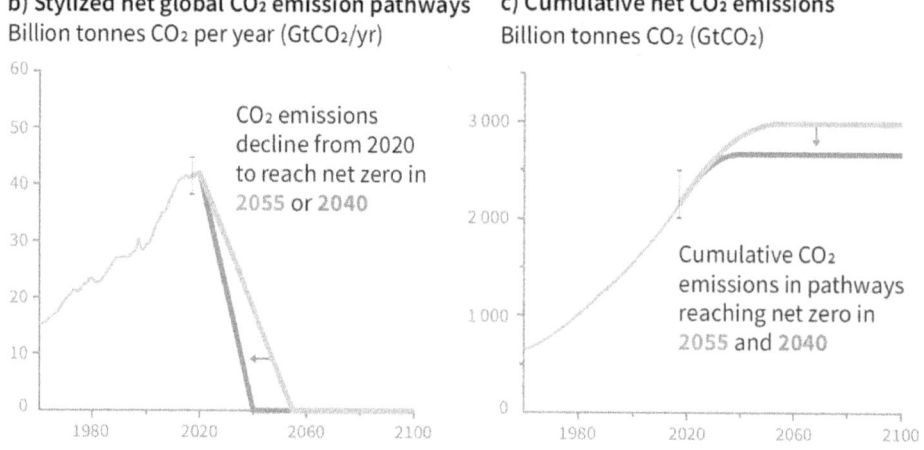

b) Stylized net global CO$_2$ emission pathways
Billion tonnes CO$_2$ per year (GtCO$_2$/yr)

CO$_2$ emissions decline from 2020 to reach net zero in 2055 or 2040

c) Cumulative net CO$_2$ emissions
Billion tonnes CO$_2$ (GtCO$_2$)

Cumulative CO$_2$ emissions in pathways reaching net zero in 2055 and 2040

Let's calculate what the world balance sheets might look like in this scenario, in 2050, 2100 and 2500.

Figure 41 - Scenario 1 – in 2050

Planetary CFO's World Balance Sheet 2050 (USD trillions) Scenario 1			% total assets
Fixed Assets			
Property			
Renewable NC (Land)			
Cropland	23.38		
Pasture land	23.06		
Forest	141.57		
Barren/wild land	1.10		
Urban land	94.48		
Oceans	152.38		
Ocean damage provision	-13.78		
Subtotal renewable NC		422.18	
Non-renewable NC		51.91	
Subtotal Property		474.09	53.1%
Plant			
Dwellings		136.96	
Other buildings		160.49	
Subtotal Plant		297.45	33.3%
Equipment			
Commercial equipment		54.57	
Military equipment		11.36	
Subtotal Equipment		65.94	7.4%
Intangible assets			
Goodwill		0.00	
Intellectual property		0.00	
Brand value, licences		0.00	
Subtotal intangible assets		0.00	0.0%
Current assets			
Inventories		53.60	6.0%
Cash and cash equivalents		1.87	0.2%
Human Capital	1,203.34		
Human Capital destructiveness provision	-1,203.34		
Net Human Capital		0.00	
Total assets		892.95	100.0%
Liabilities			
Human welfare commitment	1,711.38		
Unfunded human welfare commitment (-ve) ie asset stewardship shortfall	-818.43		
Equity of humankind		892.95	
Total liabilities and equity		892.95	

Figure 42 - Scenario 1 – in 2100

Planetary CFO's World Balance Sheet 2100 (USD trillions) Scenario 1			% total assets
Fixed Assets			
Property			
Renewable NC (Land)			
Cropland	31.88		
Pasture land	31.44		
Forest	193.05		
Barren/wild land	1.50		
Urban land	128.84		
Oceans	207.80		
Ocean damage provision	-13.78		
Subtotal renewable NC		580.72	
Non-renewable NC		51.91	
Subtotal Property			632.63	48.4%
Plant			
Dwellings		154.08	
Other buildings		180.55	
Subtotal Plant			334.63	25.6%
Equipment			
Commercial equipment		75.56	
Military equipment		15.73	
Subtotal Equipment			91.30	7.0%
Intangible assets			
Goodwill		0.00	
Intellectual property		0.00	
Brand value, licences		0.00	
Subtotal intangible assets			0.00	0.0%
Current assets			
Inventories			60.30	4.6%
Cash and cash equivalents			2.11	0.2%
Human Capital	1,874.43		
Human Capital destructiveness provision	-1,686.99		
Net Human Capital			187.44	14.3%
Total assets			1,308.41	100.0%
Liabilities			
Human welfare commitment	1,925.31		
Unfunded human welfare commitment (-ve) ie asset stewardship shortfall	-616.90		
Equity of humankind		1,308.41	
Total liabilities and equity			1,308.41	

Figure 43 - Scenario 1 – in 2500

Planetary CFO's World Balance Sheet 2500 (USD trillions) Scenario 1			% total assets
Fixed Assets			
Property			
Renewable NC (Land)			
Cropland	63.75		
Pasture land	62.88		
Forest	386.10		
Barren/wild land	3.00		
Urban land	257.67		
Oceans	415.59		
Ocean damage provision	-13.78		
Subtotal renewable NC		1,175.21	
Non-renewable NC		51.91	
Subtotal Property		1,227.12	50.9%
Plant			
Dwellings	85.60		
Other buildings	100.31		
Subtotal Plant		185.91	7.7%
Equipment			
Commercial equipment	243.48		
Military equipment	50.69		
Subtotal Equipment		294.18	12.2%
Intangible assets			
Goodwill	0.00		
Intellectual property	0.00		
Brand value, licences	0.00		
Subtotal intangible assets		0.00	0.0%
Current assets			
Inventories		33.50	1.4%
Cash and cash equivalents		1.17	0.0%
Human Capital	3,355.47		
Human Capital destructiveness provision	-2,684.37		
Net Human Capital		671.09	27.8%
Total assets		2,412.97	100.0%
Liabilities			
Human welfare commitment	1,069.61		
Unfunded human welfare commitment (-ve) ie asset stewardship shortfall (surplus if +ve)	1,343.35		
Equity of humankind		2,412.97	
Total liabilities and equity		2,412.97	

Commentary on scenario 1 (optimistic scenario)

In 2050 (figure 39) despite improvements to managing human systems, successfully tackling climate change (limiting warming to 1.5 degrees), improving the stewardship of natural capital, stabilising ocean damage and keeping population less than 8 billion, the bottom line is still getting worse. The asset stewardship shortfall has grown from USD 569 trillion in 2020 to about USD 818 trillion in 2050. Population is still growing at this point and there is still an element of inertia and overshoot, combined with the write-off of all intangibles in the first 20 years of the intervening timescale.

However, by 2100 (figure 40) the cumulative actions and improvements have started to have a significant impact on the asset stewardship shortfall, which has now passed its peak and has reduced to USD 617 trillion. This is still larger than it was in 2020, but it's moving in the right direction. Population has peaked at about 9 billion at about this time.

In 2500 (figure 41) things are looking so much better. Stewardship is working well, population has stabilised at about 5 billion, and the balance sheet looks well balanced, with about 51% of the assets being natural capital, 28% human capital, the rest being non-natural human artifacts and infrastructures. In fact, there's a _**USD 1,343 trillion** asset stewardship **surplus, contributing significantly to the ability and capacity to invest in the new era of human enlightenment and fulfilment of potential**_. Result!

Scenario 2 - "Base Case" or "Least Change" scenario

Much of the literature, studies and forecasts in this field have used, as a base scenario "Business As Usual". An immediate problem with using that approach to a base case, in the current context, is that business is not operating as usual, and hasn't been since many countries started to take climate change and other aspects of sustainability seriously. The world has already started to change how it does business, to take better account of the impacts of human activities on nature and ecosystems.

An example is Circular Economy, increasingly gaining traction as a means to reduce materials and energy used and tackle pollution and climate change. This is being discussed extensively in corporates and their supply chains.

Some Governments (eg the UK's) have committed to making their countries net zero carbon by 2050.

In light of these positive trajectories in many countries, tempered by some lack of progress against the objectives of the Paris Accord of 2015, the scenario represents falling short of the target of 1.5 degree of warming (ie the max warming is more than that). This is because 1.5 degrees is already known to be a very ambitious target, and existing commitments of all nations added together are thought to be unlikely to achieve it.

From IPCC (2018):

> "Pathways limiting global warming to 1.5°C with no or limited overshoot would require rapid and far-reaching transitions in energy, land, urban and infrastructure (including transport and buildings), and industrial systems. These systems transitions are unprecedented in terms of scale, but not necessarily in terms of speed, and imply deep emissions reductions in all sectors, a wide portfolio of mitigation options and a significant upscaling of investments in those options."

So, for our base case, let's assume such transitions are **not** achieved sufficiently well or speedily to limit warming to no more than 1.5 degrees.

What level of warming is expected, if only existing 2015 Paris Accord commitments of nations are implemented?

The UN Emissions Gap report 2019, says:

> "… even if all unconditional Nationally Determined Contributions (NDCs) under the Paris Agreement are implemented, we are still on course for a 3.2°C temperature rise."

The following graphic, from the same report, illustrates what this scenario ("Unconditional NDC scenario") looks like in relation to other possible pathways.

Figure 44 (the left hand scale is GtCO2e of annual GHG emissions)

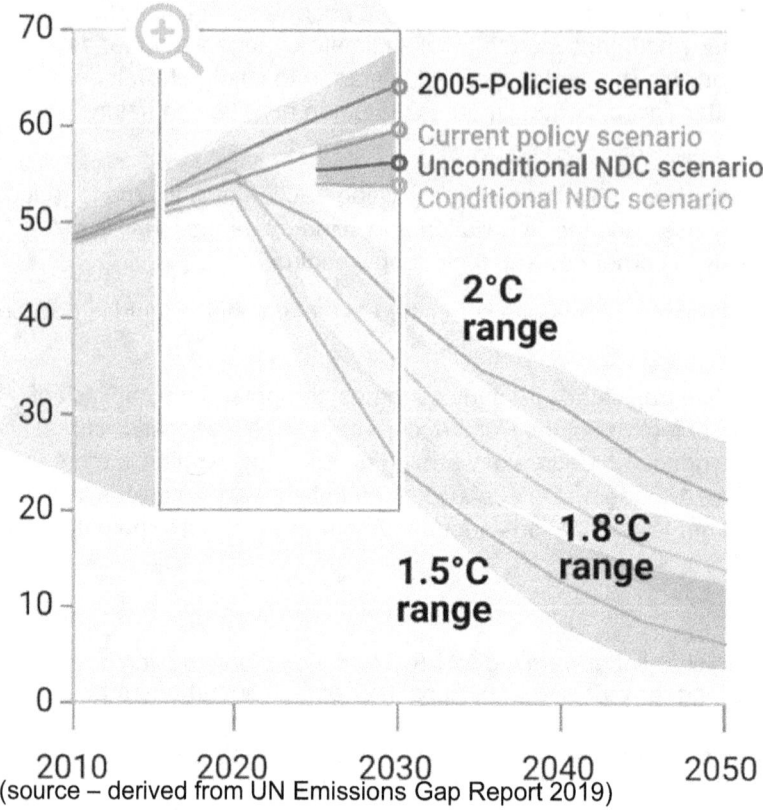

(source – derived from UN Emissions Gap Report 2019)

It seems unlikely that there will be absolutely no improvements in nations' NDC commitments in future CoP meetings. In my scenario, therefore, I assume a little progress will be made and that the maximum warming is 3 degrees rather than 3.2 degrees.

Let's calculate what the world balance sheets might look like in this scenario, in 2050, 2100 and 2500.

Figure 45 – Scenario 2 – Least change - 2050

Planetary CFO's World Balance Sheet 2050 (USD trillions) Scenario 2			% total assets
Fixed Assets			
Property			
Renewable NC (Land)			
Cropland	19.13		
Pasture land	18.86		
Forest	115.83		
Barren/wild land	0.90		
Urban land	77.30		
Oceans	124.68		
Ocean damage provision	-13.78		
Subtotal renewable NC		342.92	
Non-renewable NC		51.91	
Subtotal Property		394.83	46.0%
Plant			
Dwellings		154.08	
Other buildings		180.55	
Subtotal Plant		334.63	39.0%
Equipment			
Commercial equipment		54.57	
Military equipment		11.36	
Subtotal Equipment		65.94	7.7%
Intangible assets			
Goodwill		0.00	
Intellectual property		0.00	
Brand value, licences		0.00	
Subtotal intangible assets		0.00	0.0%
Current assets			
Inventories		60.30	7.0%
Cash and cash equivalents		2.11	0.2%
Human Capital	1,353.76		
Human Capital destructiveness provision	-1,353.76		
Net Human Capital		0.00	
Total assets		857.80	100.0%
Liabilities			
Human welfare commitment	1,925.31		
Unfunded human welfare commitment (-ve) ie asset stewardship shortfall	-1,067.50		
Equity of humankind		857.80	
Total liabilities and equity		857.80	

Figure 46 – Scenario 2 – Least change - 2100

Planetary CFO's World Balance Sheet 2100 (USD trillions) Scenario 2			% total assets
Fixed Assets			
Property			
Renewable NC (Land)			
Cropland	17.00		
Pasture land	16.77		
Forest	102.96		
Barren/wild land	0.80		
Urban land	68.71		
Oceans	110.82		
Ocean damage provision	-13.78		
Subtotal renewable NC		303.28	
Non-renewable NC		51.91	
Subtotal Property			355.19	38.1%
Plant			
Dwellings		188.32	
Other buildings		220.68	
Subtotal Plant			409.00	43.9%
Equipment			
Commercial equipment		75.56	
Military equipment		15.73	
Subtotal Equipment			91.30	9.8%
Intangible assets			
Goodwill		0.00	
Intellectual property		0.00	
Brand value, licences		0.00	
Subtotal intangible assets			0.00	0.0%
Current assets			
Inventories			73.70	7.9%
Cash and cash equivalents			2.58	0.3%
Human Capital	2,290.97		
Human Capital destructiveness provision	-2,290.97		
Net Human Capital			0.00	0.0%
Total assets			931.76	100.0%
Liabilities			
Human welfare commitment	2,353.15		
Unfunded human welfare commitment (-ve) ie asset stewardship shortfall	-1,421.39		
Equity of humankind		931.76	
Total liabilities and equity			931.76	

Figure 47 – Scenario 2 – Least change - 2500

Planetary CFO's World Balance Sheet 2500 (USD trillions) Scenario 2			% total assets
Fixed Assets			
Property			
Renewable NC (Land)			
Cropland	10.63		
Pasture land	10.48		
Forest	64.35		
Barren/wild land	0.50		
Urban land	42.95		
Oceans	69.27		
Ocean damage provision	-13.78		
Subtotal renewable NC		184.39	
Non-renewable NC		51.91	
Subtotal Property		236.30	19.8%
Plant			
Dwellings		256.80	
Other buildings		300.92	
Subtotal Plant		557.72	46.8%
Equipment			
Commercial equipment		243.48	
Military equipment		50.69	
Subtotal Equipment		294.18	24.7%
Intangible assets			
Goodwill		0.00	
Intellectual property		0.00	
Brand value, licences		0.00	
Subtotal intangible assets		0.00	0.0%
Current assets			
Inventories		100.50	8.4%
Cash and cash equivalents		3.51	0.3%
Human Capital	10,066.40		
Human Capital destructiveness provision	-10,066.40		
Net Human Capital		0.00	0.0%
Total assets		1,192.21	100.0%
Liabilities			
Human welfare commitment	3,208.84		
Unfunded human welfare commitment (-ve) ie asset stewardship shortfall (surplus if +ve)	-2,016.64		
Equity of humankind		1,192.21	
Total liabilities and equity		1,192.21	

Commentary on scenario 2 (least change scenario)

Global warming has risen to 3 degrees by 2100 before stabilising at that level. However, the permanent changes this has caused are wreaking ever more damage and difficulty. Per capita consumption has been reined in and capped. Despite this, the population continues to creep up. Human impacts on the planet and its biosphere continue to rise, reducing the amount of natural capital. The ever-present threat of collapse of natural capital, and continuing biodiversity loss, provide a constant backdrop to global conflicts, wars and economic cycles of boom and bust. The bottom line just gets progressively worse. The asset stewardship shortfall rises gradually and unspectacularly from USD 569 trillion in 2020 to about USD 1,068 trillion in 2050, USD 1,421 trillion in 2100 and USD 2,017 trillion in 2500. Nobody seems to be able to sort out the various wicked and pernicious problems. We are frogs that are slowly coming to the boil. (apologies here for those of you unfamiliar with the boiling frog anecdote).

A notable trend in the balance sheets for this scenario is that natural capital declines, over time, as a proportion of the assets, and the human artifacts and infrastructures increase as a proportion.

An alien observer, watching from space, would see the continuation of the visual changes that have occurred throughout the Industrial Revolution – a planet turning bit by bit from green and blue to various shades of brown.

Even by 2500, though, it _might_ not be too late to turn things around, providing we have tools such as species DNA records and viable seed libraries. There is still USD 184 trillion of natural capital remaining – a low but potentially viable base to build from.

Scenario 3 – an unsustainable future beyond 2050

There are so many ways this scenario could be constructed. These would probably need to include some element of backlash against carbon reduction and other sustainability initiatives and dismantling of bodies like the IPCC and the mechanisms they operate. Perhaps this scenario could include elements of societal breakdown, taking some learning points from Diamond (2011).

Let's just remind ourselves of the key variables I've decided to use for this scenario, as this scenario is so far removed from either the present state of the planet or either of the two previous scenarios.

variable	Scenario 3 – overload and collapse
Brief description	Mitigation and adaptation both fail at scale, with disastrous collapse ensuing from 2100 to 2500. Only scattered remnants of human civilisation remain. Unclear whether advanced human civilisation will ever be rebuilt in an environment permanently hostile to human existence
Warming by 2100	6 degrees
global population at 2050	15 billion
global population at 2100	40 billion (peak)
global population at 2500	4 million (after collapse) ie 0.004 billion
NPP at 2050 (2020 = 100)	130
NPP at 2100 (2020 = 100)	110
NPP at 2500	1
Natural capital index in year 2050 (2020 = 100)	50
Natural capital index in year 2100	10
Natural capital index in year 2500	1
notes	Conflict, war-damage, disease and ever more frantic use of technologies to get maximum food calories from every piece of nature result in almost complete collapse of the biome and its biodiversity – any surviving living things are constantly on the edge of extinction

Let's calculate what the world balance sheets might look like in this scenario, in 2050, 2100 and 2500.

Figure 48 – Scenario 3 – Overshoot and collapse - 2050

Planetary CFO's World Balance Sheet 2050 (USD trillions) Scenario 3			% total assets
Fixed Assets			
Property			
Renewable NC (Land)			
Cropland	10.63		
Pasture land	10.48		
Forest	64.35		
Barren/wild land	0.50		
Urban land	42.95		
Oceans	69.27		
Ocean damage provision	-13.78		
Subtotal renewable NC		184.39	
Non-renewable NC		51.91	
Subtotal Property		236.30	24.5%
Plant			
Dwellings		256.80	
Other buildings		300.92	
Subtotal Plant		557.72	57.9%
Equipment			
Commercial equipment		54.57	
Military equipment		11.36	
Subtotal Equipment		65.94	6.8%
Intangible assets			
Goodwill		0.00	
Intellectual property		0.00	
Brand value, licences		0.00	
Subtotal intangible assets		0.00	0.0%
Current assets			
Inventories		100.50	10.4%
Cash and cash equivalents		3.51	0.4%
Human Capital	2,256.26		
Human Capital destructiveness provision	-2,256.26		
Net Human Capital		0.00	
Total assets		963.97	100.0%
Liabilities			
Human welfare commitment	3,208.84		
Unfunded human welfare commitment (-ve) ie asset stewardship shortfall	-2,244.88		
Equity of humankind		963.97	
Total liabilities and equity		963.97	

Figure 49 – Scenario 3 – Overshoot and collapse - 2100

Planetary CFO's World Balance Sheet 2100 (USD trillions) Scenario 3			% total assets
Fixed Assets			
Property			
Renewable NC (Land)			
Cropland	2.13		
Pasture land	2.10		
Forest	12.87		
Barren/wild land	0.10		
Urban land	8.59		
Oceans	13.85		
Ocean damage provision	-13.78		
Subtotal renewable NC		25.85	
Non-renewable NC		51.91	
Subtotal Property		77.76	4.0%
Plant			
Dwellings		684.80	
Other buildings		802.46	
Subtotal Plant		1,487.26	76.9%
Equipment			
Commercial equipment		75.56	
Military equipment		15.73	
Subtotal Equipment		91.30	4.7%
Intangible assets			
Goodwill		0.00	
Intellectual property		0.00	
Brand value, licences		0.00	
Subtotal intangible assets		0.00	0.0%
Current assets			
Inventories		268.00	13.9%
Cash and cash equivalents		9.37	0.5%
Human Capital	8,330.81		
Human Capital destructiveness provision	-8,330.81		
Net Human Capital		0.00	0.0%
Total assets		1,933.69	100.0%
Liabilities			
Human welfare commitment	8,556.91		
Unfunded human welfare commitment (-ve) ie asset stewardship shortfall	-6,623.23		
Equity of humankind		1,933.69	
Total liabilities and equity		1,933.69	

Figure 50 – Scenario 3 – Overshoot and collapse - 2500

Planetary CFO's World Balance Sheet 2500 (USD trillions) Scenario 3				% total assets
Fixed Assets				
Property				
Renewable NC (Land)				
Cropland	0.21			
Pasture land	0.21			
Forest	1.29			
Barren/wild land	0.01			
Urban land	0.86			
Oceans	1.39			
Ocean damage provision	-13.78			
Subtotal renewable NC		-9.82		
Non-renewable NC		51.91		
Subtotal Property			42.09	45.3%
Plant				
Dwellings		0.07		
Other buildings		0.08		
Subtotal Plant			0.15	0.2%
Equipment				
Commercial equipment		0.00		
Military equipment		50.69		
Subtotal Equipment			50.69	54.5%
Intangible assets				
Goodwill		0.00		
Intellectual property		0.00		
Brand value, licences		0.00		
Subtotal intangible assets			0.00	0.0%
Current assets				
Inventories			0.03	0.0%
Cash and cash equivalents			0.00	0.0%
Human Capital	2.68			
Human Capital destructiveness provision	-2.68			
Net Human Capital			0.00	0.0%
Total assets			92.96	100.0%
Liabilities				
Human welfare commitment	0.86			
Unfunded human welfare commitment (-ve) ie asset stewardship shortfall (surplus if +ve)	92.11			
Equity of humankind		92.96		
Total liabilities and equity			92.96	

Commentary on scenario 3 (overshoot and collapse)

In 2050, this scenario doesn't seem so very different from 2020. Certainly, the asset stewardship shortfall is a lot larger, at USD 2,245 trillion. However, there are significant assets of various types providing for a population of 15 billion (much of the provision comprising large drawdowns of capital). Things are bad, and getting worse, at this point, and the damage, while possibly irreversible, has not come home to roost. Perhaps many of the climate deniers are still saying "what's all the fuss about - we're still here and growing, aren't we? This shows the environmentalists were scare-mongers".

By 2100, the picture is different. Population has grown to 40 billion and the balance sheet is showing extreme stress. The asset stewardship shortfall is now an unprecedented USD 6,623 trillion. Natural capital is even more severely depleted, and the only material assets are human artifacts and infrastructures, as this is the means by which humanity has tried desperately to keep responding to catastrophes involving lack of places to find safety, edible food, drinkable water and breathable air. It's a losing battle for survival of civilisation. The natural world is in extreme decline (and biodiversity loss has confirmed this era as a major extinction event unlike any other previous instance in geological history). Collapse of human populations and civilisation is all but inevitable.

By 2500, collapse has occurred. When the dust has settled, there are a few scattered settlements or roving bands of humans scavenging, repairing basic tools and weapons, with little prospect of regaining the technological supremacy or societal sophistication of our heyday any time soon. The balance sheet is almost moot at this point, but it shows that the main assets left are non-renewable natural capital (metals and other inorganic materials in the ground or on its surface, or in the oceans or mountainous trash piles left), and human artifacts and structures (buildings, tools, basic weapons) that are still available and in use.

Bizarrely, there is now a small asset stewardship surplus of USD 92 trillion, but this is not a consequence of good stewardship. Instead, it has resulted from a spectacular collapse of human populations.

The saddest aspect of this scenario is that it is entirely possible that it might never be possible, from the new collapsed baseline, to build a new human civilisation of any significance, and very likely that the ultimate outcome at some further point in the not-too-distant future beyond 2500 would be the extinction of the human species, as well as a legacy of a scorched planet only capable of supporting a small range of very basic species for the rest of the planet's geological history.

Sensitivity analyses on key variables

Sensitivities I will look at in very approximate ways:

- natural capital index
- population

Further sensitivities I could attempt, or leave to the reader or other researchers:

- per capita consumption
- discount rate

One way of performing this sensitivity analysis is to start with the least change scenario (as this is closest to a base case) and to alter only one of these variables, keeping the others unchanged, and see what sort of a change in the selected variable results in the scenario resembling the worst-case scenario (scenario 3 – overshoot and collapse).

Sensitivity to natural capital index

We can see, by comparing scenario 1 in 2100 and scenario 3 in 2100, that the difference in natural capital index had the effect of reducing natural capital from USD 632 trillion to USD 77 trillion.   The absolute difference in balance sheet values is minus USD 555 trillion.

Sensitivity to population

We can see, by comparing scenario 1 in 2100 and scenario 3 in 2100, that the difference in human welfare commitment stemming from a difference in population from 9 billion in scenario 1 to 40 billion in scenario 3, is that the human welfare commitment ballooned from USD 1,925 trillion to USD 8,557 trillion. The absolute difference in balance sheet values is minus USD 6,632 trillion.

By comparing these two sensitivity analyses, we can see that the scenarios are more sensitive to population numbers than they are to natural capital index. This doesn't mean that natural capital is not important. However, it illustrates the importance of both the inertia in the current state of the planet (eg the significant human population already in existence) and the significant further impact if population grows much larger in relation to the size of the (diminishing) value of natural capital.

It is the relationships between the two (nature and human populations) both in absolute numbers and per capita impacts, benefits and disbenefits, that are important.

Conclusions on this chapter

The main message from this very short and admittedly simplistic sensitivity analysis is that a focus on natural capital alone would not be enough to avert disastrous outcomes. The size of the human population and its impacts on nature are vital concerns to watch, and influence, alongside better stewardship of natural capital, to avert the worst disasters.

Fortunately, there are some obvious synergies between these two factors. For example, as people become more aware of, and active in addressing, climate concerns and the plight of nature, they're more likely to improve their own environmental and carbon footprints, to undertake work to improve and restore natural environments, and to consider such matters as their views on optimal family sizes.

Chapter 11

Summary and Conclusions

"… ideas matter – they are the cogs that drive history" (Grayling, 2009).

"There are known knowns. These are things we know that we know. There are known unknowns. That is to say, there are things that we know we don't know. But there are also unknown unknowns. There are things we don't know we don't know." (Donald Rumsfeld)

"Beyond all sciences, philosophies, theologies, and histories, a child's relentless inquiry is truly all it takes to remind us that we don't know as much as we think we know." (Criss Jami)

"I truly do not know, and that unnameable feeling that comes with not knowing: it must be worse than grief. It must." (Dexter Palmer, The Dream of Perpetual Motion)

As with any analysis such as the main subject of this book, we need to summarise, to make some conclusions, and perhaps a few recommendations.

The compilation and use of World Balance Sheets is not a new endeavour, but it is one that has been notable by its rarity over the last 150 years. This is the timeframe over which it has been within the imagination of humanity to undertake this task, as shown clearly by Mulhall. However, in that time, humanity has become obsessed with throughput (the equivalent of income and expenditure accounts) as a measure of economic and societal success, and has almost totally neglected to keep track of the most important balance sheet assets from which that success is derived, and on which it depends going forward into the future.

This book is an attempt to describe that omission and to make a tentative effort to start to set the record straight. To show that the global assets are most certainly not 'in balance' and are therefore "unbalanced". The difference, or amount by which the world is out of balance, is the unfunded commitment to provide for present and all future generations of humanity. By calculating this unfunded commitment (alternatively described as the asset stewardship shortfall), and representing it in a whole world balance sheet, we can talk about it and give more authority to voices trying to redress, or correct, the imbalance. Managing natural capital more effectively, for example by protecting and restoring nature, is one of the essential means to achieve this rebalancing, and future world balance sheets in the years, decades and centuries to come, will show how well we are doing in this task.

This is a new and emergent field of accounting. Accounting standards will need to catch up with the reality of the situation, if they are to help us avoid the worst-case scenarios of the future unfolding. Good work is being done currently, for example in a major revision to the SEEA due in 2021.

We will need an army of people to measure, monitor and revalue natural assets and flows. They are probably out there already, but they might not have all the tools or the inspiration to do this most important of tasks, for all our futures. I hope this book will help nudge things in the right direction.

The book is not intended to be an authoritative text set in stone. It's a prompt that is, in places, quite radical in outlook. It's deliberately provocative, so that it will elicit responses. The more the merrier. If it results in debate, and new thinking about old topics, then it will have achieved an important contribution. The status quo is the enemy of the new and the different. We need new and different thinking now, more than ever. As Einstein is quoted as saying:

> "We cannot solve our problems with the same thinking we used when we created them.

After writing this book, there remains an important question of completeness. This is expressed by the well-known saying "how do you know what you don't know?" The topic of the World Balance Sheet is no exception to this, and in fact presents rather a good example of it. Ecologists are frequently saying that the more they learn about the ecosystems, the more they realise they have yet to learn. Every year, species are discovered that were not known to humanity previously. There are vast tracts of ocean floor that no human has yet seen, let alone analysed for the existence, abundance and health of the ecosystems there (and the oceans cover over two thirds of the surface of the Earth).

There's so much more for us to learn and experience about the Earth and all its fantastic living inhabitants. Let's hope all of us, and innumerable future generations, get the chance to undertake that learning endeavour.

Appendix 1

Schools of economic thought through the ages

Figure 51 - Reproduced from Kvangraven I. and Alves C. (2019) (originally from Lavoie, 2009):

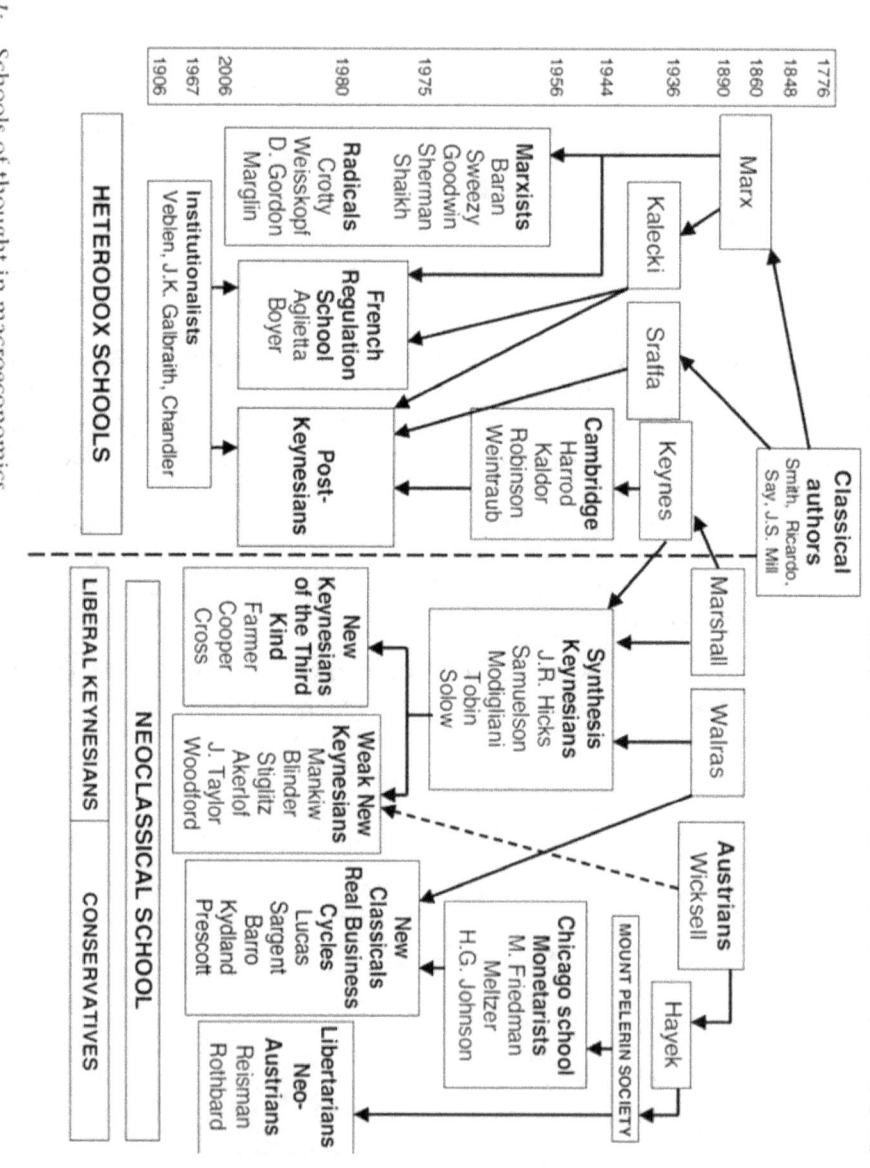

Figure 1.1: Schools of thought in macroeconomics

Appendix 2

An article about land

Excerpts are from the following source:

https://www.investopedia.com/terms/l/land.asp

-------- excerpts start ------------------------

Land

By JAMES CHEN
Updated Jun 4, 2020

What Is Land?
Land, in the business sense, can refer to real estate or property, minus buildings, and equipment, which is designated by fixed spatial boundaries. Land ownership might offer the titleholder the right to any natural resources that exist within the boundaries of their land. Traditional economics says that land is a factor of production, along with capital and labor ... Land qualifies as a fixed asset instead of a current asset.

KEY TAKEAWAYS

- Land can refer to real estate or property, minus buildings, and equipment, which is designated by fixed spatial boundaries.
- Land's main economic benefit is its scarcity.
- Land, itself, is a valuable resource, but if it comes with other natural resources, like oil and gas, its value increases.
- Investing in land for development can be costly and may come with certain risks.

More Ways to Understand Land

In Terms of Production
The basic concept of land is that it is a specific piece of earth, a property with clearly delineated boundaries, that has an owner. You can view the concept of land in different ways, depending on its context, and the circumstances under which it's being analyzed.

In Economics
Legally and economically, a piece of land is a factor in some form of production, and although the land is not consumed during this production, no other production - food, for example - would be possible without it. Therefore, we may consider land as a

resource with no cost of production. [I provide a criticism of this interpretation in the body of the book]. Despite the fact that people can always change the land use to be less or more profitable, we cannot increase its supply.

Characteristics of Land and Land Ownership

Land as a Natural Asset

Land can include anything that's on the ground, which means that buildings, trees, and water are a part of land as an asset. The term land encompasses all physical elements, bestowed by nature, to a specific area or piece of property - the environment, fields, forests, minerals, climate, animals, and bodies or sources of water. A landowner may be entitled to a wealth of natural resources on their property - including plants, human and animal life, soil, minerals, geographical location, electromagnetic features, and geophysical occurrences.

Because natural gas and oil in the United States are being depleted, the land that contains these resources is of great value. In many cases, drilling and oil companies pay landowners substantial sums of money for the right to use their land to access such natural resources, particularly if the land is rich in a specific resource.

… Air and space rights - both above and below a property - also are included in the term land. However, the right to use the air and space above land may be subject to height limitations dictated by local ordinances, as well as state and federal laws.

… Land's main economic benefit is its scarcity. The associated risks of developing land can stem from taxation, regulatory usage restrictions … and even natural disasters.

------- excerpts end ----------

My response to the UK Government Consultation - August to October 2020 - on

"Due diligence on forest risk commodities"

The consultation is a first step in the right direction. It sets out the proposed new legislation as a means to make supply chains more sustainable, by requiring large companies to undertake due diligence on their (global) supply chains regarding the sustainability of the harvesting of commodities (eg timber) from forests. However, inevitably this will initially fall short of being optimum for sustainability. This is because it is currently expressed in a form that represents a type of "weak sustainability".

Thresholds (for the scope of the legislation) should be set to cover a specific proportion of the amount of forest risk commodities involved in the UK economy. Those thresholds and proportions should be reviewed and revised every few years, and progressively tightened until the point of diminishing ecological returns.

I believe in "strong sustainability" and would recommend moving as swiftly as possible from the initial position to a position where the sum total of the world's natural capital is maintained and improved to a point of being optimal. This will go beyond many nations' existing laws, and will need to be backed up by new international laws.

Appendix 4 – SDG Synergies and Trade-offs – Figure 52

Length shows strength of connection

The overall size of the coloured bars depict the relative potential for synergies and trade-offs between the sectoral mitigation options and the SDGs.

Shades show level of confidence

The shades depict the level of confidence of the assessed potential for Trade-offs/Synergies.

Very High · · · · · · Low

(source = UN Emissions Gap Report 2019, originally Figure SPM4 in IPCC (2018))

References and Bibliography

Abenezer A. and G. Ing-Marie (2014) *Economic incentives for carbon sequestration: A review of the literature*

Accounting for Natural Capital (2018) from the Government Dialogue on Natural Capital

Admiraal, J.F. Wossink, A. de Groot, W.T. and de Snoo G.R. (2013) *More than total economic value: How to combine economic valuation of biodiversity with ecological resilience.* Ecological Economics, 89, pp.115-122

Ahlroth et al (2019) *Increasing the use and usefulness of Natural Capital Accounting for decision making*

American Meteorological Society (2017) *State of the Climate report 2017*

Anderson V. (2018) *Debating Nature's Value – The concept of 'Natural Capital'*

Archer D., Kite E., Lusk G. (2020) *The ultimate cost of carbon*

Bassens (2020) *Placing Cities in the Circular Economy: Neoliberal Urbanism or Spaces of Socio-ecological Transition?*

Bazhanov (2020) *A comment on Hamilton 2016 - measuring sustainability in the UN System of Environmental-Economic Accounting*

Beheshti S. (2018) *Holistic Product Design Education to Promote Sustainable Systems*

Bellassen et al (2014) Carbon sequestration: Managing forests in uncertain times

Bennett M. and Xu J. (2007) *China's Sloping Land Conversion Program: Institutional Innovation or Business as Usual?*

Bezemer, D. J. (2010). *Understanding financial crisis through accounting models.* Accounting, Organizations and Society, 35(7), 676–688. doi:10.1016/j.aos.2010.07.002

Bowe et al (2017) *The inescapable truth: Brexit, business and natural capital*

Boysen, O., Jensen, H. G., & Matthews, A. (2016) *Impact of EU agricultural policy on developing countries: A Uganda case study.* The Journal of International Trade & Economic Development, 25(3), 377-402

Brealey, R. A., & Myers, S. C. , Marcus A. J. (1995 and 2003). *Fundamentals of Corporate Finance* (International ed.). McGraw-Hill/Irwin.

Brown M. et al (2017) *Sustainability, Restorative to Regenerative*

Burke et al (2019) *How to price carbon to reach net-zero emissions in the UK*

Calver D. (2020a) *Peak XXXX : Infinite Possibilities on a Finite Planet*

Calver D. (2020b) *People or Planet: Towards a Regenerative Economics*

Capitals Coalition (2020) *Improving nature's visibility in financial accounting*

Clark C. (1971) *Economically optimal policies for the utilization of biologically renewable resources*

Clark C. (1973) *The economics of overexploitation*

Clark C., Munroe G. (2017) *Capital Theory and the economics of fisheries - implications for policy*

Climate Commission (2020) *How carbon pricing can help Britain achieve net zero by 2050*

Cohen F. Hamilton K. Hepburn C. Sperling F. Teytelboymthe A. (2017) *Wealth of nature* - INET paper

Cohen et al (2018) *Is Natural Capital Really Substitutable?*

Costanza, R., R. d'Arge, R. De Groot, S. Farber, M. Grasso, B. Hannon, et al. (1997) *The value of the world's ecosystem services and natural capital. Nature 387 (6630): 253.*

Costanza R. and Steffen W. (2005) *Sustainability or Collapse? An Integrated History and Future of People on Earth*

Costanza et al (2013) Beyond GDP: *Measuring and achieving global genuine progress*

Costanza, R., R. de Groot, P. Sutton, S. van der Ploeg, S.J. Anderson, I. Kubiszewski, S. Farber, and R.K. Turner. (2014) *Changes in the global value of ecosystem services. Global Environmental Change 26: 152–158.*

Costanza et al (2020) *Investing in Nature as the true engine of our economy - A 10-point Action Plan for a Circular Bioeconomy of Wellbeing*

Couix Q (2019) *Natural Resources in the Theory of Production: The Georgescu-Roegen / Daly versus Solow / Stiglitz Controversy*

Cresswell P. (2010) blog entry http://pc.blogspot.com/2010/03/family-tree-of-economics.html

Cullen et al (2017) *Understanding Financial Accounts (OECD)*

Czech B. (2008) *Prospects for Reconciling the Conflict between Economic Growth and Biodiversity Conservation with Technological Progress*

Czech B. (2013) *Supply Shock: Economic Growth at the Crossroads and the Steady State Solution*

Czech B. (2020) *Best of the Daly News*

Daly H. (1991) *Steady-State Economics*

Daly H. (2011) *Ecological Economics - Principles and Applications* - Second Edition

Daly H. (2013) *From a Failed Growth Economy to a Steady-State Economy*

Dasgupta, P. (2007) *Human well-being and the natural environment*

Deutsch H. (2020) *World Balance Sheet: Global Assets at a Glance*

Devine E. (1898) *Economics*

Diamond J. (2011) *Collapse – How Societies Choose to Fail or Survive*

Dietz, R., Jones, N., O'Neill, D.W., (Editors), (2010) *Enough is Enough: Ideas for a sustainable economy in a world of finite resources*

Dolfsma et al (2013) *Interdisciplinary Economics*

EEA Guatemala Policy Brief (2019)

Eichner A.S. (1987) *The Macrodynamics of Advanced Market Economics*

European Union (2017) *Taking stock: progress in natural capital accounting* In-depth Report 16 produced for the European Commission, DG Environment by the Science Communication Unit, UWE, Bristol.

Eurostat-OECD (2015) *Eurostat-OECD compilation guide on land estimation*

FAO (2011) *Review of the state of world marine fishery resources*

Fenichel E. and Abbott J. (2014) *Natural Capital: From Metaphor to Measurement*

Fleurbaey, M. and D. Blanchet (2013), *Beyond GDP: Measuring Welfare and Assessing Sustainability,* Oxford University Press, Oxford.

Friedman M. (1977) *From Galbraith to Economic Freedom*

Fuller J. (2018) *The shifting sands of how to account for goodwill continue to try the standard-setters and users of accounts. Jane Fuller looks at the history and points out the problems* – online ACCA article downloaded 18 September 2020

Fullerton J. (2015) *Regenerative Capitalism*

Fullerton J. (2019) *Finance for a Regenerative World*

GRI (2020) (Global Resource Initiative) *Final Recommendations Report*

Gaffney, Mason. (2008). *Keeping land in capital theory: Ricardo, Faustmann, Wicksell, and George.* American Journal of Economics and Sociology 67, no. 1:119–41.

Godley W. and Lavoie M. (2012) *Monetary Economics – An Integrated Approach to Credit, Money, Income, Production and Wealth*

Grant A. (1870) *Graphic Representation of the Laws of Supply and Demand, their Application to Labour, Part I*

Groom and Hepburn (2017) *Looking Back at Social Discount Rates: The Influence of Papers, Presentations, Political Preconditions and Personalities on Policy*

Gruber et al (2007) *The Oceanic Sink for Anthropogenic CO2*

Guardian Newspaper (25 November 2015) *Between Debt and the Devil by Adair Turner review – should the government start printing money?*

Hamilton K. and Hartwick J. (2005) *Investing exhaustible resource rents and the path of consumption*

Hamilton K. and Hepburn C. (2017) *National Wealth*

Harris et al (2021) *Global maps of twenty-first century forest carbon fluxes*

Hartwick J. M. (1977) *Intergenerational Equity and the Investing of Rents from Exhaustible Resources*

Hawken P. Lovins A. and Lovins L. (2010) *Natural Capitalism: The Next Industrial revolution*

Hayek F. (1944) *The Road to Serfdom*

Helm D. (2015) *Natural Capital – Valuing the Planet*

Helm D. (2019) *Green and Prosperous Land: A blueprint for rescuing the British countryside*

Helm D. (2020) *Net Zero: How we stop causing climate change*

Hepburn et al (2014) *Resilient and Inclusive Prosperity within Planetary Boundaries*

Hotelling H. (1931) *The economics of exhaustible resources.* Journal of Political Economy 39, no. 2: 137–75.

Hensher P. (2020) *A beginner's guide to avoiding bad policy mistakes in the anthropocene*

Hoshi T, Takatoshi I. (2012) *Defying gravity: How long will Japanese Government Bond prices remain high?*

Hudson M. (2015) *Killing The Host*

Hopkins J. (1833) *John Hopkins's Notions on Political Economy* (London: Longman, Rees, Orme, Brown, Green, and Longman, 1833).

Hynes, W., P. Love and A. Stuart (eds.) (2020), *The Financial System, New Approaches to Economic Challenges*, OECD Publishing, Paris, https://doi.org/10.1787/d45f979e-en

IMF (2020) *World Economic Outlook*

Intrilligator (1971) *Mathematical Optimisation and Economic Theory*

Jackson et al (2016) *Towards a Stock-Flow Consistent Ecological Macroeconomics*

Jackson T. and Victor P. A. (2019) *LowGrow SFC: a stock-flow-consistent ecological macroeconomic model for Canada.* CUSP Working Paper No 16.

Jorda O. et al (2016) *Macrofinancial History and the New Business Cycle Facts*

Kadir M. (2000) *Mental health and life stress of retired people* - The Bangladesh Journal of Psychology

Kant, S., 1999. *Endogenous rate of time preference, traditional communities, and sustainable forest management.* Journal of Social and Economic Development II, 65–87.

Kering (2019) – *Kering Environmental Profit and Loss methodology 2019*

Khan A. (2012) *Understanding Global Supply Chains and Seafood Markets for the Rebuilding Prospects of Northern Gulf Cod Fisheries*

King S., Ferrier S., Turner K., Badura T. (2019). *Discussion paper 11: Research paper on habitat and biodiversity related ecosystem services.* Paper submitted to the

Expert Meeting on Advancing the Measurement of Ecosystem Services for Ecosystem Accounting, New York, 22-24 January 2019 and subsequently revised. Version of 15 March 2019

Krznaric R. (2020) *The Good Ancestor*

Kvangraven I. and Alves C. (2019) *Heterodox Economics as a Positive Project: Revisiting the Debate*

La Notte A. and Rhodes C. (2019) *The theoretical frameworks behind integrated environmental ecosystem and economic accounting systems and their classifications*

La Notte et al (2019) *Capacity as virtual stock in ecosystem services accounting*

Lavoie (1992) *Towards a new research programme for post-Keynesianism and neo-Ricardianism*

Lavoie (2009) *Introduction to Post-Keynesian Economics*

Lavoie (2012) *The post-Keynesian economics of credit and debt*

Lavoie (2014) *Post-Keynesian Economics – New Foundations* - e.g. chapter 1 - Essentials of heterodox and post-Keynesian economics

Lawn (2001) *Toward Sustainable Development: An Ecological Economics Approach*

Leach M. (2017) *Why did the Big Society fail?* From the Local Trust website (downloaded June 2020)

Lungu I. (2017) *Neocolonialism or Balanced Partnership? Reframing agricultural relations between the EU and Africa*

Lyytimäki J. and Pitkänen K. (2020) *Perceived Wellbeing Effects of Ecosystems in Finland*

Man (2019) *Retirement, predictive factors of retirement and retirement adjustment*

Manley J., van Kooten C., Moeltner K., Johnson D. (2005) *Creating carbon offsets in agriculture through no-till cultivation: A meta-analysis of costs and carbon benefits*

McCoy S. et al (2013) *Alcohol Production as an Adaptive Livelihood Strategy for Women Farmers in Tanzania and Its Potential for Unintended Consequences on Women's Reproductive Health*

McFalls J. (2007) *Population: A Lively Introduction, 5th Edition*

McLaughlin E. et al (2014) *Historical wealth accounts for Britain: progress and puzzles in measuring the sustainability of economic growth*

Mechanical Markets (2017) *The Shape of Supply and Demand Curves in Rapidly Clearing Markets*

Mill, John Stuart (1848) *The Principles of Political Economy*. Book 2, Chapter 2, §6

Moore J. (2015) *Capitalism in the Web of Life. Ecology and the Accumulation of Capital*

Moore J. (2017) *The Capitalocene, Part I: on the nature and origins of our ecological crisis*, The Journal of Peasant Studies, 44:3, 594-630

Mora et al (2015) *Suitable Days for Plant Growth Disappear under Projected Climate Change: Potential Human and Biotic Vulnerability*

Mulhall M. G. (1881) *Balance-Sheet of the World For Ten Years 1870 - 1880*

Mulhall M. G. (1884) *A Dictionary of Statistics*

Mulhall M. G. (1896) *Industries and Wealth of Nations*

Murison Smith F. (2019) *Economics of a Crowded Planet*

Murison Smith F. (2020) *A Planetary Economy*

Natural Capital for Governments (2018) - Government Dialogue on Natural Capital

Nikiforos et al (2017) *Stock-flow Consistent Macroeconomic Models: A Survey*

Nobre (2018) *The Amazonia Third Way Initiative: The Role of Technology to Unveil the Potential of a Novel Tropical Biodiversity-Based Economy*

Office of National Statistics (2019a) Dataset – *The UK national balance sheet estimates* – published November 2019

Office of National Statistics (2019b) *UK natural capital accounts methodology Guide* – published October 2019

O'Neill, D.W., Dietz, R., Jones, N. (Editors), (2010). *Enough is Enough: Ideas for a sustainable economy in a world of finite resources.*
    The report of the Steady State Economy Conference. Center for the Advancement of the Steady State Economy and Economic Justice for All, Leeds, UK

Ord T. (2020) *The Precipice*

Orr et al (2020) *Liberty and the Ecological Crisis* (2019) Published by Routledge

Palley T. (2007) *Financialization: What It Is and Why It Matters*

Pearce D. (1988). *Economics, equity and sustainable development. Futures, 20,* 598–605

Pearce, D. and Atkinson, G. (1993) *"Capital theory and the measurement of sustainable development: an indicator of "weak" sustainability."* Ecological Economics, 8 (2). pp. 103- 108

Pettifor A. (2019) *The case for the green new deal*

Pickles E. (2011) *Armchair auditors are here to stay*

Polansky S. (2015) *Confused at the Crossroads*, BioScience, March 2015 / Vol. 65 No. 3

Pozsar, Zoltan & Adrian, Tobias & Ashcraft, Adam B. & Boesky, Hayley, (2013) *"Shadow banking,"* Federal Reserve Bank of New York Economic Policy Review, 19 (2), pages 1-16

Rambaud A. (2016) *Towards a finance that CARES*

Raihan et al (2019) *A Review of Emission Reduction Potential and Cost Savings through Forest Carbon Sequestration*

Randers J. (2012) *2052: A Global Forecast for the Next Forty Years*

Raworth K. (2017) *Doughnut Economics: Seven Ways to Think Like a 21st-Century Economist*

Read et al (2014) *A Price for Everything – The Natural Capital Controversy*

Rewilding Europe (2019) *Three-Year Strategic Plan 2019-2021*

Ruffing et al (2010) *The Right Target: Stabilize the Federal Debt*

Ryan-Collins J. et al (2017) *Rethinking the Economics of Land and Housing*

Samuelson, Paul A., and William D. Nordhaus (1985) *Economics.*

Schneider, F., Kallis, G., Martinez-Alier, J. (2010) *Crisis or opportunity? Economic degrowth for social equity and ecological sustainability.* Introduction to this special issue. Journal of Clean Production. 18, 511–518.

Schularick, Moritz, and Alan M. Taylor (2012) *Credit Booms Gone Bust: Monetary Policy, Leverage Cycles, and Financial Crises.* American Economic Review 102(2): 1029–61.

Schumacher E. (1973) *Small is Beautiful - Economics as if people mattered*

Scott G. et al (1995) *Success and failure components of global environmental cooperation: The making of International Environmental law*

Scott W. (2011) *Financial Accounting Theory* - Sixth Edition

Sills E. et al (2014) *REDD+ on the ground - a case book of subnational initiatives across the globe*

Skaggs, N. (2003) *H.D. Macleod and the origins of the theory of finance in economic development.* History of Political Economy, 35, 361–384.

Spash C. L. and Ryan A. (2012) *Economic schools of thought on the environment: investigating unity and division*

Spencer R. (2013) *"Costing the earth"* at https://www.icaew.com/-/media/corporate/files/technical/sustainability/costing-the-earth-oct-13.ashx?la=en (accessed 09/11/2020))

Statistics Finland (2014) *National Balance Sheets for Non-financial Assets Finland Final Report*

Steffen, W., Crutzen, P. J. & McNeill, J. R. (2007). *The Anthropocene: Are humans now overwhelming the great forces of nature? Ambio, 36(8)*, 614-621. http://dx.doi.org/10.1016/j.gloenvcha.2015.09.017

Steffen et al (2015) *The Trajectory of the Anthropocene - The Great Acceleration*

Steinberger et al (2020) *Providing decent living with minimum energy: A global scenario*

Stern, D. (2004) *The rise and fall of the environmental Kuznets curve.* World Development 32:1419–1439

Sterlin J. (2019) *The Civilicene and its Alternatives Anthropology and its Longue Duree*

Stiglitz J. (1974) *Growth with Exhaustible Natural Resources - Efficient and Optimal Growth Paths*

Stiglitz, J., J. Fitoussi and M. Durand (eds.) (2018) *For Good Measure: Advancing Research on Well-being Metrics Beyond GDP*

Stone R. and Brown A. (1962) *A Computable Model of Economic Growth*

TEEB (2013) *The economics of ecosystems and biodiversity for water and wetlands.* London and Brussels, Institute for European Environmental Policy (IEEP) & Ramsar Secretariat.

TEEB (2018) *Measuring what matters in agricultural food systems*

The London Group (2018) *EEEA 2020 Revision Issue Final July 2018*

Turner A. (2016) *Between Debt and the Devil - Money, Credit, and Fixing Global Finance*

UK National Accounts Blue Book (2019)

UK Sea Fisheries Report 2017 – published by the Marine Management Organisation (2018) – a UK ONS publication

UN (2014) SEEA - *System of Environmental-Economic Accounting 2012— Experimental Ecosystem Accounting*

UN (2018) SEEA - *The Role of the System of Environmental Economic Accounting as a Measurement Framework in Support of the post-2020 Agenda*

UN (2019) SEEA - SEEA EEA Revision - Expert Consultation - Working group 5: Valuation and accounting treatments - Discussion paper 5.2: *A framework for the valuation of ecosystem assets*

UN (2020) SEEA - *Revision of the System of Environmental-Economic Accounting 2012—Experimental Ecosystem Accounting (SEEA EEA) Global Consultation on Chapters Cover Note*

UN (2020b) - UNEP/FAO Factsheet (Feb 2020) *The UN Decade on Ecosystem Restoration 2021-2030*

UN Emissions Gap Report 2019

UNEP (2015) *Outcome Evaluation of Barcelona Convention UNEP MAP Five Year Programme of Work 2010-2014*

UNEP (2018a) *Inclusive Wealth Report 2018*

UNEP (2018b) *Inclusive Wealth Report 2018 – Methodological Annex*

UNESA (2016) *ODA Issue Brief*

Vaden et al (2020) *Decoupling for ecological sustainability - a categorisation and review of research literature*

Van der Ploeg, S. and de Groot R.S. (2010). *The TEEB Valuation Database – a searchable database of 1310 estimates of monetary values of ecosystem services.* Foundation for Sustainable Development, Wageningen, the Netherlands

Victor P.A. (2008) *Managing without growth. Slower by Design, Not Disaster.* Edward Elgar, Cheltenham, U.K.–Northampton, MA, USA.

Victor P.A. (2011) *Growth, degrowth and climate change: A scenario analysis* Ecological Economics, doi:10.1016/j.ecolecon.2011.04.013

Victor P.A., Rosenbluth, G. (2007) *Managing without growth.* Ecological Economics 61, 492–504.

Volans (2020) *Procuring a Regenerative Economy*

Vom Hau M. et al (2006) *Colonialism and Development - a comparative analysis of Spanish and British colonies*

Vox Science and Health (2019) *Brazil's Amazon rainforest destruction is at its highest rate in more than a decade*

Wang B. et al (2017) *Policy-driven China's Grain to Green Program: Implications for ecosystem services*

Wapshott N. (2011) *Keynes / Hayek: The clash that defined modern economics*

WAVES (2014) *Natural Capital Accounting in Action - Guatemala forests*

WAVES (2019) *Towards Natural Capital Accounting in Guatemala – Synthesis Report*

WEF (2018) *Harnessing the Fourth Industrial Revolution for Life on Land*

White D. J. and Hagens N. J. (2020) *The Bottlenecks of the 21st Century*

World Bank (2006) *Where is the Wealth of Nations? Measuring capital for the 21st century.*

World Bank (2018) *Changing Wealth of Nations 2018 - building a sustainable future – (Lange, Glenn-Marie, Quentin Wodon, and Kevin Carey, eds. 2018. Washington, DC)*

Zari M. (2009) *Towards a sustainable future: Adopting a regenerative approach to development*

Zhou S. (2009) *Modified hierarchical Bayesian biomass dynamics models for assessment of short-lived invertebrates: a comparison for tropical tiger prawns*

Index

G

M

market-traded 137
Marxan 168
matched 64
matching 180
material 5, 77, 94, 104, 111, 122, 144,
146-148, 157, 160, 172, 205,
222
materiality 6, 83, 180
materially 15, 130, 205
materials 69, 112, 119, 121, 136, 144,
157, 212, 222
math 80, 187
mathematical 15, 121, 188, 236
mathematically 69, 74, 181
mathematics 2, 25
maths 89
MATOPIBA 171
mature 197
maturing 100
maturity 82, 159, 187
maximal 96
maximisation 138
maximise 168
maximum 74, 98, 138, 203, 213, 218
measure 11, 14-16, 45, 91, 114, 122,
145, 148, 158, 159, 168, 225,
226, 240
measured 11, 36, 46, 47, 51, 53, 83,
97, 100, 126, 128, 130, 137,
145, 147, 153, 159
measurement 5, 16, 65, 111, 118, 130,
134, 147, 156, 159, 165, 168,
170, 172, 173, 178, 234, 237,
239, 241
measurements 5, 47, 156, 158
measures 11, 16, 17, 21, 26, 38, 45,
51, 72, 100, 112, 125, 129, 134,
139, 142, 144, 147, 151, 158,
159, 165
measuring 14, 25, 101, 115, 116, 159,
168, 169, 232-234, 237, 240,
242
media 61, 164, 240
mega-macro 10
Merchandise 36
meta-analysis 237

Meteorological 73, 76, 232
methodological 164, 202, 241
methodologies 14
methodology 5, 7, 15, 35, 47, 48, 52,
53, 60, 63, 156, 164, 170, 174,
176, 236, 238
methods 15, 26, 29, 35, 44, 49, 51, 53,
55, 58, 65, 67, 78, 88, 111, 114,
116-118, 124, 135, 136, 138,
142, 160, 162, 168, 169, 174,
191
metrics 4, 11, 25, 26, 240
Mexico 170, 171
mineral 46, 126, 127
minerals 108, 229
minimal 205
minimising 12, 168
minimum 38, 67, 168, 240
mining 144
ministers 195
Ministry 183
mitigation 81, 111, 198, 203, 212, 218
model 4, 12, 14, 53, 67, 100, 130, 137,
143, 187, 201, 205, 236, 240
modelled 188, 197
modellers 197
modelling 142, 143, 170
models 104, 105, 130, 142, 168, 232,
238, 242
modernisation 10
molecule 188
monetary 13, 16, 58, 64, 88, 99, 104,
111, 115, 117, 119, 134, 154,
157, 159, 165, 166, 168, 170,
180, 235, 239, 241
monetisation 135
monetised 5, 156
monetising 104, 157
money 4, 20, 48, 98, 112, 113, 120,
122, 137, 149-154, 181, 184,
185, 229, 235, 240
money's 152
monopoly 138
moral 19
morally 118
mortal 36

O

objectives 13, 25, 39, 47, 67, 78, 82, 98, 134, 172, 212
objectivity 23
obligation 93, 129
obligations 14, 16, 113, 135
obllvlon 191
ocean 63, 64, 73, 74, 76, 77, 211, 226
oceanic 76, 235
oceans 19, 63, 64, 66, 73-77, 80, 81, 89, 108, 191, 222, 226
ocean's 75
Odum's 197
OECD 16, 50, 51, 133, 234, 236
offset 89, 198
offsets 237
offsetting 11, 55, 67
optimal 18, 77, 125, 126, 224, 230, 233, 240
Optimisation 236
optimising 49
optimism 191, 197
optimist 191
optimistic 6, 46, 190, 191, 203-205, 207, 211
optimization 169
optimizing 81
optimum 76, 77, 138, 230
option 60, 135
options 144, 212
Orangutan 168
organisation 21, 29, 52, 133, 164, 165, 175, 241
organisations 2, 50, 118, 171, 186
organisms 107, 126, 173
organization 4, 164, 165
organizations 4, 171, 232
Ospreys 124
outflow 60
out-flows 120
outgoings 185
outlier 66
outliers 88

output 24, 26, 39, 91, 96, 100, 111, 112
outputs 14, 47, 79, 108, 134, 136
overexploitation 98, 122, 139, 233
over-exploitation 72, 152
overexploited 47
over-exploited 12, 115
overfished 77
over-fishcd 77
overfishing 74, 77
overload 203, 218
overreaching 154
overshoot 18, 48, 211, 212, 219-223
overshooting 18, 143
over-simplified 54
oversimplify 204
overuse 116
owed 101
owned 48, 135, 141, 164
owner 23, 127, 129, 132, 141, 174, 175, 185, 228
owners 105, 113, 114, 129, 132, 141, 174, 179
ownership 14, 48, 126, 132, 142, 174, 175, 228, 229
owning 121, 141

P

paid 36, 60, 113, 119, 179, 181
pandemic 10, 12, 89, 91, 207
Paradox 147, 150
Paris 212, 236
Accord 13, 212
Passive-use 135
pasture 64, 66, 83
pastureland 64, 65, 74, 83, 89
pathway 12, 151, 198, 205
pathways 13, 192, 194, 206, 207, 212
paying 67, 136
payment 99, 132, 175, 179, 181
payments 48, 132, 175, 181
peace 125
peak 2, 98, 203, 211, 218, 233
peaked 61, 211
peaking 98

T